Every Father's Daughter

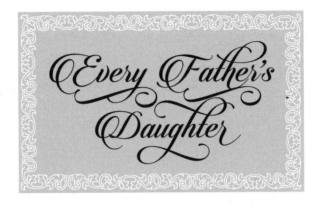

Every Father's Daughter

Twenty-four Women Writers Remember Their Fathers

Selected and Presented by
Margaret McMullan

With an Introduction by
Phillip Lopate

McPherson & Company
KINGSTON, NEW YORK

Published by McPherson & Company, P.O. Box 1126, Kingston, NY
12402. Book and jacket design by Bruce R. McPherson.
Typeset in LTC Californian. Printed on pH neutral paper.
Manufactured in the United States of America.
1 3 5 7 9 10 8 6 4 2   2015 2016 2017 2018 2019
First Edition

Library of Congress Cataloging-in-Publication Data
[Works. Selections]
Every father's daughter : twenty-four women writers remember their
fathers / selected and presented by Margaret McMullan ; with an introduction by Phillip Lopate. – 1 Edition.
    pages cm
Includes bibliographical references.
ISBN 978-1-62054-013-8 (alk. paper)
  1. Fathers and daughters. 2. Parent and child. 3. Interpersonal
relations. I. McMullan, Margaret, editor.
HQ755.85.E964 2015
306.874'2–dc23
                                                    2015001996

ACKNOWLEDGEMENTS AND CREDITS
Many thanks must go to William Baer for his sound editorial advice and guidance;
Jessica Woodruff for her editorial assistance; Pat O'Connor for being as thrilled as
we were with each new acquisition; Tena Heck for bringing order back to our home;
Maria Zamora and Miraia Vergara for their steadfast goodness and efficiency; Melvin
Peterson for his generosity; Carlette McMullan; Michael Martone, Ian Morris, Ann
Abadie, Gregg Schwipps, Steve Yates, Jennie Dunham, Ron Mitchell, and Mary Laur
for all their help with this project; Robert Anderson, Sarah Dabney Gillespie, James
O'Connor, Ned Jannotta, Richard Levy, Robert Fix, Jim McKinney, Annette Peck,
Tracy Grace, Nancy Kwain, Martha Ann Aasen, Paul Wilson McMullan, and Jimmy
Young for their stories about my father; Christine Chakoian for her calm wisdom;
and Madeleine McMullan for her appreciation.

All photographs are the copyrighted property either of the authors or the photographers
cited and are used by permission. All rights reserved.

PAGES 301-302 CONSTITUTE A CONTINUATION OF THIS COPYRIGHT PAGE.

For my father
James M. McMullan (1934-2012)
and for all our fathers

CONTENTS

Foreword by Margaret McMullan 9
Introduction by Phillip Lopate 17

ABSENCES

No Regrets Jane Smiley 23
Christmas From Now On Patricia Henley 33
My Father's Daughter Bliss Broyard 37
Secrets of the Sun Mako Yoshikawa 51
Sol's Exodus Nancy Jainchill 67

LOST & FOUND

My Dad Jill McCorkle 79
My Father's Bible Joyce Maynard 87
Masters in This Hall Melora Wolff 97
Crossing State Lines Jessica Woodruff 117
The Memory I Chose Jane Friedman 129
Waiting for My Father Barbara Shoup 137
The American Father Maxine Hong Kingston 147

PRESENCES

Life Saver Ann Hood 167
Reading My Father Alexandra Styron 173
Gifts Nancy McCabe 191
Oxygen Susan Neville 207
What He Worked For Susan Perabo 219
Do You See What I See? Antonya Nelson 225
Daddy's Dime Store Lee Smith 229
Balloons Johanna Gohmann 235
A Relationship of Words Lily Lopate 243
Burning the Trees Jayne Anne Phillips 255
My Fathers Bobbie Ann Mason 263
Working for a Living Alice Munro 267

Contributors & Acknowledgments 295

Foreword

A FTER A PROLONGED illness, my father died on a chilly spring day when the lilacs had just started to bloom. In that last month of his life, when he could no longer talk, we learned to communicate in other ways. I cooked for him, fed him, clipped his nails. He thanked me by putting his hand on my head. What there was to say, we had already said. In those last days, I read essays, poems and stories to him. I read other people's words. What I read to my father and what I wanted to read after he died became the genesis of this anthology.

My father was born the eldest son of four in 1934 in Lake, Mississippi, and raised in Newton, Mississippi. He broke his nose playing high school football and went on to attend the University of Mississippi in Oxford. As an undergraduate, my father once had drinks with William Faulkner at the Peabody Hotel in Memphis. They were both waiting to catch a train that would take them back to Oxford. They got to talking about horse trading. Learned either from people or books, my father knew about empathy. He never made fun of people. His narratives about people were underlined with dignity, grace, honor, and humor. I like to think that my father learned about character from the master that night at the Peabody. I often told him if he hadn't gone into finance, he'd have been a writer.

About a year after he graduated from college, he broke up with a girl from the Mississippi Delta, and, to recover, he visited his sister in Washington, D.C. She threw a party, served a vodka punch, and my father met an exotic Ingrid Bergman beauty named Madeleine. That night, after the party, my father told his sister, that woman, Madeleine, was the woman he wanted to marry. Three days later my father proposed marriage in a car he borrowed from Senator James Eastland, staring at Eastland's cigar stubbed out in the car's ashtray as he did so. He spoke no more than he needed to. When I think of my father in the time before he became my father, he seems marvelously determined and ready to get the hell started with his life. My father always appreciated a straightforward narrative.

It took a certain amount of imagination and courage to marry my mother, Madeleine, a woman who had escaped the Nazis in Vienna, Austria, and who worked for the CIA in Washington. She was nothing like any woman he had ever known. She became the love of his life; he hers, and they stayed married for the next fifty-four years. Once, a man who knew my parents told me, when he heard the way my mother say my father's name—*Shimmy* for *Jimmy*—he knew how difficult it would be to find a woman who would say his own name in that *in-love* way.

After my sister and I were born, and after a short period selling farm equipment at his father's International Harvester tractor store in Newton, my father joined Merrill, Lynch, Pierce, Fenner & Smith in Jackson, Mississippi, as an account executive in 1961.

One evening, my parents attended an outdoor Joan Baez concert in Jackson. It was about 1964 and my father loved Baez, and that night he laughed when he saw her stick her tongue out at *Look* and *Life* magazine photographers. People parked in a big, open field, and afterwards, a young man from out of state couldn't start his station wagon. My father offered a jump-start. The two spoke briefly. *Where was he headed?* my father asked. *Meridian.* My father told the young man he grew up near there. The station wagon started and the two went their separate ways. Later, my father recognized both the station wagon and the young man in the newspapers. The young man my father recognized was Michael Schwerner, one of the Civil Rights workers murdered in Philadelphia, Mississippi. The FBI found the burned-out station wagon before they found the bodies.

There were other factors beside the nightmarish racial conflicts that led my father away from Mississippi, a place he loved more than any other place. His decision to leave wasn't easy. But in the end, my father was ready to get us away from the violence, the hate, the confines, restrictions, and, some would say, advantages of growing up in a state amongst all his extended family.

My father survived and even thrived away from the South, in Chicago, despite the snowstorms and the impossible Dow-Jones industrial average of the 1970s. He found his footing in that perilous place, nicknamed The Windy City, the city where Binx felt "genie-souls perched on his shoulder" in Walker Percy's novel *The Moviegoer*. Maybe my father found his own genie-soul there, somewhere within Chicago's muscular skyline and market fluctuations.

In the 1980s, I moved from Chicago to New York to write the entertainment pages for *Glamour* magazine. One February, my father called to say he was coming to town on business, and I told him to pack his tux. I had special tickets to a CBS Records party. The invitation they sent was printed on a white glove. This was 1984.

Our cab let us out on the street because the road was blocked off to the Museum of Natural History. Behind police barricades, crowds of people stood outside in the sub-zero weather. My father put on the white glove with the invitation printed on the palm. When he held up his gloved hand, the police allowed us through, and the sea of people parted. Once inside, my father shook hands with Michael Jackson and Brooke Shields, who stood together inside a dinosaur skeleton. We were all there to celebrate the historic success of the album "Thriller." Years later, whenever my father told friends about that evening, what he stressed more than anything was how the NYPD let us through because of that one white glove. He laughed and said he never felt more powerful.

I knew my father in many ways—in the south and in the north, through the stories he told me, the places we visited, the food we ate, and through the music we listened to—anything by Johnny Cash, Hank Williams, Emmy Lou Harris, and George Jones, way before they became hip. But I knew my father best when we talked about books. When we talked about a book, any book, he talked easily and about anything. When we talked about a book, we always talked about important things.

My father read more than any other non-writer I've known. His favorite authors were William Faulkner, William Shakespeare, James Lee Burke, Eudora Welty, and John Updike. He also loved Alice Munro, Gore

Vidal, Henry Miller, Patti Smith, Bruce Chatwin, among countless others. Because I loved my father and because he introduced me to most of these authors and because they really are great writers, my father's favorite authors became mine; my favorite authors became his. Reading and talking about what we were reading was a way my father and I had of staying close, even when we weren't living nearby. Eventually, probably because of my father's love for the written word and talking about literature, I quit my job at *Glamour* to become a writer and a teacher.

I remember when we both read and talked about Philip Roth's *Patrimony* while my father's own father was not well. It helped my father to read a nonfiction narrative about a father and a son struggling together during a difficult time. Reading Roth's book allowed us to talk about the fact that there was no way my father could care for his father, who still lived in Mississippi. My father paid for caregivers, but he said he could not see moving back down with my mother to do the intimate hands-on work Roth wrote about. I took the opportunity then to tell my father flat out that it would be my honor and privilege to care for him, should he ever need that kind of care. He laughed then and said that certainly would not be necessary.

My father and I became literary groupies together. We often attended The Oxford Conference for the Book in Oxford, Mississippi, where he had the opportunity to meet writers he admired, among them Lee Smith and Bliss Broyard. They were two of the first writers to respond to this project with such enthusiasm so that we could include their wonderful essays in these pages. One night after dinner at the conference, we were outside on the square, and my father got to telling a story about how Barry Hannah's uncle Snow Hannah shot Red Alexander during a card game in Forest, Mississippi. "Shot him," my father said. "But didn't shoot him dead. That took a while." One of the writers there, Mark Richard, turned to me and said, "Have you used this yet?"

Most of the young adult novels I wrote set in Mississippi (*How I Found the Strong*, *When I Crossed No-Bob*, and *Sources of Light*) had everything to do with my father's stories and both of our growing-up years in the south. In so many ways, his memories became my memories.

My father was always deeply involved in my life, especially my writing life. He was the first person I called with every success – a first story sold, an award, a first book contract, and that great two-book deal. He always had the best, unquestioning, gleeful responses. It was all so *good*. He didn't know much about my profession, but as a businessman, he understood both failure and success. A friend of his once compared him to a wrestler. Pinned down or felled, my father never stayed down long on the mat. He fairly *bounced* up, ready for more. He wanted me to be that way as a professional writer.

When my father was diagnosed with inoperable brain cancer in June of 2010, he told me he didn't want a lot of weeping and wailing. "Let's just take this as it comes," he said. "Let's not get all emotional. When I was 45 and I had my first heart bypass, I asked myself *Why me?* Well, now, I'm 75. Why NOT me?"

We were careful with words. We didn't use the C word. It was "mass" or "images" and sometimes "spots." We stayed positive. We thought of the next meal. We considered dessert. We talked about what we would read next.

"My balance is off." That was his only complaint and it was hardly a complaint; just a statement of fact. He even said it like, *so what? I'm not 100%, but so what?* For him the days were always "beautiful." I always looked great. My food tasted wonderful. People were so nice. *What should we read today?*

When he fell the third time, and he said in his bed at the hospital, "This room sucks the memory out of me," that was when he made the decision to go home and spend the rest of his time surrounded by family, camellias, good food, music, and the literature he loved.

His particular illness is known to change people. Patients can become mean, angry, even violent. But my father retained his calm, his graciousness, his dignified, gentlemanly manner friends still recall. He thanked every nurse, caregiver, and visitor. He said he hoped he wasn't a bother when I helped him walk. When he could no longer walk, he apologized to my husband, who lifted him into his wheelchair. As debilitating as his illness was, my father never disconnected with who he was, who he had been, and the stories that shaped him.

Time took on a sacred quality. Consequently, stories and good writing played a big part in my father's final days as they had in his life. Every morning we began with the paper, reading from the opinion pages of the

New York Times. By noon we were on to Henry Miller's *Book of Friends*, stories by Mark Richard, Alice Munro, William Faulkner, Willie Morris, or Eudora Welty. Then lunch, a nap, tea, the PBS news hour with a glass of wine through a straw, dinner, a little poetry and an old movie. One night W. H. Auden led to a Marilyn Monroe movie followed by Gerard Manley Hopkins' "Pied Beauty," ending the evening with that wonderful last line: "Praise him."

When my father began to forget, I stopped beginning sentences with, *Remember when...* He often spent a morning sitting up in bed, hand on chin, two fingers on his lips, thinking. Great literature helped my father make sense of his life and his feelings in a way that nothing else could. In this way, I think that my father was a very realized man. He lived his life and he considered it too.

During his last few weeks, my father and I both spoke less and less. Having little use for our own words, we found comfort and solace in the words of others. As he lay dying, all the talk of symptoms, ability and inability, therapists, caregivers, insurance, and healthcare gave way to other, preferable narratives as we read and read and read. I read out loud from all the authors he loved, until his last breath, letting the words and sentences hover in the room for as long as they would stay, like so many invited friends come to say good-bye.

After my father died, I couldn't read or write, perhaps because, in the end, my father was unable to read or write. I didn't know it then, but I was looking for a collection of intensely personal essays, written by great women writers telling me about their fathers and how they came to know their fathers, a collection which might help me make some kind of sense of my own very close relationship with my father. I wanted to know from women, replacement sisters, if they had similar relationships with their fathers as I had with mine. Or, if their relationships were altogether different, I wanted to know how exactly these relationships were different. I wanted to know if the fact that my father was southern had anything to do with anything. I suppose, more than anything, I just wanted to know that I wasn't alone in my love, my loss, my loneliness. I wanted to read this anthology, but it did not exist. Writers write the book they want to read. Editors do the same. This book came out of a need, my own, personal, selfish need.

Eventually, I contacted the authors I loved and admired—some of them friends, some of them friends of my father's. I never wanted this to feel like an assignment, but I suppose it was. I simply asked these women to tell me about their fathers. They took it from there. For some authors, the idea of writing about a father just clicked, and they wrote their essays, often within days of the request. We all have stories about our fathers, even if it's a bad story or a non-story, it's a story. If you write, you will read these essays and feel the need to write your own.

I kept my father's tastes very much in mind during the difficult but joyful process of selecting essays for this book. This collection reflects my father, and, of course, other fathers as well. These essays are a sort of collage or mosaic of fatherhood and all the ways daughters communicate or don't with their fathers. Of course, there's a long list of wonderful women writers not included here—this anthology really should extend itself into another volume.

How we as daughters come to know our fathers is the organizing principle in these pages. Essentially, these essays are about daughters wanting to know, failing to know, but always, always *trying* to know their fathers. And often, the search to know doesn't end, not even with the father's death. A father's death, in fact, might instigate another search or further investigation, as Jill McCorkle writes about in her moving essay, "My Dad," and we are moved to tears by the big-heartedness of a father who doesn't want to destroy the ramshackle yard barn his now-grown daughter turned into a playhouse.

What does the father represent? For Martin Luther, our fathers are godly to us: how we see our fathers has a lot to do with how we see, or don't see, God; for God manifests himself in the father.

Our culture is rich with images and ideals of what makes good mothering, but our idea of what makes good fathering is more abstract. Is this because we don't expect much from a father? We know what is NOT good fathering. A good father does not drink away all the money or shoot at people. He does not scar his wife or his children for life. But what does a father do right? And is his idea of right our idea of right? Such questions emerge as you read Jane Smiley's "No Regrets" and Jessica Woodruff's "Crossing State Lines."

There are many kinds of fathers represented in this collection—shadowy, attentive, absent, abusive, overpowering, loving, charming, gentle, violent, and cruel. Some fathers are a mixture. There are recurring themes here, too: the fact that a father is often seen as a link to the outside world, to the marketplace, to *out there*, is balanced against a daughter's need to please and be loved. In myth and even in history, women tend not to murder their fathers, literally. They tend to care for them.

This anthology had to include Alice Munro's gorgeous essay "Working for a Living," which I read to my father in that last month of his life. My father loved anything by Alice Munro, and we especially appreciated this stunning essay because of Munro's nuanced writing, but also for the complex dynamics between the father, mother, and daughter as they work to raise, kill, and skin foxes in Canada.

Like many of these writers, I know I'll be writing about my father always. Our stories don't stop, even when lives end. Reading these essays was both painful and uplifting. I am amazed at my own pleasure. Reading these writers recollecting their fathers helps me call up my own father. And I remember him all over again, and in my mind, he lives. These are essays my father would have loved. I still can't believe I won't see him again, standing in a room, straightening his tie, or putting on his hat, the dimpled kind he held by the crown and pinched between his thumb and forefinger when he put it on or when he took it off to put on the hall closet shelf. I still can't believe I won't be able to discuss this book with him.

Living through my father's dying, I realized that his death was not at all the end of him, not in my mind, not in my memory, certainly not in my dreams, where he comes to me often. I still see him cutting his roses and camellias. I still see us planting the vegetable garden. He is forever selecting the suit he will wear to work, the night before. I listen for his voice. I feel him beside me.

On what was to be his last day, I picked gardenias and camellias he had grown and put them in a mint julep glass beside his bed. I found his mother's old Bible, a tiny yellowed one with most of Genesis missing. I scooted a chair up close to his face, laid the book open on his bed, held his hand, and began reading about tender mercies.

PHILLIP LOPATE

Introduction

WHAT IS IT about the relationship between
fathers and daughters that provokes so
much exquisite tenderness, satisfying communion, longing for more, ide-
alization from both ends, followed often if not inevitably by disappointment, hurt, and the need to understand and forgive, or to finger the guilt
of not understanding and loving enough? The bar is set very high from
the start: fathers tend to find their young daughters infinitely cute, adorable, incarnating the essence of all that draws these men to the feminine,
without the intimidating judgmental scrutiny and moral character of the
adult women who are now their partners in parenting. Later, once these
daughters reach adolescence and beyond, they may scrutinize their fathers in equally excruciating detail, but that is another story. Then, too,
the very fact that sexual release is out of the question between fathers
and daughters (except in horrific circumstances) means there is no ceiling, no brake on the romantic fondness that may develop between them.
Hence the ache that often accompanies the love.

Our language has a word for being dotingly enamored of one's wife
(uxurious) and a word for loving one's father (philopatric), but not, so
far as I can tell, one for the love of fathers for their daughters. Speaking
as the father of a daughter, I can testify that there may be no comparable
affection as intense or all-consuming. That does not mean that I fail to
note her flaws, or can rise above irritation in the face of her intermittent
panics, tantrums or self-absorptions. It simply means that I adore her.

Do fathers and daughters understand each other? Yes and no. We
see from Shakespeare's greatest play, *King Lear*, that even the most lov-

17

ing filial loyalty tie may be misconstrued. Reading the superbly written, empathic, insightful set of personal essays in this volume by daughters about their fathers, which run the gamut from portraits of successful businessmen and civic-minded heroes to shady con artists and failures, from the most patiently paternal to the most neglectful, I am struck by the persistent note of missed connection. These father figures, even the most loving and devoted, often seem so strangely distant, so abstract and unreachable. Perhaps because I experience myself as perfectly ordinary and transparent, on a day-to-day basis, including those moments when I interact with my daughter, I am flummoxed by the mystery and remoteness with which the fathers here seem to be imbued. As a father, put on the defensive, I am tempted to ask, paraphrasing Freud's famous question, "What do these daughters want?"

Some of the distance may simply be accounted for by the differences between men and women—what used to be called, euphemistically or not, "the battle of the sexes." Some of that distance may be ascribed to the generation gap: many of the fathers described here belonged more to that generation that fought in World War II or the Korean War and came back home taciturn about their war experiences. It is noteworthy how often the fathers are characterized as movie-star handsome, especially from the looking-up angle of girlhood; and how many of these matinee idols subsequently took to drink. Meanwhile, their daughters were coming to consciousness in a different order.

The world of their fathers is a bygone world, quaint and unquestioningly patriarchal.

~

We are living in an era when some biologists and feminists speculate whether men will even be necessary in the future. The roles of men and women are mutating from the old rigid patterns, mostly for the good, but we may ask: What then is the role of fathers vis-à-vis daughters in our present culture? First, to be present—or, in the case of divorced parents, present enough to offer another model of beingness to daughters than that of her mother. Of course, a girl can grow up into a confident young woman without a father or male figure present, as we see from many children of single mothers and lesbian couples. Still, there is something to be said for the old-fashioned family pattern. The sensitive, alert girl-child will know how to extract life lessons from even the most taciturn of fathers, be he the strong silent or weak silent type. The father may be a purveyor of cultural knowledge, like the Mozart-loving subjects who keep popping up in this anthology. The father often takes on a protective role, which the growing daughter may find comforting and reassuring—until she doesn't. The father may also indulge his daughter more than his spouse might, or give her more freedom to take risks. Many mothers see the world outside the home as filled with predators, and try to imbue their daughters with fine-tuned wariness. A father, himself a member of that dubious male species and therefore less likely to indict his entire sex, may convey a more benign regard for life beyond the domestic sphere. Certainly for previous generations of daughters (less so today, when women are accepted into more professions) the father was a bridge to that bigger world, and part of his glamour derived from access to those stimulating, if potentially more dangerous, environments. How many of the fathers described here, awkward and passive at home, suddenly sprung to life in their occupational milieus!

Some of the essays honestly portray a daughter's competition with her father's workplace, or her rivalry with the other siblings or her mother for the father's undivided love. She may have winced at the easy camaraderie her brothers had with her father. She may have rejoiced, however discreetly, at the sense that she was "getting" her father's inner nature more than her mother had. Not a few of the authors here opted for the role of Daddy's Girl, proudly bonding with the father over the mother.

It is not an easy thing, under any circumstance, to write about loved ones. There are boundaries of privacy to consider. It is so difficult to get the exact distance, the proper perspective: to appreciate a family member without sentimentalizing or idealizing, to be truthful about a parent's defects without indulging in "Daddy Dearest" exposés.

The writers in this collection seem to me scrupulously fair in their attempts to portray their fathers' complexities and their humanity. The hardest thing, perhaps, is to see a parent not just through the scrim of one's filial relationship, but as having an autonomous existence. I am reminded of something the essayist B. K. Loren wrote:

"In your little role as the offspring, you do not get the luxury of watching your parents become their own, oddly whole human beings with quirks and jaggedly adorable imperfections. As soon as you no longer depend on them, you blame them, and as soon as you learn that blaming them for who you are or whatever pain you feel is ridiculous because you are just fine the way you are and pain accompanies every ecstasy of life anyway, just at that moment, you wake up and see that your parents have entered into a whole new territory called old age. You cannot go there. You cannot meet them. You cannot enter."

Beyond old age is a territory even more inaccessible, which the writer is not permitted to enter. Many of the essayists here write of seeing their fathers disappear into that terra incognita; and their regret becomes suddenly, keenly irreversible that they did not ask enough questions or listen enough to these men when they were alive. The distance between the dead and the living is notoriously unbridgeable, which may explain the ghostly absence-presence of the men portrayed here.

Finally there is a simple but profound division, beyond gender or generation or mortality, which exists between writers and non-writers. The contributors to this collection are professional authors, some highly acclaimed, and their fathers (with but a few exceptions, such as Alexandra Styron and Lily Lopate) were not. The writer is always looking with wonder and bemusement at those who have opted not to render existence in words on the page. Are such unbookish creatures, who go to their graves without written testimony, ever knowable at all, at least from the standpoint of those who spend their lives scribbling away? Did these particular fathers get a chance to read any of their daughters' books? If so, were they proud? Chagrined? Baffled? Are they watching from on high even now, and, if specters can read, perusing and mulling over their daughters' eloquent turns of phrase? We can only hope they will or would be pleased at these (for the most part) loving literary tributes. The rest of us are free to eavesdrop in on the poignant father-daughter exchanges which follow, with pleasure and enlightenment.

Absences

If I could make a patchwork quilt of all the correspondence I received while assembling this anthology, Jane Smiley's e-mails would be among those at the center. When I approached her, Jane responded within a few days with this remarkable essay, which tells us as much about the savvy women in Jane's family as it does about her troubled father. "I do hope you like it," she wrote, unaware yet that I would be blown away. The title came later. "No Regrets" was one of Jane's favorite songs in college. Listen to the epic Edith Piaf version, and recall her powerful, righteous tone as she belts out, "All the things that went wrong. For at last, I have learned to be strong." Jane, of course, is the prolific, Pulitzer Prize-winning author of A Thousand Acres.

⌒ JANE SMILEY

No Regrets

OUR FAMILY abounded in tall, handsome
veterans of the Second World War. My un-
cle Hal had been an Army photographer—his job was to lie in the belly
of U.S. bombers and take pictures of the bombings, to make sure that
the targets had been destroyed. My uncle Carl flew planes in the Pacific.
My absent father was said to be cut from the same angular, dark-haired,
hypermasculine pattern. The war may not actually have been a constant
topic of conversation in my childhood, but it seemed to be, at least to me.
These men stood up straight, as if still in uniform, spoke in loud voices,
as if still giving orders.

But around the time of my first birthday, in 1950 my father was placed
in a veterans' hospital with some sort of mental disorder which may have
been schizophrenia or may have been P.T.S.D. or may have been something else. For a year and a half after my father went into the hospital,
I lived with my mother's parents in St. Louis while my mother stayed
in Michigan, attempting to understand their future, her future, and my
future, and so my father became a fictional character—portrayed by my
mother in detail and with a tragic air. He was uniquely handsome ("Gregory Peck"), brilliant, and charismatic. He went to West Point and chose
the cavalry—but the cavalry was disbanded, so they put him in the tank
corps, except that he was too tall for a tank. He turned to the Army Air
Force, but because he was too tall for a plane, he invented a way of refuel-
ing planes in air. When they tested his "hypodermic method," one of the
testing planes crashed and the pilot was killed. While he was working
out the kinks, the British came up with another method, and he found

himself back in the infantry. He was sent to Bavaria to organize and aid the sea of refugees then flooding from the east, and there he met my mother, who was serving in the Women's Army Corps. The army and the war provided the grand backdrop for my father's dramatic episodes of bad luck, but he did not fit in there.

When my father did visit, when I was four, he filled our one-bedroom apartment with his resonant voice and his six-foot-four frame. I found it strange that he was there in bed with her (where I often nestled or played or chatted) and strange to see his things on the bathroom counter. I felt a hovering shift in the atmosphere that denoted that things would soon be done differently around here, and an answering feeling of dread. My father didn't have a lot to say to me, but one morning he called me over to him when I came out of the bathroom, turned me around, and pulled down my pants to see if I had wiped myself properly. The rest of the visit remains hazy—maybe because the hygiene incident was so vividly unprecedented. I do remember him showing us how to work the new television.

My parents were divorced shortly after the visit, but my mother continued to tell me about the dashing genius of my father. His uncle, a Michigan State legislator, had gotten him into West Point after misadventures elsewhere. At West Point, he was almost cashiered for insubordination several times. At the end of the war, he got a general discharge instead of an honorable discharge. When my mother and he ended up in Los Angeles in the late forties, he could not find a job—my mother earned their daily bread. The implication of this latest fact might have been that his problem was unusual. Though unemployment among war veterans was generally high, perhaps potential employers could sense he would be hard to handle and arrogant. But another possibility was always there in my mother's stories—maybe he was just too good for them. When I was ten or eleven, she found a photograph from the newspaper announcement of their marriage. Since she'd been working for that newspaper at the time, it was a large picture, full length. She looked like Ingrid Bergman and he looked like, yes, Gregory Peck. The article was dated December 7, 1948. This time, she told me how he had wooed her with ideas for all sorts of brilliant inventions, which he had lost interest in prematurely. It was he who had bought my innovative baby bottles—they were right out of "Popeye," the nipples at the end of long hoses. For a long time, we did have a few items around the house that he'd thought were brilliant, for example a record player for 45s—33s, he thought, were going nowhere. Really, though, he preferred the wire recorder to the tape recorder, fidelity and purity over convenience. As for my mother's aspirations as a writer, my father told her that writing was for "second-rate minds"—a novel, for example, could never be as well-written as The Army Field Manual. She seemed to forgive him this prejudice—he was just so compelling.

~

My mother got full custody of me, and I later learned that my father had a habit of driving to St. Louis, then up and down my grandparents' street, hoping to see me. My grandmother was adamant—she sent him away. I remember his arriving only one time. Perhaps I was seven. I was happy to see him in spite of the toilet-training incident. He was still handsome and still had that fictional extra dimension that my now domesticated uncles lacked. I sat on his lap on the front porch of my grandparents' house for a bit while he chatted with my grandfather in the other chair. My grandmother watched from just inside the screen door, and then he walked down to the street and got into his car.

As the years went by, I stopped listening to stories about my father, stopped paying attention to the murmurs of compassion for me as a fatherless girl. I took my uncle to father-daughter night at school and I viewed the fathers of my friends with some skepticism—they seemed tall and vapid, much less dynamic than the mothers. Thinking of my father made me nervous, but I did visit one set of cousins. They were nice; they had a boat; they were well behaved and circumspect. When my uncle, my father's youngest brother, spoke, he made pronouncements rather than jokes. The relationship went nowhere.

The traditional Freudian interpretation of how boys and girls grow into sexuality is based on Greek myths—Oedipus, Electra—but as soon as I read those myths (in 8th Grade, Edith Hamilton's *Mythology*) I sensed that they had nothing to do with me, child of divorce. I did have a complex, though, one I call a Tom Sawyer complex. The great boon of my childhood was my older boy cousins. Jody was almost three years older (born in November, 1946) and Steve was two years older (born in July, 1947). They were dynamic and handsome, and I couldn't take my eyes off them.

My grandparents' house was where we gathered, and my grandparents let the boys run free. My grandfather had grown up a bit wild in the eighteen-nineties and nineteen-hundreds, and though our parents recalled him as very strict, by the time we came along, those days had passed. My grandfather was more interested in playing golf and making jokes, and my grandmother liked baking and gossiping with her friends and neighbors. Their house was comfortable rather than stylish, filled with my grandmother's crocheting and embroidery. If my grandmother ever yelled at us, I don't remember it—the most she ever did was throw her hands into the air and tsk. My grandfather had a hotter temper, but, especially with the boys, he was playful and teasing.

~

The boys climbed on roofs and clambered up trees; they put pennies on the railroad tracks and firecrackers under tin cans. They threw water balloons out the front window of my grandparents' house and they sledded down the steepest hills. They told me things (that I could not, in fact, marry my mother, that everything on the back of a cereal box was true; what a Communist was, that a bird ate seven times its weight every day) and showed me things (a German helmet my uncle Hal brought back from the war with a hole where the shell fragment went through, the difference between a flush and a straight, why you couldn't get a plain hamburger at MacDonald's). They took me places (to the swimming pool, on the RoundUp at the carnival, downtown to the drugstore, to their friends' houses where strip-poker was being played—sort of). They propounded theories, fell asleep in front of late movies, stayed up all night. They were always on the go, but they were always nice to me, maybe nicer to me as their cousin than they would have been if I had been a pesky little sister.

When I was eleven, my mother remarried. My stepfather was portly and kind, too old to have fought in the war. He was far more successful than my father would ever be. What he did in the world—run a small petroleum company, oversee his own children as well as his birth family (he was the oldest, he had a mentally handicapped brother), travel to the Middle East and Venezuela, build a house for my mother, and allow me to buy my first horse—was saintly but not mythic. I am sorry to say that this image of kindliness and success did not form the iconography of my desires.

~

My new stepbrother, Bill, though, was the same age as my cousins, just as good-looking, but with a Catholic twist—he wore his hair in a ducktail with long sideburns, he smoked, and he was always working on the engine of his '56 Chevy. He was as wild as they come, a good girl's dream older brother, who climbed out of the upstairs window when he was grounded, had passionate girlfriends who called and came over day and night, and wore a permanent half-smile, as if the joke of existence was always being freshly told. The Tom Sawyers were a threesome now, brawny and daring, handsome and on the move. If one didn't have a motorcycle, then another one did. The cops, the narrow escapes, the pieces of good luck, the sparkling blue eyes, the irreverent laughter were features of all their adventures.

When I left home to go to college, I was thrilled to discover that Tom Sawyers abounded, and they were neither cousins nor stepbrothers. Just like the boys back home, they had theories and ambitions. If they were not in trouble at the moment, they recently had been in trouble, so they had stories to tell. And just like my cousins, they never even thought of restricting my freedom. There was a girl in my dormitory who told me that her boyfriend wouldn't allow her to come out of her room unless her hair, clothing, and make-up were perfect—slavery. I wore what I wanted to wear and if that included belting my navy surplus jeans with a string, well, I liked the effect. My boyfriends egged me on: Let's do live in a Marxist commune and talk political theory day and night, let's do work in factories or hitchhike to Cape Cod or drive a clunker from New York to St. Louis. Let's go to Europe for a year with only our backpacks. Let's work on an archaeological dig. Let's get lost. Let's do drive the motorcycle a thousand miles (including a mere six hours from St. Louis to Cleveland) and when it gets stolen, let's hitchhike home. Let's live in a ramshackle cabin and forage for heating wood. Let's take the band on the road, let's live on two-hundred and sixty dollars a month, let's drive to California and up the coast to Oregon and back home. Let's get pregnant, let's start a family, what could go wrong?

Eventually, I became gainfully employed and the author of two novels. In the fall of 1983, one night when my husband was away and my daughters had been put to bed, I was unaccountably seized with thoughts of my father. I went to the phone and called information for the town where he lived, and tricked them into giving me his address. The next day I sent him *Barn Blind* and *At Paradise Gate*, my first two novels. I toyed with enclosing a note, decided against it. I didn't know what to say, for one thing, and I wasn't sure how big a step I wanted to take toward acquaintanceship, for another. I was a little relieved when there was no response, and I forgot about it until two months later, when I got a call telling me that my father had died, leaving me his only heir. The caller was a woman my father had known—the circumstances of his passing were mysterious. His friends suspected that he had starved himself to death, as he was prey to numerous anxieties about food. Or, they thought, maybe the hospital had let him die because he refused treatment. His abode was a mobile home, so full of books and pamphlets and other debris that it sagged on its foundation. Did I want to come and go through all the stuff?

I did not. I felt even less about the death of my father than I expected to feel—not only no sense of loss, but also no curiosity. And by the way, a copy of one of my books was found in his bed. He had been reading it the night they took him to the hospital—this struck me as eerie, but not moving. I knew he was a curious man—I gave it no more meaning than that.

In the end, they sent me his car. It was a Datsun, full of little gadgets that plugged into the cigarette-lighter socket. A pair of his flip-flops, very large, was under the seat. The carpeting was sandy. It was as if he had just gotten out of the driver's seat and gone into the house, a patch of Florida in the midst of an Iowa winter. I sold it and bought a station wag-

on, but not before retrieving from the trunk a steel file box full of photographs, some identified and some mysterious—was my father's father
really the youngest of twelve? Really the son of a photographer from Rock
Island, Illinois, who seemed to have taken the photos (including several
of himself tipping his hat to the camera). The possible great-grandfather
had the look—tall, lean, bald, bespectacled. The most mysterious photo
in the box was of a weather-beaten, unsmiling fisherman, taken in Nova
Scotia. Was that where they came from—Glasgow to Canada to Illinois,
hardscrabble all the way, until one of them, the youngest with his arm
around the dog, married into a dynasty?

All the Tom Sawyers settled down. Bill became an accountant. Steve
became an editor. Jody completed his service in the Navy and went to
work organizing large construction projects. They replaced their wild
ways with self-knowledge and responsibility. Their avatars, the ones I
married and had children with, made similar transitions. White haired
now, but still fun and funny. Our children are the same age that I was
when I was glorying in our freedom.

A few years ago, after several decades of not saying much about my
father, my mother remembered another story. They were living in Los
Angeles. My mother was pregnant with me. They were walking down
the street, and he suddenly grabbed her hand and took her into a Catholic Church, where he went up to the altar and knelt down. My mother
was both surprised and alarmed—normally my father was vociferously
opposed to religion, his acknowledged deities being science and technology. But he knelt there for a fairly long time, and seemed to be praying.
When he stood up, he took her to him, and said, "You have been given to
me as my handmaiden."

I can easily imagine my mother, looking like Ingrid Bergman, recoil-
ing from this role. My grandparents hadn't raised their ambitious oldest
daughter to be anyone's handmaiden. But I was about to be born, my
mother had committed herself. Maybe she thought it would all turn out
okay. And it did, though not in a way that anyone could have foreseen.

Because, my father gave me two precious gifts. One of them was his
height. The height was the surprise. All through elementary school, I
was the same size as my friends, sometimes a half an inch taller or short-

er, sometimes a couple of pounds more or less. I fit in with the crowd in the most obvious ways. When they weighed and measured us at the beginning of seventh grade, I was about the same as the other girls, five-foot-one and a hundred pounds. Two years later, I was six feet tall and a hundred and twenty-five pounds. My mother was so worried that she sent me to a growth specialist and he estimated what was to come. He was right—between ninth and tenth grade, I grew another two inches and gained twenty pounds, and then I stopped and awakened from a growth-induced haze. I can't say I minded being so tall. There were models my height—I had a picture of Veruschka on my mirror. She and Vanessa Redgrave were a two-person example for tall girls of how to get ahead. Usually, Veruschka and Vanessa were photographed alone, in a park, on a street or forest road, so that's what I thought tall girls did— they made their way, free and strong.

But my father's gift of absence—I've come to realize that that was even more precious. Because I have children of my own, I have theories and beliefs about raising children, and one of them is that a man who pulled down his daughter's pants to check her hygiene would have had a role for me to play (maybe handmaiden, maybe something else) and a standard for me to live up to. He would have seen me as a reflection of himself, and as his self became more desperate and disorganized, his demands on me would have intensified—the world is full of men who, once they have lost power over their colleagues or their lives, redouble their power over their families. He would have made sure that I knew that I was female, and that females have limited capacities and defined roles. He would have disdained my failure to grasp, say, algebra, and my devotion to the Bobbsey Twins and Nancy Drew. Unlike my grandparents, he would have not been wise enough to leave me alone, and unlike my mother, he would have been idle and looking for a project.

About a year ago, one of my cousins on my father's side said that he, his sisters, and another cousin were coming to California and would like to meet me. I was cool to the idea, but I did think that the metal box of old photos belonged more to them than it did to me.

We met in Los Altos over a long breakfast, and they were not only charming, but affectionate and supportive of one another. I admired them. They had, indeed, suffered the difficult childhoods that my grand-mother had been determined to protect me from, but they had also ben-efited from years of therapy and years of scrupulous honesty. And they loved my father, who had befriended them and saved them when their own parents, his sister and her husband, failed them. To them, he was kind, good-natured, and funny. And my cousin told me a story about visiting my father in Florida, where he was living. They were all in their teens. One day, he took them to his favorite beach, and after they laid out their towels and umbrellas he went over to a tree and set his loaf-ers at the base. Into the heels of his loafers, he put a few nuts, then he called out. I don't remember the names he used, but let's say Lucy and Desi—something amusing like that. Pretty soon, a pair of gray squirrels appeared in the upper reaches of the tree, looked at everyone. My father backed away, and the squirrels skittered down the tree, ate the nuts in the shoes, and also a few more that he gave them by hand. A nice man.

I enjoyed this story, but even so, I don't feel that I missed anything. I know from my own experience as a parent that sometimes it takes disap-pointment and heartbreak, as well as a little distance, to disabuse you of your cherished notions of who you are, who your child is, and how you might "mold" him or her. When my father knew me, he seems to have been both confused and very sure of himself, a fearsome combination.

The Tom Sawyers made chaos and distracted my mother, stepfather, grandparents, aunts, and uncles. This gave me the private space of being a comparatively good girl, where I thought my own thoughts and came up with my own ideas. A girl who is overlooked has a good chance of not learning what it is she is supposed to do. A girl who is free can grow up free of preconceptions. Sometimes, from the outside, my work and my life look daring, but I am not a daring person. I am just a person who was never taught what not to try.

My dad and I first read Patricia Henley's work in The Atlantic, so when she was teaching at nearby Purdue University, I invited her to my university to give a reading. We've been friends ever since. I treasure, in particular, Patricia's collected stories Friday Night at Silver Star, which I gave to my dad for Christmas one year. Her essay here focuses on a time when, as a young girl, Patricia waits for her father before Midnight Mass. In fact, it feels very much as if the author waits for him still, and they are forever in the present tense of this piece. Patricia said her father worked away from home when she was a child, and, consequently, she does not have many photos of him. In this family photo with her brother Michael, and sister Nancy, a young Patricia stands in their front yard, to the right of her father. She's not sure about the small child peeking out the window behind them. Patricia's friend, Elizabeth Stuckey-French, took the recent photo of Patricia outside a bar in Oxford, Mississippi.

Christmas From Now On

WE LIVE IN Terre Haute. I am standing outside our house on 20th Street in my new circle skirt—shiny and brown and gold. A delicate light blue design is woven into it. A nylon net petticoat attaches to the underside. My sweater is blue. I wear clunky snow boots and a paisley scarf, what my aunts from the old country call a babushka, ties under my chin. A heavy snow coat completes my ensemble, but nothing can spoil the joy of that circle skirt. It is not a hand-me-down.

I am waiting for my father to come out. We are going to Midnight Mass together. There is a full moon or almost full. The snow sparkles. I am eight years old and for the first time in my life I am fully aware that I am brimming with wonder. Before Mass we pull up to Johnny Rowe's Liquor Store on South 7th Street. I am allowed to go inside. Johnny and my father and my mother grew up on the south side, in the 'twenties and 'thirties. They went off to war during World War Two, which is not so far away in time. This is 1955. Johnny pulls a bottle of liquor from beneath the counter and he and my father drink shots and talk. I am content to be in my circle skirt among the shiny bottles of liquor, listening to the sound of their murmuring male conversation. When we leave the store, the light goes out, and Johnny snaps down the blind over the door.

After Mass, we drive to my grandmother Cowgill's two-room house on an alley between 5th Street and 6th Street. She answers the door clutching a robe shut, her hair thin and gray. She is delighted to be a part of the surprise. Presents for me and my five brothers and sisters are cached in her little house. We are each allowed to request one present.

Mine is a real miniature sewing machine. There are also gift-wrapped bundles of flannel pajamas that my aunts have sewn for us. My father and I load the presents into our car and we drive the icy streets and when we arrive home, the tree in the picture window shines bits of colored light on the snow.

Everyone is asleep except my mother. Our house is very small. Our parents sleep in what was intended to be the dining room. My brother David's crib is near their bed. We are oh-so-quiet. It would be a disaster if anyone woke up—everyone still believes in Santa but me. My mother sits at the kitchen table with a glass of beer and saltines and cream cheese in front of her. They drink Sterling Beer, which is bottled in quarts. It is sentimental for my father. When he was stationed in Manila at the end of the war, he and his buddies opened up a shipment from the States and the crates contained Sterling Beer, made in Terre Haute. She pours a beer for my father.

We put out the presents. My mother doesn't like to do it. She's too tired to do it. I get into my PJs, as my father called them. I am too excited to go to sleep. I read by flashlight as my sisters Nancy and Mary Ruth sleep beside me in a double bed. Again, I listen to the murmur of adult voices. What my parents say doesn't register with me, but I like the sound.

I wish that I had listened more intently. My sense of wonder did not extend to them, not really. It was about the moon and the snow and that blue design in the skirt. I wish I still had that circle skirt. I wish I could talk to Johnny Rowe's children or grandchildren to see what they remember. I wish my parents had lived to see their children happy in their lives. If wishes were horses, beggars would ride, my mother used to say. My father died 25 years ago on December 23rd.

My father and I were both impressed with
Bliss Broyard's confidence and talent when we
first heard her speak at The Conference for the
Book in Oxford, Mississippi. At that time, the
campus statue of James Meredith had recently
been defaced and boys in pick-up trucks were
driving around the square with confederate
flags flying. Bliss was remarkably honest and
forthright about all the aspects of race. She
joked, laughed, and spoke eloquently about her
own bi-racial heritage that day at my father's
alma mater, the University of Mississippi, still
so fraught with racial tensions. A version of
Bliss's essay here is also included as a chapter
in her memoir One Drop: My Father's Hidden Life—A Story of Race and Family
Secrets. Melodie McDaniels took the recent
picture of Bliss. The other family pictures are
from Bliss's personal collection.

the sheets like a security blanket. We both shake our heads and mourn the shortage of decent young men out there these days. We both secretly believe that my charms belong to another era, a better and more refined world, his world. In his day, no doubt, I would have been a smash. At least this is my fantasy of what he is thinking.

Where do I meet these men? Mostly they are my father's friends. And since he died six years ago at the age of seventy, I have been transfigured from being my father's daughter into a young woman friend of these men in my own right.

Vincent, the oldest of my father's friends, lives in Greenwich Village, still carrying on the same sort of life he and my father led when they were young there together. There is Davey, the youngest of my father's friends, who over the years was his summer playmate for touch football and volleyball and beach paddle and who is now a father himself. Mike was the closest to my dad, serving as his primary reader during his long career as a writer and book critic. When Mike and I talk on the phone, he seems to miss my dad as much as I do. Finally there is Ernest, my father's most contentious friend. My dad used to say that he had to befriend Ernest, otherwise Ernest wouldn't have any friends at all, although I think he secretly took pride in being able to tolerate his pal's notorious crankiness.

Though the ages of these men span more than twenty-five years and they come from a variety of backgrounds, I think of them as natives of a singular world, a world belonging to the past and a particular place: Greenwich Village, where my father's friendships with these men—if not actually born there—were consummated. Like any world, it has its own language and culture. There is a hip, playful rhythm to the conversation and an angle of the observations that makes everything appear stylized, either heroically or calamitously. In this world, folks don't walk, they swagger; they don't talk, they declaim. Women are crazy, beautiful, impeccably bred, tragic. They are rarely boring. No one had much money, but happiness, as my father liked to say, could be bought cheaply. A man's status is determined by his wit and intelligence and, most of all, his successes with women. A woman's status is a product of her beauty and her novelty, not a fresh kind of novelty because that would imply innocence—and you couldn't have too much innocence if you were with this crowd—but the kind of novelty that places you on the cutting edge of things. To be described as modern is a high compliment.

Of course, nostalgia has smoothed out these memories to make them uniform and sweet, and the world that I know from my father's stories is pristinely preserved in my mind as though it were contained in one of those little glass spheres that fills with snow when you shake it. I imagine, though, that by stepping in I can unsettle this scene with my presence and make it come back to life; then I will find a world that is more cozy than the one I live in, a world that is as reassuring and familiar as those winter idylls captured under glass.

~

Vincent has lived in the same apartment on Perry Street for over forty years, and as I walk up the five flights to visit him, the years slip away behind me. Everyone lived in four- and five-floor walk-ups in the old days, Vincent has told me. All cold-water flats.

~

"Your father and I once went to a party at Anaïs Nin's, and I rang the bell and flew up the five flights as fast I could. Your dad had briefed me that Anaïs gauged her lovers' stamina and virility by how long it took them to reach her floor without puffing."

This is a story I heard from my father, though many of the stories Vincent tells me about the old days I have not. Those are the ones I have come to hear.

Vincent's apartment is decorated with things collected from his years traveling the world as a cruise director on ships. Geometric Moroccan tiles and bits of Persian carpet and copper-colored patches of stucco cover every inch of the walls. Through a beaded curtain is his bedroom, where tapestried form a canopy over a daybed heaped with Turkish pillows. The tub located in the entrance hall is concealed by day with a sort of shiny green lamina which, when you gaze upon it, is reminiscent of an ancient Roman bath. Also off the entrance hall is the toilet, concealed only with a thin strip of fabric. Once, after I'd used it, Vincent asked me if I noticed how the base was loose. I hadn't.

"Well, it's been like that for almost forty years," he explained. "Once I loaned the apartment to your dad so he could take a girl he'd met some-where private. Afterward, the toilet was a little rocky. I asked him what the hell he was doing in there, and he told me they were taking in the view." Vincent took me back into the bathroom and pointed out the Em-pire State Building, barely visible between two other buildings. "I won't have the toilet fixed," he said, "because I love being reminded of that sto-ry." I headed down the stairs with Vincent's laughter trailing behind me.

Should a daughter know such things about her father? Should she have an image of him that she must rush past, one that is a little too vivid and too private to be promptly forgotten? It is easy to become embar-rassed by such stories, to let my own paternal memories sweep them under some psychic rug, but my father's past is like a magnet I can't pull myself away from. This is my history too, I argue to myself. I've had my own sexual adventures, my own versions of making love on a shaky toi-let, an aspect of my life that I have been sure to share with my father's friends. I have paraded a host of boyfriends past them, have brought along young men to their apartments, or out to dinner, or for an evening of dancing. When the fellow gets up to fetch another round of drinks, I might lean back in my chair and watch him walk off.

"So," I'll say offhandedly, "I'm not sure I'm going to keep this one. He's bright and successful too, but maybe not quite sexy enough."

"You are your father's daughter," the man answers, laughing, which is just what I'd hoped to hear.

Of course, with my own contemporaries I am never so cavalier. I have argued on behalf of honesty and respect in relationships. I have claimed to believe in true love. I will even admit that I am looking for my own version of a soulmate (although I can confess to this only in an ironic tone of voice, all too aware of its sentimental implications). Nevertheless, this desire runs in me alongside a desire for a successful writing career, children, and a house in the country with dogs and flower beds and weekend guests visiting from the city—a lot like the kind of life my father left New York to build with my mother, a move that shocked many of his friends.

All of my father's friends share a boyish quality, one that is often de-lightful with its playfulness and vitality but that contains an underside too: a sort of adolescent distrust of any threat to the gang. A silent pact was made never to grow up. And though I wouldn't be here if my father, at the age of forty, hadn't managed finally to break free of this hold to marry my mother, I carry on this pact with his friends in spite of myself.

Some of these men eventually did marry and have children now themselves, have daughters who one day, no doubt, they hope to see married. If I would let them, they would probably wish for me a similar simple and happy fate. But I don't want to be seen in the same light as their daughters. Just as they knew my father as a friend first, rather than a dad or husband, I want them to view me as their friend rather than my father's daughter. Otherwise, I would never learn anything about him at all. I search out these men to discover the man behind my father, that is who I've come to meet.

Besides all this, these men are exceptional, and to be accepted by them my aspirations must be sophisticated, more rarefied and imaginative than my dreams of a husband and house in the country.

Once out for dinner with the contentious friend, Ernest, we argued about the value of monogamy in relationships. Over the years, Ernest has taken me to some of New York's finest restaurants. Everywhere the maître d's know him by name, probably because he is the worst kind of customer: he demands special dishes which he then complains about, is rude to the waiters, and usually leaves a shabby tip. I put up with his behavior for the same reason a parent puts up with a misbehaving child in a restaurant—to challenge Ernest would only egg him on. What I had forgotten was that in conversation he is the same way.

His expression grew increasingly pitying and snide while he listened to my argument for monogamy, which—best as I can recall—went something like this: monogamy in a relationship engendered trust and trust was the only means to a profound intimacy, not the kind of combustible sexual intimacy that Ernest favored (I added pointedly), but the kind that requires a continual commitment of faith, not unlike the effort to believe in God. And the rewards of this type of intimacy—the compassion, the connection—were infinitely greater. Trust was the only route to a person's soul!

I was only about twenty-five at the time, and while my line of reasoning was hardly original and smacked somewhat of piteous posturing, I remember being pleased that I was able to unfold my rationale in a composed, yet passionate manner. Sometimes when I was talking with my father or his friends, I would grab panic-struck for a word only to find it out of my reach. By the end of my speech, Ernest looked amused. He dabbed at his mouth with his linen napkin and sat back in his chair. "I had no idea you were so bourgeois," he said. "How in the world did your father manage to raise such a bourgeois daughter?"

"Bourgeois" was one of those words that floated through the air of my childhood, occasionally landing on a dinner guest or neighbor or the parent of one of my friends. I wasn't sure when I was young what it meant, but I didn't miss how efficiently the term dismissed the person as though he or she had been made to vanish into thin air.

For weeks after that dinner with Ernest, I carried on an internal debate with myself about the value of monogamy and, more fundamentally, wondered from what source I had formed my opinions on it: Was this something that my father believed, if perhaps not in practice, then in theory? Was I falling into a conventional, clichéd way of thinking? Or did I actually believe the stance I'd taken with Ernest for the very reason that it was not my father's position. This was not the first time I had tried to locate myself behind his shadow.

Although my father was a critic of books by profession, he could be counted on to have an opinion on just about anything. At a gathering back at my house following his cremation, I sat around the dining room table, reminiscing with a group of family friends. We began listing all the things my father liked, and after one trip around the table, we ran out of things to say. Then someone offered up "thick arms on a woman," and someone else jumped in with "kung fu movies and cream sauces," starting us on a long and lively conversation about all the things my father disliked. What surprised me during this discussion (besides the welcome relief it provided to that bleak day) was how many of my own opinions were either my father's—or the exact opposite. I remember thinking that rather than having a unique personality, I was merely an assemblage of reactions, a mosaic of agreements and disagreements with my dad—a feeling that has reoccurred intermittently since. I keep hoping to find the line where he stops and I begin.

~

Vincent keeps scrapbooks. He has scrapbooks from his travels, scrapbooks from his days in Cuba where he first encountered the Afro-Cuban music that became his and my father's passion, scrapbooks from his youth with my dad in New York City. Sometimes before heading out to dinner or to a club to hear some salsa band, Vincent and I will have a drink in his apartment—we always drink champagne or sherry—and flip through these books. One evening I pointed out the pictures of people I didn't recognize. Vincent became irritated when I didn't know their names. Machito. Milton. Willie.

You must know who these people are! How can you have not heard these stories? You should have paid more attention to your father when he was alive, he scolded. Are you listening to what I am telling you? Your father was a beautiful man! He lived a beautiful life!

Nostalgia made us quiet when we were out on the street. Vincent was nostalgic for a past that seemed in danger of being forgotten, and me—I was nostalgic for a history that both was and wasn't mine.

Vincent had worked as a tour guide on and off for most of his life and he walks very fast. That evening, I let him lead me around by my elbow. He rushed me across the intersections, hurrying me along in a variety of foreign languages: vite, rapido, quick-quick-quick. He began to talk as we twisted and turned through the labyrinth of streets, pointing out various buildings and explaining their significance: there was an illegal nightclub here where we went to hear Machito drum, you had to know the code word to be let inside; this was where your dad had his bookstore and Milton and Willie hung out talking, talking, talking about books. We turned a corner to arrive on a quiet, tree-lined street. He pointed out the top floor of a brownstone. Your dad lived there for a while.

He had a girlfriend in the next house over, and rather than walk down the five flights to the street and then up another five flights to her apartment, he would climb across the roof to her window like a cat burglar.

I pointed out the steep pitch of the roofs and said that my dad must have really liked the girl to put himself at such risk. "Oh, he wasn't afraid of risks," Vincent answered knowingly, and I had no idea at that moment whether this assessment was true or not, a realization that brought tears to my eyes. After a moment, I remarked quietly that men didn't do that anymore—climb over rooftops for a woman—at least none that I'd ever met.

～

Only when a parent dies does it seem that a child gains a right to know that parent's life. While my father was alive, his life, as it should have, belonged to him. Besides, we were too involved with each other for me to step back and gain some objective view. But now that his life contains both a beginning and an end, it seems possible to shape some complete picture. I can't help regretting, though, that so much of my information must come secondhand. Perhaps Vincent is right. I should have paid more attention to my father when he was alive. Perhaps if I had asked him more questions about his past, I could have learned these things from him myself. Perhaps if he had lived longer, if we had moved on from being father and daughter to being friends, we would have arrived at some understanding of each other, or rather I would have arrived at some understanding of him that would allow me to incorporate such anecdotes like a splash of color into the portrait I held of him rather than their changing the portrait completely.

But when my father was alive, I was too busy trying to figure out what he thought of me—another question that I now lay at the feet of his friends, as though he had handed off his judgment like a baton in a relay race.

At another, earlier dinner with Ernest, I watched him as he studied my face. I hadn't seen him in a few years, and I knew that since our last encounter I had evolved from looking like a girl to looking like a woman.

"You've grown up to be attractive," he finally decided. "For a while there it seemed that you wouldn't. Your features were so sharp and you were always frowning. You should keep your hair long, though. It softens your face."

～

I wish I could say that if my father had been present he would have reprimanded Ernest for this cold comment, but I know that he wouldn't have. Over the years I came to learn that being my father didn't limit his ability to assess me critically. He had opinions about my hairstyle, he picked out the clothes that he thought best brought out what he referred to as my "subtle appeal"; he noticed anytime I gained a few pounds. And while I realize now that in his world a woman was as powerful as her beauty, that doesn't lessen the hurt caused by such impartial opinions.

At times with these friends I have felt like an impostor or a spy, trying to lure them into a conversation where they will unwittingly reveal some assessment of me my father had shared with them, or that, since they knew him and his tastes and were able to observe us with the clarity of a spectator's view, they will reveal some insight about our relationship that remained hidden from me. On occasion, I have just asked point-blank what it is I want to know.

Recently I had a wedding to go to in the Long Island town where my dad's youngest friend, Davey, now lives with his wife, Kate, and their three teenage children. Davey has been in my life for as long as I can remember. And my father was in Davey's life as long as Davey can remember. They first met in the summer of 1950 on Fire Island. Davey was a chubby, cheerful boy of four, and my father was a trim, athletic bachelor of thirty. It's hard for me to picture the start of this friendship; nevertheless, during the ensuing summers on Fire Island, the man and boy became friends. They would remain close friends until my father's death. Davey spoke at my father's memorial service, recalling how when he was sixteen he helped move my parents from one five-story walk-up in Greenwich Village to another a few blocks away. Theirs was a friendship sealed by carrying books, he said. Throughout my childhood, Davey visited us each summer on Martha's Vineyard, and he and my father would write in the mornings (Davey eventually became a successful playwright) and then the two men would head to the beach for an afternoon of touch football or beach paddle, or they would just stroll and talk.

During this recent visit, Davey and I strolled on the beach ourselves and talked about our writing. He had been feeling discouraged recently about the unsteady progress of his career. I had just finished a graduate school degree in creative writing and was nervous about reentering the world with this new label of writer. We had walked a short distance when Davey mentioned that his back was bothering him and asked if we could sit down. We lay on the sand, a bit damp from the previous night's rain, and looked out over the choppy ocean.

A few days before, TWA flight 800 had crashed not far from where we lay, and earlier that day bits of fuselage and an airline drinking cup were found on a neighboring beach. Groups of people searched along the shoreline—airline officials, family members, curiosity seekers. Davey talked about his own kids, how well they were all doing, how different they were from one another and from him and Kate. It was clear in listening to him how much he respected and loved them, but I was surprised at how objectively he was able to assess their talents and weaknesses. I asked him what my father thought of me.

"Well, of course he loved you," he said, and then looked away toward the beachcombers. I could see that my question had upset him. Perhaps he was wondering if his children would ever ask such a thing. I was searching too, there on that beach, but my debris was not the result of some tragic, sudden accident; rather, my father had died slowly from the common illness of cancer when I was twenty-three, an age when most children are letting go of their parents in order to establish their own independence. I was lost somewhere between missing my father and trying to move past him. Davey looked back at me and said again with a surprising urgency in his voice that I must believe my father loved me. And I do, but in an abstract way, believing in my father's love the same way that I believe that all parents must love their children. What I am searching for is the shape of that love. These men are bright men, observant and persuasive. They are my father's friends, after all. I want them to make elegant arguments, peppered with indisputable examples and specific instances of the how and why and where of that love.

When all this searching makes me too weary, I call Mike. He is a psychologist and a writer too. Besides his interest and insight into human nature, he has most of Western literature for reference at his fingertips, which makes him wonderful to talk with. Over the years, even when he and my father lived in separate states, my dad would read to him the first drafts of almost everything he wrote. I can remember my father stretched out on his bed for an hour at a time, laying in the dark room, telephone in hand, chatting with his pal. Their talk was filled with elegant phrasing, animated starts and stops, black humor, and the sort of conversational shorthand one develops with an old, close friend. When signing off, my father would say, "All right, man, work hard and I will too."

I called Mike up recently with some gossip about the size of an advance for a book written by one of his colleagues. Mike is working on a new book and with one kid about to enter college and another following closely behind, he's hoping for a sizable advance himself. Before long we have moved on to the subject of his new book: how difficult and necessary it is to console yourself to the disappointment of life and the world. Doesn't scream best-seller, I joked, since no one likes to admit to this truth. I talked about how this disappointment often feels like a large white elephant in the corner of the room that no one will acknowledge, and how that denial makes you feel like you're crazy. Given the choice between feeling crazy and feeling disappointed, I don't understand why more people don't opt for the latter.

"You're exactly right, Blissie," Mike agreed. "That's just what I am trying to get at."

I was stretched out on my own bed now, watching the afternoon shadows lengthen down my wall. Talking with Mike was like walking down a familiar path that leads toward home. Here is the oak tree; around the bend is the stone wall. Talking with Mike was almost like talking with my father.

Both men shared a predilection for cutting through hypocrisy and looking past denial. They viewed the world with a bittersweet affection, appreciating the shadows of life's events as much as the events themselves. I once asked my dad why all the great stories were sad ones. Most good stories are mysteries, he said. The author is like a detective trying to get to the bottom of some truth, and happiness is a mystery that can come apart in your hands when you try to unravel it. Sadness, on the other hand, is infinitely more resilient. Scrutiny only adds to its depth and weight.

I don't ask Mike what my father thought of me. Mike's a shrink, after all, and he knows that I'm the only one who could answer that question.

What I realize when I am with the older men in my life is that the older man I want most is my father, and no amount of colorful anecdotes, no amount of recreating the kind of outings he might have had with his pals, can conjure him up in a satisfying way. Grief, like sadness, is too resilient for such casual stand-ins.

After I finished talking with Mike, I remained lying on my bed. Out-side my window it was dark, and I hadn't bothered to turn on the light. I was thinking about how it is an odd time to get to know your father, after he has died. And it is odd to get to know him through his friends. I wondered why I should assume that they knew him any better than I did. If some aspects of his life before I knew him were mysterious to me, certainly the reverse was true as well: there are parts that only I know about. Would his friends be surprised to learn that when I was a baby, after my bath, my father would carry me around the house seated naked in the palm of his hand, holding me high up over his head like a waiter with a tray? Or that he would spend afternoons tossing my brother and me, torpedo-like, from the corner of the bedroom onto my parents' bed, the far wall piled high with pillows? Before each toss, he would inspect our teeth to make sure they were clenched so we wouldn't bit our tongues. Would his friends be surprised to know that when I was in college he would sometimes call me up in the middle of the day because he was feeling lonely in the empty house? Or when standing over him in his hospital bed, my throat chocked with all the questions I realized there wasn't time to ask and his mouth filled with a pain beyond articulation, he suddenly seized my hand and raised it to his lips? "You're my daughter," he assured me. "You're my daughter."

When my father and I went out dancing together, we didn't dance the old dances, as Vincent and I tried to do when we went to hear a salsa band. Vincent had great hopes for my talent as a dancer, since my father was a good one, but as he attempted to lead me across the floor, I kept over-anticipating his moves. The slightest pressure of his hand would send me off in a new direction.

My dad relied on me to introduce him to the new music, the new dances. Competitive as always, he wanted to be sure that he could keep up with the times. In our living room, the rug pulled back and the coffee table pushed aside, I blasted "Word Up" by Cameo. I led the way across the smooth wooden floor, shouting out the lyrics, my hands waving in the air, my hips bumping left and right. I can still hear his encouragement as he followed along behind me. With my eyes closed, in the quiet of my dark bedroom, his hoots rise out of the silence.

49

When I read "Secrets of the Sun" in Southern Indiana Review, I immediately contacted Mako Yoshikawa to ask if I could include her essay in this collection. Here, we witness the Japanese work ethic in overdrive, and perhaps, get a better understanding of Karōshi, or death from overwork. Mako's father, Shoichi Yoshikawa, was an internationally recognized physicist, but he was so absent from her life, Mako is forced to play psychological detective in order to figure out who he really was, and, as a result, perhaps better know herself. After her father's death in 2010, Mako began writing essays with a view toward completing a memoir. Her father is the beautiful child standing on the chair.

MAKO YOSHIKAWA

Secrets of the Sun

M Y FATHER'S memorial service was held in
December of 2010, in a Hyatt hotel on the
strip mall–lined highway that connects the prettiest and most idyllic of
all college towns, Princeton, to the rest of the world. Outside, where a
parking lot went on almost as far as the eye could see, a cold fitful rain
fell. Inside, the air was musty and stagnant, and despite valiant stabs at
elegance—a red carpet, an oversized chandelier, and a mirror covering
one wall—the gathering place looked all too clearly like what it was,
an overcrowded multi-purpose conference room. My father, Shoichi Yoshikawa, had been an eminent physicist and an international leader in fusion energy research in America and his native Japan, and he had worked
at his Princeton University lab for more than forty years before being
pushed into early retirement in 2000. But he was arrogant and disagree-
able, famously bad at working with others, and my sisters and I considered ourselves lucky that as many as fifty-odd mourners—neighbors,
friends, and colleagues, as well as our mother, who had flown in from
England for the weekend—had turned out for the event.

On the center table, alongside a few flower arrangements, we had
placed two framed photos. Shoichi had died at seventy-six, and in his
last decade he had been skinny in all the wrong places and bloated everywhere else. His gaze was unfocused and his hands shook; although he
had inherited a fortune as well as a parking lot in Tokyo from his father
in Japan, he hated to spend money, and tended to dress in clothes he had
bought by the boxful from the flea markets he loved to frequent—ill-
fitting, cheaply made shirts and slacks from a wide assortment of eras

and styles. In the first photo, which was taken about a year before his death, the unhealthy color and puffiness of his face has been magically transformed into the rosy glow and plumpness of prosperity. He wears a beautiful navy suit jacket, a crisp white shirt, and a red power tie, and his white hair is glossy and full; he gazes up and to his right, serenely, a small smile on his lips.

In the second photo—unearthed by us from the chaos of his home, the same cramped, University-owned ranch house we had grown up in—he is maybe three years old. Dressed in a kimono, he stands on a chair, clutching its back for support. His hair is cut in a bowl shape; his ears stick almost straight out; his eyes are wide-set and alert.

You can see the quality of his kimono in the fineness of its design, which is abstract and swirling; the seat cushion he stands on is covered in rich brocade and would do an emperor's posterior proud.

He had had a long-term heart condition, but his death, a month earlier, was unexpected, and I had been taken aback at the thickness of the fog I found myself in afterward—indeed, at the fact I was in a fog at all. In his younger days my father had been capable of charm and even sweetness, but even back then he had a vicious streak that could catch you out, and over the years he became increasingly violent and abusive at home. In 1982, when I was 15, my mother finally left him, moving my sisters and me out during one of his long trips to Japan, and after that I saw him rarely.

He was a manic depressive, but unhappy beyond his depressive spells. Despite some professional success, during his last three decades he had been deeply, poisonously aware that what he had done was a fraction of what he, a man of singular gifts, could have achieved. By contrast, the failures of his personal life—his turbulent first marriage to my mother; his second, marginally less dysfunctional marriage to a woman who had died; the long string of short-term girlfriends, lovers, and flings that had followed, and his all-but-nonexistent relationship with his daughters—seemed to disturb him little, if at all.

By the day of the memorial I knew that the fog I was in could not be grief. Pity, more like, along with confusion and probably guilt. My father was someone I had loved and feared as a child, hated as a teen, and foresworn as a young adult. In my early thirties, when my first novel had finally been accepted for publication and I was brimming over with good will to all, I contacted him and we reconnected, eventually falling into the schedule—cards at birthdays and Christmas, and lunch or dinner every three to four years—we maintained until his death. He was over 60 by then, with most of the arrogance and fight beaten out of him, and as we built up a small store of stilted conversations about science fiction, his latest travails with women, and the quality of the Japanese food we were eating, I began to see him as more broken than monstrous.

Now, in my mid-forties, I was close to my mother, secure in my friendships, fulfilled by my writing and teaching career and, after a number of failed relationships and many years of being single, finally happily married. I would not miss my father, I told myself at the memorial, nor would I wish him back. And I was right about that—but it was grief, even though it was months before I could recognize it, even though I reach for the subjunctive now to name its source: the man he could have been, a relationship he and I might have had.

Seven of my father's colleagues had asked to eulogize him, and eager to fill seats, my sisters and I had said yes to all of them. At the service they stood up one by one, aging men in crumpled suits, and spoke with almost palpable nostalgia of the same heady time: the nineteen-sixties and 'seventies, when their lab, a top center for fusion research, overflowed with bright young men fired by the conviction that the discovery of a limitless, non-polluting energy source lay within their grasp. And in that company, they said, Shoichi Yoshikawa stood out—the best, most daring and dazzling thinker of them all, and the most idealistic, too. One speaker said that while they had all cared about the hope that fusion offered, my father's commitment and passion had put them to shame. According to another, in the early sixties Shoichi had turned down a career in the budding field of computers, despite his certainty that it was the wave of the future, because he'd been equally sure he could create a clean energy source and had deemed that the more vital step for mankind.

I felt a pang—I had never thought to ask my father why he had chosen fusion or, for that matter, physics—and I wondered, too, if the speakers felt bitter as well as wistful about the years they had devoted to their cause. But sitting in the front row in a good black jacket with my hair pinned up, my mother's mother's locket at my throat and my own carefully crafted eulogy clenched tight in my hands, I could pay little heed to their words. I knew few specifics about my father's work. If I had visited the lab in its heyday, I could not recall it. I did poorly in high school algebra, a failing for which he punished me with two pale blue knots along my jawline and a bump the size of a sand dollar on the back of my head; and I grew up to be a novelist with a ham-fisted grasp of numbers: when I asked about his research, he greeted my questions with impatience laced with contempt. What I did know was that my father had hungered for glory, and that the Nobel Prize was the goal around which he built his life. His colleagues were taking advantage of the eulogist's license to exaggerate and, even, manufacture positive attributes, as I, the last speaker, was about to do.

I had been with my mother and sisters through the weekend of the memorial. Afterward we dispersed: my mother back to England, where she lives with my stepfather, and my sisters to California, where they work—one as a yoga teacher with a thriving practice, the other as a director in a high-powered internet company—and raise families. I stayed on the East Coast, where I live with my husband, a filmmaker, and teach and write.

Through the winter I could not sleep, relax, or think well. It was well into spring before I understood there might be a way out. Part of what was bothering me was that my father had never cared about my sisters and me, not in comparison to his work. But what if his colleagues had been telling the truth? If I could believe that my father's devotion to physics and fusion had been born out of hope and idealism rather than a desire for the Nobel Prize, the memory of his indifference, I thought, might trouble me less. Surely it was one thing to be thrown over for the possibility of personal glory, and quite another to be sacrificed for the world and all its future generations.

~

While writing my father's eulogy, I had asked my mother for anecdotes that would convey his commitment to physics, and she had told me, her laughter shaky, how he had gotten out of bed in the middle of their wedding night to work on an equation. At the memorial I retold the story, concluding with the one completely truthful line in the speech: "That's a man who loved his work."

That the man's devotion to his wife fell a little short—that the anecdote hinted at the divorce that lay in their future—I left for the audience to infer. In 1952, when she met Shoichi at her parents' lavish summerhouse at the foot of the Nagano mountains, my mother was a nose-to-the-grindstone high-school student who had never seen the point of boys. Shoichi was a striking eighteen-year-old, tall with a shock of black hair and enormous, arresting eyes, but she, just sixteen, already prized intellectual and creative work above all else, and it was to his brilliance that she lost her heart. She had fallen hard, and although not much to look at she was willing to do what she needed to get him: While he pursued a doomed relationship with another girl, she wrote long, eloquent letters, and when that relationship ended she was there for him. She followed him to America, where they married, and she stayed with him for twenty-two years—through a series of breakdowns, his diagnosis of manic depression, his slide into alcoholism, a long string of professional disappointments, his bursts of rage and violence, and his envy of her successes as an artist and a writer—because a part of her never stopped loving him, but also because she never gave up on his potential as a physicist.

Yet when, soon after leaving him, she began to regret the decades she had wasted, it was his career that she blamed. In my mid-twenties I was a graduate student in literature, perpetually at loose ends, with a hankering, as yet unacknowledged even to myself, to write novels instead of analyzing them. Having located what I thought was the source of my restlessness, I turned to my mother one Christmas break for advice. Plain as a teenager, she had turned into a fine-boned beauty, and after the divorce, with her pick of men, she had found and married a well-read, warm-hearted international executive, a true soul mate. She was painting in her studio in the dramatic modernist house in Princeton they had bought and decorated, only a few miles but a far cry from my father's, and when I confessed my anxiety about not being able to find a man, she didn't take her gaze off the canvas.

"You'll be fine, with or without someone," she said. "Just don't marry a physicist."

~

Growing up, my father seemed destined for greatness. Born in Tokyo in 1935, he showed unusual intelligence and curiosity as an infant. His parents, people of culture and discernment as well as wealth, were descended from samurai, minor aristocracy; their sprawling house in Tokyo, filled with art and music, survived the war intact. Young Shoichi was the eldest son and his family, nursemaids, and tutors doted on him; his father, a scientist, and his grandfather, a doctor, encouraged and nurtured his interest in science and math. In grade school Shoichi was cheerful and outgoing, well liked by both boys and girls despite an increasingly intimidating intellect. His head seemed too large for his body and he was disarmingly bad at sports. His grin, bright and sudden, took up his whole face.

He received the highest score in the country on the qualifying exam for Tokyo University, the most prestigious college in Japan. There he garnered awards, honors and, finally, the offer of a full fellowship to MIT. When he decided to accept it, a couple of Japan's most prominent newspapers ran articles about the "brain drain" that was stealing minds such as his to America. In three years he completed his doctorate with a dissertation on plasmas—clouds of disassociated atoms, sometimes called the fourth state of matter after solids, liquids, and gases—and in 1961, at the age of twenty-seven, he began working at Princeton University's Plasma Physics Laboratory.

At PPL physicists, engineers, and technicians endeavored to create energy through nuclear fusion, a process that took as its model the sun and the stars. In contrast to fission, which split the atom, fusion would merge the nuclei of two hydrogen atoms to form a single nucleus of helium. The new nucleus would weigh less than the original two, and the difference in the mass would be released as energy. Whereas fission required the mining of uranium as well as massive, lethally unstable processing plants to enrich it, fusion would need only hydrogen isotopes extracted from seawater, an essentially inexhaustible supply. It would not result in pollutants, nuclear waste, or greenhouse gases, and its production facilities would not hold materials that could lead to an environmental disaster.

My father worked on what were and still are fusion's two central conundrums: how to produce and sustain the high temperatures, more than a million degrees Celsius, necessary for a fusion reaction, and how to safely contain the reaction once it was underway. His lab was founded in the belief that the solution to these problems lay in plasma, which out of all the states of matter allows atomic particles to move the fastest, thus increasing the chances of fusion occurring. In the nineteen-sixties, scientists and engineers were constructing different fusion reactor machines around the world, and in one of them, the Russian-designed tokamak, magnetic fields held the hot plasma inside a bottle shaped like a donut, which would accommodate the particles' movement while containing it at the same time. According to the obituary submitted by the lab, my father had been among the first in the country to appreciate the advantages of the tokamak concept, championing the construction of one at PPL as well as another in Japan. He also designed and led investigations to figure out why plasma had been lost in earlier models, and in 1968, at the age of thirty-three, he invented a new kind of magnetic bottle, the Spherator, to contain fusion plasmas.

Solid achievements, if not the greatness his childhood seemed to presage. Yet they came at a steep price. Overwhelmed by stress, my father drank to excess. Working long hours on little sleep, as on his wedding night, he wore himself out. Acutely aware in his twenties and thirties that physics is a young man's game, he spoke often about blowing his brains out before he turned forty. He resented and, at times, hated us, his family, for taking up his time and preventing him from becoming the scientist he could have been. Every October for years, long after fusion had been widely deemed a bust, he was in a torment of anticipation and anxiety in the days leading up to the announcement for the Nobel Prize in Physics; weeks passed before his rage and despondency afterward ebbed.

∼

Although my mother had not seen or spoken to my father for more than twenty-five years when he died, no one knew him better in his twin incarnations as prodigy and disappointment. In early June I visited her and my stepfather in their grand manor house outside of Bath, and the morning after I arrived she took a break from her latest book project, a narrative history of Japanese World War II veterans, to stroll around her garden with me. The sky was an unsullied blue and the flowers in full bloom; my mother, though thinner than she should have been at 74, in good spirits.

She paused when I asked why Shoichi had chosen to work on fusion. Then she said that despite what we had heard at the memorial, it wasn't computers but theoretical physics that he had been tempted to choose over fusion. His advisors at MIT had told him he would be more temperamentally suited for it, since it would entail working alone more than with others. He should have listened to them, she said; who knows how much happier he would have been. "But your father—" She threw a glance at me and stopped.

I gazed back, stricken, suddenly certain she was about to say that Shoichi had thought fusion the surer route to the Nobel. "But my father what?" I said.

"Your father—" She hunched her shoulders, and then dropped them. "He believed in fusion," she said. "He thought it would happen, and sooner rather than later."

For a moment I was still, longing to believe her, wondering if I could. "Is that true?" I said.

"I know it's hard for you to believe." Her head was half-turned and I could not see her eyes. "But he was a good man, deep down."

I looked away. *He's good inside:* It was a line I hadn't heard for decades. Before their marriage began to disintegrate, she had deployed it regularly as both apology and excuse.

My father had been hard on my sisters and me, but he had reserved his worst for his wife. One night, in a rage over the success of her first book, he had torn up four of my mother's paintings, knocking her onto the floor whenever she tried to stop him. Afterward, with one hand pressed to the rapidly swelling lump along her hairline, she collected the scraps with the help of my sisters and me. By the end of the week she had pasted two of the paintings back together. One she threw away;

the other, a mountain landscape, hangs in a back hallway in her and my stepfather's home, its joins visible only as hairline cracks.

Yet in the weeks after his death, my mother had wondered whether she should have stayed, and if she could have saved him.

He was the first man she had ever loved. Perhaps objectivity was beyond her; perhaps she was lying to me, or herself, about the man he had been. Either way, I could not trust what she said.

~

In 1961, when my father began working at the Plasma Physics Laboratory, fusion energy research was cresting. It had started in America in the nineteen-fifties, when innovations such as dishwashers and vacuum cleaners were making their way into homes, and it took off in the 'sixties, when the space program stoked America's imagination and its love affair with science and technology was at its peak. Through the 'seventies, the Arab oil embargo as well as belief in fusion's possibilities continued to fuel media attention and funding, with articles about it appearing regularly in the major newspapers.

As late as 1983, three years after my parents' divorce, when I was a moody sixteen-year-old more interested in French existentialism than fashion, *Vogue* had a full-page photo of my father standing inside his lab's tokamak, alongside a breathless write-up. "A modest proposal: solve the world's energy crisis by developing a safe, clean, practical, commercially viable method of producing electricity. That's what scientists at Princeton University's Plasma Physics Laboratory set out to do, and today—astonishingly—they're very, very close." The tokamak resembles a giant tractor tire festooned with string; my father, standing inside what would be the rim, looks handsome and confident, his arms folded and his feet braced, the bloat of alcoholism not yet apparent in his face.

But only a year or two later the excitement was gone, drained by a string of well-publicized failures. By the mid-eighties, which is when I remember it best, my father's lab seemed quiet and a little sleepy, a place where smart men dutifully toiled. The optimism was leaking out of them by then; funding was drying up and they were beginning to suspect that if their lab did achieve its goal, it would not be in their lifetime. The problem was not that they had been wrong. My father's and the other physicists' ideas were sound: By bringing two hydrogen atoms together, they could, and did, create energy. Yet the energy required to produce the conditions for the reaction was always more than they could create. For all practical intents and purposes, they had failed.

My last visit to the lab was in 1987. I was a know-it-all college student lit up with anger at my father, and I can't tell now if it was my attitude or an actual change that made the equipment, which had once seemed shiny and impressively gigantic, look clunky and as outdated as my old heavy one-speed bike.

~

In New York in late June, in the bookshelves-lined Upper West Side apartment, my stepfather's, that my husband and I were staying in for the summer, I caught up on recent developments in my father's field. I was not expecting much. Just days earlier, a *Times* article focusing on the Lawrence Livermore National Laboratory in California, the site of "the world's most ambitious nuclear experiments," had openly scoffed at fusion, and fretted about the possibility of radioactive material leaking from the facility. "Some scientists question whether ignition will ever be possible" had been its sobering conclusion.

But my research revealed that the experiment, which involved large lasers bombarding pellets of hydrogen in mini-bursts, had supporters as well as detractors. I also learned about a second project that was being run and financed by the EU, Japan, China, India, South Korea and Russia as well as the United States. Known as ITER, or the "International Thermonuclear Experimental Reactor," the consortium was in the process of constructing the world's largest and most powerful tokamak in the south of France.

Both projects faced considerable obstacles. At Livermore, the laser needed more power than expected to ignite the reaction, and how to contain the radioactive tritium was an unsolved problem. As for ITER's project, which still lay years in the future, the issue was how to keep the plasma stable long enough to heat the hydrogen and squeeze energy from it. In one article's words, "According to the old quip, a practical fusion reactor will always be about twenty years away." Still, each project had top-notch scientists and funding that ran into the billions, and from what I could gather, the recent meltdown of the Fukushima nuclear power plant in Japan was providing added impetus to the research, at least for now. My father's lab might be limping along, its budget reduced to a pittance, but the quest to make fusion a reality was not over yet.

I was almost at the end of my stack of articles, reading yet another sentence extolling fusion energy's virtues—*its plants can't melt down; they won't produce long-lived, highly radioactive waste, and fusion fuel cannot be easily weaponized*—when something clicked.

Fusion fuel cannot be easily weaponized, but the fuel used in fission reactions can be. As, of course, it had been, by the Manhattan Project in 1945.

My father had been nine when the bomb destroyed Hiroshima and Nagasaki. In grade school he had learned about the flash, bright enough to be literally blinding and filled with so much radioactivity it vaporized human beings, leaving only a shadowy imprint in their place; the pressure wave that followed, collapsing entire buildings; the blast of heat that left everything in its wake in flames; the second pressure wave which, moving in the other direction, swept away anything still left standing; the mushroom cloud that bloomed over the scenes of apocalypse and, finally, the black rain of radioactive particles. As a child he saw photos of the devastated cities and heard about the hundreds of thousands who had been burned, injured by falling debris, and poisoned by radiation.

By all accounts he had been a sensitive and highly intelligent child, and nine was an impressionable age. How had he first learned that the humble atom had been responsible for the almost supernatural force of those bombs—the radio, a schoolyard rumor, or a teacher who recognized his precocity? No, it must have been his father, the scientist, who took him aside and explained. He was blunt, as he tended to be, and Shoichi, who would be celebrated in later years for his powers of concentration, would have listened intently, not missing a word.

Perhaps Shoichi found that afterward, he could not stop thinking about the photos of the piles of concrete rubble, the twisted and melted steel girders, and the miles of razed wooden homes that he had seen in the papers. Perhaps he, a bright and hopeful boy, wondered at the power of the atom, and eventually began to dream about mastering and harnessing its force for more peaceful and productive ends; perhaps those images helped shape a career.

I wrote to four of the scientists who had spoken at the memorial. *Could my father's experiences during the war have inspired his research into fusion energy?* I asked, citing Hiroshima and Nagasaki. *Or is that completely farfetched?*

Three didn't know, but thought it possible. The fourth, a Japanese colleague, wrote that he himself had been born well after the war. *But I am sure that having lived through its terrors, Yoshikawa-san was very much influenced by it,* he said. *That could be the reason he chose to pursue the peaceful utilization of fusion as his life work.*

～

I grew up listening to my mother's stories about the war. She was four when it started and seven when she, her mother, and two of her siblings left their home in Nagoya and moved to the countryside, away from the frontlines. Food was scarce: In one story, her ten-year-old sister swings upside down on the monkey bars, her hair falling forward, and my mother sees a sizable bald spot on the side of her head. Yet they managed, catching and cooking the insects that fed on rice plants—*they eat so much rice,* my grandmother explained, *they're practically the same thing*—and searching the mountains for akaza, an edible weed.

The few times I asked my father to talk about the war, his face grew grim. Instead of stories I got facts, haltingly delivered: that on his fifth birthday, his mother died of pneumonia. That Japan attacked Pearl Harbor just twenty months later. That his father made the decision to keep him in Tokyo through the war, where bomb scares as well as actual bombs were constant. That he was often sick, and so malnourished his stomach swelled.

The war had clearly informed my mother's career. The book she was working on involved trips to Japan as well as extensive research and long and numerous interviews with veterans. Before that there was a collection of essays about British POWs who had been incarcerated and tortured by Japanese soldiers. And before that a novel, her first book in English, which traced the fortunes of a Japanese family from the late eighteen-hundreds to post-war. Surely it was not unreasonable to think that my father's career choices had also been shaped by his wartime experiences.

And if that was the case—if my father had elected to work on fusion because he wanted to transform war's horrors into something good, if he had tried to solve the global energy crisis in order to help save the world—then my mother had been right about him after all. He had been good, deep down—perhaps in a different way than even she could have guessed.

I reread the e-mail from my father's Japanese colleague one last time and then checked the clock. It was just past one, not yet suppertime in England. My mother picked up on the fourth ring.

As I explained, the words tumbling out, all I had recently learned, she was quiet. Turning the revelation over in her mind, I assumed, but when I finished and she began speaking, her voice was measured, with just a hint of surprise.

"I thought you knew," she said. "I thought you had figured out that connection." Of course the war had influenced his career choice. It was only logical, she said: After all, Hiroshima and Nagasaki had affected him—they had affected every single person in Japan—in so many ways.

It was my turn to be silent.

These days, she continued, she often found herself thinking about the bomb—something to do with her age, perhaps, or the fact that she was the only Japanese person for miles around. Or maybe it was just her current project. The wire hummed. "Even if your father didn't think about the war everyday," she said, "some days he must have."

She had been writing when I called. I pictured her, tiny, fragile, and still beautiful, sitting in her study with its spectacular views of the garden, her head tilted toward the phone and her feet propped up on her desk, papers and books in neat piles around her.

"But your father," my mother continued, "I wouldn't call him an idealist." She spoke slowly, thinking it through. "He wasn't working to save the world."

His motivations were pure, she said, just not in the way I had thought.

He had worked on fusion because it was the question that intrigued him the most—and small wonder, she said, imagine trying to solve the secrets of the sun!—and one he thought he could solve.

I looked out the window, at the brownstones, the treetops, and the sliver of the Hudson that the view afforded.

"What your father wanted above all else," my mother said, "was to unravel the mysteries of the universe. What he wanted was to find truth."

She sounded solemn, and I realized that for her—as, perhaps, for me—a quest to know was no less noble than a quest to save the world.

I glanced down again at the letter in front of me.

Despite what she had said, my mother's view of my father did not contradict what his Japanese colleague had written. My father had been drawn to fusion because he wanted to make the world a better place— by creating an alternative energy source, but more crucially by solving one of the mysteries of the universe and so adding to the store of human knowledge. That he had done so for his own reasons—because truth was both beauty and bliss to him—did not detract from the fact that he was an idealist, albeit of a very special kind.

Outside the Hudson winked in the sun.

Had my father's work been worth it? To him, yes. What I thought about it was another question, and one I was not quite ready to resolve.

~

Almost a year has passed since then. The first anniversary of his death, in November, came and went; winter ended, and then spring, and I'm still of two minds about my father's work. In my most generous moments I celebrate his life with Camus' words on that toiler par excellence, Sisyphus: "The struggle itself toward the heights is enough to fill a man's heart." I say that my father did right, that outcomes are always uncertain and we must truck on regardless—because that's the only way anyone will ever accomplish anything, but even more importantly because the work itself, the joy of the day-to-day doing of it as well as the hope of creating something great, is what lifts us. In those moments I'm glad for my father that he had the satisfactions and bliss of his work, and I'm proud of him, too.

But most of the time I'm not that pure-minded. When it comes to my father, at least, work as an ideal is too abstract. I dream of traveling back in time—a concept that he loved, both as a sci-fi fan and as a physicist—and grabbing his younger self by his flea-market lapels and telling him to *give it up, your work will come to nothing. Stop torturing yourself and everyone else; make time for your kids before it's too late.*

In my dream he looks back at me, his eyes dark and expressionless, and I come to and realize that I, like my mother before me, am blaming work for the choices and actions of the man.

My editorial partner, Phillip Lopate, told me about a memorable essay he read one summer at the Bennington Writing Seminars in Vermont. When I approached the author, Nancy Jainchill, she sent me that earlier version called, "Oh My Poppa," a title hinting at old world heartache. In Nancy's loving and painfully honest lament, we meet her father, the Orthodox Jewish father from Palestine, the loving, caring, judgmental, terrified, Old Testament father wearing a fedora. Nancy sent several old family photographs of her father, but I was especially moved by the one here, where it's 1957 and they are outside on a lovely day, sitting in a metal chair and she is ten years old, comfortable in his lap. They both look so pleased to be together.

NANCY JAINCHILL

Sol's Exodus

CANAL STREET was dark, silent and empty, except for the occasional rumble of a truck. I was shouting into the lone payphone. The anonymous operator didn't care that my father was lying on the floor and that he had peed on himself. But suddenly I did. In my mind, once again, he was my father the hero, born in Palestine in the early nineteen-hundreds. That made him a *sabra*, and that made him special. As a little girl, I'd be eager for the sound of his key in the door, signaling his arrival home from work, and I'd run to him. "Daddy, daddy." In winter, his overcoat held the chill from the outdoors as he lifted me in his arms. He'd remove his ever present fedora, placing it on a wooden hat rack.

When I was six and seven and eight, during our best years, he was the perfect daddy. Sunday mornings began with the two of us reading the newspapers in the living room. My father bought the *New York Times* and the *Mirror* at the luncheonette which was less than a block from our apartment building on the upper West Side of Manhattan, and which neighbored the Riverside Funeral Chapel where all the Jewish New Yorkers were memorialized. He would sit in one of the easy chairs and I'd be on the floor nearby. The *Mirror*, which had more pictures and talked simpler than the *Times*, doesn't exist anymore, but every Sunday morning on the last page of the *Mirror*'s magazine section there was a true murder story. Although I was a scared kid, sleeping with a baseball bat by my bed, every Sunday I read the piece. Mostly, they had a resolution—although occasionally the murderer was still walking around. The crimes happened in faraway states like Wisconsin or Montana, the distance mak-

67

ing the story less frightening, less likely that it could happen to me. I might carry a lurid image around for the rest of the day, a woman's head found unattached to a body, with shoulder-length blonde hair, or a body stuffed into a refrigerator of a forsaken house.

Finished with the *Mirror*, I'd crawl into my father's lap to study the bridal section of the *Times*. Those days, brides were mostly blonde, with posed lips, their faces framed by gossamer veils.

Pointing at the portraits, I'd smile and ask, "Who's the prettiest bride?"

Examining each picture, we'd announce our first choice, not always agreeing. But that didn't matter. We had a routine. Leaning close enough into me that I could breathe his Old Spice, my father would kiss me on the cheek. "You're prettier than all of them." And it didn't matter that I didn't believe what he said.

Snuggled safely against his soft belly, I loved him.

Having established that I was the prettiest, we'd ready for our Sunday walk. Sitting on the edge of the bathtub, my arms resting on the sink ledge, I watched him shave, my legs swinging back and forth against the side of the tub. He'd smile into the mirror. "Just a few more minutes, Bubula" (little darling).

A clean swipe of skin appeared with each stroke of the razor. Finishing, he'd splash his face with Old Spice, which was the scent of kisses. At the door, in winter he'd wrap his two-tone, cashmere scarf around his neck.

~

Now waiting for someone to answer my 911 call, that smell came over me, and I felt how soft his face was right after he had shaved. I remembered how he would take my hand in his hand that was strong enough to hurt someone, and he would rub my palm against his face to feel the softness of his freshly shaved skin. Still, it is one of the softest things I've ever felt: if I could capture and preserve a touch I would hold onto that moment of my hand rubbing up against his cheek.

I was proud that he was a *sabra*. To me this suggested that he was brave and different from other fathers. But he rarely spoke of the past.

On one of our Sunday morning walks, I asked him what it was like in Palestine.

"I spoke Arabic, Turkish, German, Yiddish, Polish, Hebrew and… English." He sounded pleased, this was a good memory. "We all went to school together. Then things changed. Then I always had to be looking over my shoulder."

I felt the warmth of my hand in his as we walked. "One day," he said, "I was sitting on the top of a hill and I felt movement behind me. I turned around. It was a Turkish boy and he was getting ready to throw me over the side of the hill."

Looking up at him, I saw my father as a rough-and-tumble boy in a rough-and-tumble land. This was the image I wanted of him, to replace who he had become. I saw strength and adventure, a courageous boy who crossed the ocean by himself. For a brief period, when I was eleven or twelve, I became a Zionist. I read Leon Uris' novel, *Exodus*, four times. There was no separation between Paul Newman, who played Ari Ben Canaan in the movie, and my father. I envisioned myself in Israel by their side.

～

Then I turned thirteen and everything changed. We began to argue. It started with verbal war. Having lost my Zionist sentiments, I would pick fights with him over Israel.

"Maybe we have to share Israel."

"We're the chosen people." If we were walking, he might stop and turn to me. "Israel belongs to us."

He may have given up religion, except for the biannual visit to the synagogue on Rosh Hashonah and Yom Kippur, the Day of Atonement, but he hadn't given up his Jewish identity.

"That's ridiculous," I protested. "What makes us chosen?"

"You don't know what you're talking about," and his voice would rise.

"That's why we're so hated, because we're obnoxious." My father was no longer a *sabra*, and I became anti-Semitic.

My mother would appear if she were nearby and heard the arguments escalating: "Nan dear, please don't get your father upset. Please, please don't fight with your father. His blood pressure."

"It's not my fault if he can't control his damn blood pressure." I'd fix my eyes on her, not yielding.

I began waiting for him to die. My mother told me he'd have an early death and I'd be the cause. I waited.

Soon I was disappearing with my friends, and had boyfriends, and the battles intensified. The critical explosion happened when I was sixteen. I was going out with a bad boy—again.

"You are not going out with that boy," my father shouted. "Didn't he leave you at that party and I found you in front of our building with some freak with long hair?" My father had come downstairs looking for me, because I was so late coming home. He circled us several times, making sure it was me, his daughter, talking with this weirdo, who had gotten me home safely from the East Village after bad boy had abandoned me.

The bad boy's last name was Epstein—Jewish—but that didn't matter. He was a greaser—his dark hair slicked back, he wore a black motorcycle jacket and went to Brooklyn Tech, not to Stuyvesant or Bronx High School of Science, where the good boys went. His upper lip seemed to be in a perpetual curl and he barely said hello to my parents when he came to the apartment.

"I am going out with him on Friday."

"You're a slut," my father's hands clenched in a fist. "You're nothing but a slut."

"I am not. I'm going out with him." I fought not to cry. I wasn't giving in, even though inside I wondered about this boy. He could be nasty— not a nice Jewish type. My father and I were standing in the middle of my pink bedroom, facing each other.

Then he came toward me and his hands reached for my neck. I grabbed at them as they tightened, and I began squawking, trying to speak. His hands, the same hands that held onto my hand as we took our daddy-daughter Sunday walks.

Once my father spanked me after we got home from a walk, because I had been dawdling as we crossed the street. Now, his hands were wrapped around my neck, not letting go, just as they didn't let go of my hand, making sure that I got across safely.

Why did my mother walk by my room at that moment? Because the shouting had stopped? Because she needed something from her bedroom and happened to be walking past my room? "Sol, are you crazy?" and she pulled him off me. I was crying then, and I watched as he retreated from my bedroom. Neither of us said "I'm sorry."

～

So when I returned to New York seven years later to live on my own with a roommate in New York City, I still didn't trust our relationship. I refused to join my parents, my roommate and her father, since the dinner plans had been decided without me. I wasn't going to do what my mother wanted me to do—or my father. I wasn't fighting like I used to, but I wasn't giving in. And I wasn't about to have my father think I had returned to New York because he asked me to—that I was finally doing what he wanted, like going to dinner and pretending everything was okay.

"Nan, dear, why don't you come with us?" My mother, as was typical, spoke for both of them. "It won't take long and you have to eat." She and my father stood by the doorway. He was in the background, dressed in his customary attire—a shirt and tie, and his fedora—meticulous as he used to be on our Sunday walks. His slacks, as usual, wore a neat crease down the middle. He was a gentleman. In the picture I have of him on my desk shelf, looking down at me, slightly smiling, his eyes twinkling behind the dark-framed glasses, his top coat collar is turned up, the rim of his fedora tipped down. There is no hint of his struggles to hold onto me.

I hadn't given in when I moved to New Germany, Nova Scotia, several years before, and he wanted me to come right home. The letter from my father arrived around my twenty-third birthday. In florid, curving letters he wrote, "Nancy Darling, It's time for you to come home. I love you and I want you to come home. Your loving father." Every word looked as though it began with a capital. The letter took three weeks to reach me at the Canadian outpost where I was trying out another lifestyle. I had been there only a month and I wasn't scheduled to leave so soon.

My father didn't want me going to Nova Scotia just as he hadn't wanted me to move out to Berkeley, California, from New York City. He didn't want me doing anything I had been doing for the past ten years.

~

The two flights of stairs to the loft were steep, my father was over-weight, and his blood pressure was often volatile, even dangerous. I greeted my parents at the door upon their return from dinner, and he appeared shaky, his face sweat-wet.

"I don't feel well." He walked over to the only chair there was in the vast unfurnished space, a small wooden desk chair on wheels, set low, as if for a child. Not for a grown man. Sliding off it, his legs splayed out awkwardly, I thought the size of the chair had unbalanced him, made him lose his seating.

I heard my mother's voice. "Sol, Sol, get up, Sol." The same tone of voice she had used earlier, urging me to go to dinner with them. It rang out even more than usual in the hollow space of the loft.

Only a few minutes passed before I realized that my father wasn't getting up, and the problem wasn't the chair's size. Someone went over, straightened out his legs, and put a blanket beneath his head. I was afraid to go near him, afraid of what I might see. Afraid he was dead. I had heard his disappointment that I wasn't going to have dinner with them. I had pushed him away when he tried to kiss me good-bye.

Now, lying on the bare wood floor, my natty father had urinated on himself.

We didn't have a telephone yet so I raced down the stairs to the pay phone on the street, my heart beating like thunder. Would my father have been okay if I'd gone to dinner? Was this it? Just like that.

I didn't want to cry. I was wishing, now, that I'd known my father when he first came to this country, when he was a *sabra*, when he had hair and it was black, and his adventure was only beginning. I wish I'd known him before he shuffled when he walked. Before he lay on the wooden floor of the loft, nearly dead.

~

He had told me so little. I knew he came to the United States through Ellis Island and that his brother, seventeen years older, was waiting on shore for him. But I saw my Uncle Willie only a few times. My father was distant from his family, maybe his own choosing, or maybe in reaction to my mother's comments. She didn't like it that Uncle Willie and his family lived in Brooklyn. In those days Brooklyn was another country to Manhattanites like my mother—Brooklyn was lower class. He also had a sister, twenty-five years older, but I don't recall he ever visited her.

In one of the few stories my father shared, he said that his name was originally DeZenziel, a Portuguese name, which had been changed to Jainchill. DeZenziel, the sound fills my mouth, and I conjure up images of dancers and passion, and the soft shush of the language sliding over the body.

There was a time—at a restaurant—he began talking about himself. I watched his face, to see how he felt.

"The first time I left to come here from Palestine," he said, "I turned around and went home. I was leaving from Alexandria." He paused, and took a forkful of his apple pie.

I was interested in him then, instead of angry. "What made you go back?" I listened to his voice, trying to hear if he was sad, or proud, or nostalgic.

"I missed my parents. The next year I left for good. I was sixteen and I took the boat from Haifa."

"How did you feel? Were you scared?"

"It was exciting. I wanted to get here. You know this is the best country in the world." I wanted him to say more, but he grew silent.

I wish I'd asked him if he knew he would never see his parents again.

～

I have a sepia-toned photograph of my father—he looks about twelve years old—standing between his parents. His father is dressed in the traditional Orthodox Jewish garb. His long, black cloth coat reaches to the floor of the photo and his face is covered in a full grey beard extending below his neckline. I can detect that he has *payot*, long uncut sideburns, curled around his ears, and he wears a black, round-brimmed hat. My grandmother sits, her ample bosom resting on an equally generous lap. Her head is covered, as dictated by religious law, not allowing a married woman to show her hair. My father also has *payot* and wears the traditional garb of Orthodox Jewish men; he has no beard, which means he hasn't started shaving yet. All three stare straight forward, unsmiling.

His father, Lazar Yakov, came from Zambrov, Poland and owned a kosher slaughter house and butcher shop in Jerusalem. With so little information I imagined that he began and ended his days with prayer, and that my father was taught to do the same; that his mother, Rivka, spent her days sweeping away the dry brown dust, the street an interruption of the desert. I imagined that Rivka was ready with the evening meal at sundown, when Solomon returned from Yeshiva and Lazar had finished his day's work. Years later I find out that she was ultra-Orthodox, and fasted twice a week to give to the poor.

My father never spoke about his parents or discussed his religious upbringing. He made the voyage to America, leaving them forever. And he dismissed a religious practice that was a way of life, of thinking, of being. Until I found the picture after his death I had no sense of what he'd rejected.

~

Thirty years after he died I obtained a copy of the ship's manifest, the log of passengers it transported to the U.S. This first page of my father's new life documented the human cargo for the SS France. My father, Solomon, is the twenty-fifth entry on page 312. If I've read the information correctly, the ship departed Le Havre on February 9, 1920, reaching New York on March 6th. His surname, Jainchill, is misspelled, the first "I" missing.

The manifest tells a different story: my father was Syrian, born in Poland, and he migrated to Palestine. His recorded age is seventeen, a year older than his actual age, in order for him to be admitted to this country. His age continued to fluctuate over the years. The manifest says he was a student, and that he paid his own passage—fifty-five dollars. My father was one of the 225,206 immigrants processed that year, one of the last years that Ellis Island was used as a Federal immigration station. Subsequently, I learn he was born in Palestine, as he said. And that his parents' surname was Yankel. Sounds like Jainchill. Not like DeZenziel. Maybe, I tell myself, the "facts" aren't really so important; my father was who he was, however I wanted to write his story, a story that occupies the first pages of my own narrative.

This man who was always well-groomed, traveling as a steerage passenger, confined to the lowest decks of the ship, with only the most basic amenities—I can't picture his experience.

After living in the United States for a while, he began calling himself Stanley. Maybe he thought Stanley sounded more American. I don't know. I don't know if he was afraid or lonely. I know that after living with his brother Willie in Brooklyn, he rented a room at the Mayflower Hotel in Manhattan. My father enjoyed eating and drinking, so there must have been years when he was out and about before being introduced to my mother by a mutual friend. Their dates began under the gold clock of the Biltmore Hotel, after he had changed into a clean shirt in the men's bathroom at Grand Central Terminal. My mother told me that after I was born they bought the Frank Sinatra record, *Nancy with the Laughing Face*, and they would dance to the music in the living room, holding me in their arms.

Mostly, he was awkward in the father role. He didn't do much with me when I was growing up, but on Sundays, past the early years of our walks, when I was learning how to ride a bicycle, he'd run behind me, holding onto the back of the seat, so that if I tipped one way or the other, he could right the bike. But, keeping up with me had to be hard for him. Old for his years, he lumbered when he walked. I didn't like training wheels, the way you could easily become unbalanced with them, even if you couldn't really fall down. So my father ran behind me.

~

It was almost midnight when we arrived at the hospital. Seated in the back of the ambulance with him, I felt as though the spinning red light on the car's roof was attached to my head, my eyes going round and round. The first two weeks, we were told, were critical; the doctor didn't know how much he'd recover. When my father emerged from his coma, he was speaking Arabic, probably his first language, suggesting to me, how alone he had been all these years. Again, he was the *sabra*, the boy with an uncommon, even courageous past.

For a brief time he was able to shuffle down the hospital hallway, holding onto the pole which carried his vital fluids, but then he went away again, into a world more silent and unseeing than any before. His hands lay limp and still. I thought about the kid on the hill in Israel, and the dreams he must have had. And how endings so rarely meet our expectations.

After eight months my father was transferred to a nursing home in the Bronx; he was never coming home. Did he sense that? Did he realize he was being taken someplace that was an hour subway ride away from everything that had been familiar to him? I wondered if he was lonely, encased in his deepening silence, in a room with no remembrances of his other life.

Tuesday was my day to visit. I hated the hour-long subway ride and I couldn't wait to leave, to get back to my everyday existence and away from his dying. I'd spoon-feed him, crying as the cottage cheese dribbled from his mouth. "Damn it," I'd yell, "Eat, please eat. Please, Pop, eat."

Once, I smacked him across the face. I wanted him to come back from the faraway place where he now lived. I wanted to know him better and it was too late. Oh, I knew he liked Dannon prune-flavored yogurt and sweet breads. I knew he loved music, and was an armchair conductor. He watched Ed Sullivan, while I preferred Steve Allen. At home, though, mostly, he'd sit by himself in the living room and read the newspaper, often falling asleep, the pages spread across his lap.

Now, his big brown eyes, round like a cow's, stared straight ahead.

~

When my father died, he took with him the incomplete pieces of his life—two names, two birthdays, a dismembered family. I had his name inscribed on the Immigrant Wall, and in 2007 went to Ellis Island to see the wall, and to walk through the buildings where he had walked. I wanted to bring back the *sabra*, the young man with courage and fire I never saw.

I have the scarf that he always wore, cashmere, two-tone—one side burgundy, the other black—soft like his freshly shaven skin. And I have a few of his letters, including the one that found its way to me that August in Nova Scotia. "Nancy, darling, come home."

Lost & Found

After Lee Smith sent me her essay about her own father, she told me in no uncertain terms that I really should, no, I absolutely had to contact her friend and North Carolina neighbor Jill McCorkle. Say no more, I thought. I have loved Jill's writing every since I read *July 7th*. Lee Smith and Jill McCorkle are two writers who speak to the very heart of my father's southern roots and mine. Jill's funny, poignant essay here is about the author and her mother, but most of all, it's about Jill's dad, a man who just can't bear to tear down his daughter's childhood playhouse. Jill sent a number of charming pictures from her family photo album, but I loved this bright snowy one with her father and her sister during a younger time, when there were no shadows hovering over them. Jill's husband, Tom Rankin, took the recent picture of Jill.

JILL McCORKLE

My Dad

WHEN MY DAD was diagnosed with lung cancer and told that at best he had six months to live, he said: "I am sixty-four years old and I have had a good life." He never said the words "death" or "dying," but in these last three months of life he did talk a lot about what he missed (not being able to lie on his left side to read as he had done his entire life) and would miss (his grandchildren growing up, their graduations and weddings and trips to the beach). Shortly after being diagnosed, he removed his glasses and never wore them again. I think he must have wanted us to blur, my mother and sister and me blending as we came and went among old friends and neighbors who came to say good-bye. I think it was probably easier to confuse us with the people he said were waiting for him there at the end, those people over just beyond the corner. By then, he had given up his worry about becoming addicted, and morphine coursed through his body. He often spoke in eloquent metaphor, once about the new tax law that everyone just had to accept: There is no way around it. It doesn't matter who you are or where you live or what you have ever done, you just have to accept this law and follow it. He said he wished he had a train and could go around and pick up everyone he had ever loved. He asked me to lift my son—then just under two—up as high as I could so that he could see his whole body. He said that he was sorry if he had ever let us down. And on one of his last clear days, he simply said: "You [meaning the collected group of us] are my heart. That's all that there is."

~

This was twenty years ago but I think of his words often. I had dreaded and feared this moment my entire life. My dad had suffered severe depression and been hospitalized several times during my childhood, and so I had always been preparing myself to lose him again. It was an experience that left me feeling split in two, my mind and heart seeming to function independent of the other and this shocked me. My heart was breaking—I was a grieving child—and yet, my mind was allowing me to pay bills and take care of my children and read manuscripts for the classes I would fly back to Boston to teach the week after he died. More so, I found myself completely mystified and fascinated by the miracle of the human body, watching as it began to shut down, like someone moving through a house and turning off the lights, preserving energy for those most vital parts. Conserving and protecting the heart. I watched my dad's limbs darken and thought this is the shadow of death and wondered if this process had anything to do with the origin of that phrase, wondered where in my fiction this image of the darkening house might appear. If he were my character, how could I possibly reveal the whole life there in front of me. What would I choose to tell?

I could tell one of my earliest memories—an Easter Sunday when I was no more than four. I wore a dress sewn by my dad's mother, white with an appliquéd train, a rickrack track running from shoulder to hem. The memory is enhanced by a few family color slides, daffodils in bloom, a green rolling lawn, a tall brick hospital building. Spring was my dad's hardest time, the warm rise of sap and blooms that most people welcomed were a harbinger of dread and discomfort that threatened to sweep in and carry him off like the tide. This was one of those bad springs. He came outside into the sun and sat with us there; he wore a blue bathrobe and gave my sister and me a card he had bought in the gift shop. The part of the memory that is clearest to me is when it was time to leave, someone—I don't even know who—told me to wave good-bye to my Dad. They told me to count up six floors and wave back to him and I saw his figure there behind a window that had bars on it.

There were items in our home associated with his time in the hospital. A brown vinyl-covered bench he had made in a woodworking class. A jewelry box for my mother, the image of a crocus hammered into copper and attached to the felt-lined box with little tiny nails. He had also hammered out the picture of a horse's head that my mother praised and hung on the wall of the den, a tiny pine-paneled room where my sister and I had found many animals and faces in the knotholes, most memorable being the one I loved—a slender deer with large brown eyes—and the scary one I tried not to see because it looked like one of those angry trees in the *Wizard of Oz*. My mother was never sentimental about keeping things, a balance to my dad, and yet that jewelry box stayed on her dresser for years and years.

~

When I was watching my dad die, I was aware of wanting to commit to memory the shape of his face, his hands and feet. My mother always loved to tell how she once dated a boy who had the ugliest feet she had ever seen, so ugly it made her feel sick and have to go home. Well, she then said and laughed, nobody on this planet earth has uglier feet than your daddy and his didn't bother me a bit. This was an anecdote told as proof of her great love for him, and it was also a lesson about how you never knew how or when your tolerance for something might change, say okra, or having to dry your clothes at the laundromat. She said my dad's feet looked like flounders and teased that he needed to be careful when surf fishing so nobody gigged him.

He loved to fish and waited all year for that week we would pack up and head to the beach. One summer, he told me that when the alarm clock rang, I should run to the fridge, grab the paper bag he had in there and run as fast as I could the mile down to the point of the inlet where he was going to be all set up fishing. I felt very important to be depended on for this fishing mission, not knowing that there in those pre-Playmate cooler days, I was not only the son he didn't have but also his St. Bernard. The bell rang and I raced to deliver two cold Falstaffs at appointed times of the afternoon. He also let me fish with him, giving me my own rod and reel and outfitted tackle box when I turned seven. He told me that if you just sit on the beach and stare at the ocean and think—maybe drink a beer or two—that someone (most likely my mother) would come by and wonder why you weren't doing anything. "This is why I fish," he told me. "And this is why if they ever start biting too much, I stop baiting my hook." He had a pole holder and just sat there in his low sand chair, puffing on his pipe and staring at the ocean, occasionally checking the tip of his pole to see if anything was happening. And he would say things like: this would make a good story. Here's a good movie idea. Then he would begin telling an elaborate plot that usually had at the heart of it an honest hard-working man who for whatever reason was misunderstood by society.

His childhood pictures are labeled so that his name is sometimes Jonny then Johnnie and then Johnny. In the ones where he is smiling his lips are clamped tight, not to showcase his dimples as you might think, but to hide the crookedness of his teeth, a habit set for life even when no longer neces-sary. Then there are a lot of pictures where he's not smiling at all, a solemn gaze not unlike the way he looked at the ocean, head ringed in pipe smoke.

My parents attended first grade together and my dad once walked her home because she had forgotten which way to go. They had always known each other but didn't begin dating until they were sixteen. He was a kid who got let out early in elementary school because he knew the lessons and made good grades (my mother had to stay) only to later, in high school, have to stay back two years past when he should have graduated because he went to the pool hall instead of school. He had a pet goat named Popeye and often blamed his tardies and absences on the goat getting loose. So, what happened between point A and point B? I spent a lot of time trying to figure that one out, to pinpoint exactly what happened or when, so that if indeed I was just like him, as I was often told, I might see it before it saw me. This was a man who came in to tell our bedtime story and system-atically looked under the beds and in the closet, forever cementing in my mind the idea that something could be there. Might be there.

I could tell that his father was an alcoholic but you've heard that story a million times, and so I would add that his mother was a brilliant seamstress who made wedding gowns with intricate bead work, and that his dad was a kind-hearted world weary butcher who once showed up drunk at a high school function where my dad sat holding my moth-er's hand. I could tell how my dad got up and left the group of kids he was sitting with and went to get his dad and carry him home. I could make the story a little richer by adding that this is not something my dad ever told himself but a story that was told about him; how people from all walks of life showed up at his funeral, several saying how they often chose to wait in a longer line at the post office so he would be the one to wait on them; that like his father, he was very kind and also pretty easy on the eyes. I could tell you how when my mother insisted he participate in the disciplinary process that he took my sister and me in a room, closed the door, told her she needed to stop being sassy and told me I wasn't supposed to paint and hammer things without getting permission first, and then told us that he was going to clap his hands together and he wanted us to start crying and act like we'd been spanked.

I could tell how my dad once—while working at a local textile mill—brought home the wooden crate that a knitting machine had been shipped in with the idea he would cut out a door and a tiny window and turn that 8×8 box into a storage shed. The flat roof was covered in heavy tin and in the summers it was like a sweat box, but as soon as he had fixed a door, I began moving in—slowly at first, a few things in the corner and then more and more—a blanket where my old battered Tom Cat could come and collect himself before heading off again, a child-size rocking chair and tea set, a doll or two, things my sister complained about in that room we shared, things like Buzzy, a large rubber snake I kept in a big jar of water on my dresser, named for a teenaged boy I thought was cute though I never would have told anyone. She had drawn that invisible line down the center of the room so many times, I could see it in glaring neon. Anything in danger of spilling over into dangerous territory went straight to the playhouse. I stacked bricks for a fireplace and drew an enormous fire on cardboard and my dad just stepped back and let me. I remember my mom asking "what about your storage shed?" but I have no idea what followed, just that my dad handed over the key to the padlock and told me it was mine but that I should never light candles in there and that I had to keep the window open on really hot days. He took the old metal bike plate that had my name on it and nailed it by the door.

The first Christmas I had the playhouse, I got the serrated steak knife from my tackle box and set off for the little strip of woods that separated our neighborhood from I-95. I was not supposed to go near the interstate and I wasn't allowed to use sharp objects. The hatchet I had favored and the saw had been taken and placed out of my reach with severe consequences attached if touched. But the steak knife was mine—placed in my tackle by my dad. I selected a little three foot pine tree and sawed away until I was able to snap the tree and carry it home. It filled the corner of the playhouse and was decorated almost entirely with aluminum foil. Then I made invitations and wrapped gifts and much to my sister's horror, had a party that required the whole family to come out there and squat in that 8×8 box to see how I thought Christmas should be done. And this went on for the next several years, each party a little longer and more festive than the one before it—Little Debbie snacks cut and arranged on teeny tiny plates and the Coca-Cola flowing.

I asked them to read aloud from various Christmas stories and asked that we all sing at least one festive song.

The year I was ten and in the fifth grade, we had the party as always. It had become an event, one always prompted by my dad asking if I knew what time it was. "You know what time it is, right?" he asked, and I got my knife and went to get a tree and make the invitations. But some time early that year, my big old cat got hit by a car and then it seemed everything clicked into a new gear and all ran together. My dad had a job at the post office and my parents were adding a master bedroom where the carport had been and so by spring I would have my own room and as if by magic a puppy appeared, found by the youngest boys in the neighborhood. I had been begging for a dog for years and told my parents I had prayed for him and here he was. I said that now I would always believe—I prayed for a dog and here he was. I didn't acknowledge that I knew I was being manipulative and suspected they knew I was being manipulative and still they let me keep him. Smoky, a dog who lived for the next sixteen years and was my dad's closest companion and fishing buddy once I was off doing other things.

"You know what time it is don't you?" my dad asked one year right after Thanksgiving but I was mostly interested in my new poncho, some suede-fringed boots and a boy named Danny who I wrote notes to and sat with at football games. I spent my nights there in the comfort of my own room—yellow walls and white furniture—writing in a diary and listening to Tiny Tony's Nightbeat on WTSB and then WOWO Fort Wayne Indiana which was as far as my transistor radio could pick up late at night.

"You know what time it is don't you?" It was years before I realized how many times my dad had asked me that question. In fact, it did not hit me until I was a freshman in college. He kept calling me one whole afternoon. It was spring and I had just played tennis with some friends. It was hot and the big window fan in the dorm window was set on high, my roommate was under her hair dryer so the music was extra loud—Fleetwood Mac or Boz Scaggs—that was the year. There was an impatient hulking boyfriend pacing around downstairs while waiting for me to come and go wherever it was I was going. And on the phone there was my dad telling of termites and rotten wood and how he couldn't bear to tear down my playhouse but knew that he had no choice. He said it was breaking his heart but he didn't know what else to do. Did I want to speak to Smoky while he had me on the phone? Should he wait for me to come home and see it again?

"It's okay" I told him. "Really, I understand. It's okay." "But it's your house," he said. "You'll never see it again."

He called about three more times and I walked as far as the phone cord would stretch and looked out the window and across the road where I could see daffodils and tulips and dogwoods in bloom. He said he took pictures. He boxed everything up and put it in my room. He was saving the piece of wood where I had painted my name. It's okay, I kept saying. It's time. There's nothing else to do.

But he didn't want to let go. He wanted me to keep having that party. He wanted us all there together. I don't remember what I did or thought or said the rest of that day, only that that time I spent on the phone with my dad lodged in me right beside that dress with the train appliqué, only to return on that final day when we had been encouraged by the hospice nurse to tell him that it was okay. It's okay to let go. He had given us such gifts there at the end—wishes for all the events he was going to miss, apologies for all the things he hadn't been able to do; this man who had lived his whole life in fear, faced death without a visible trace of it. Blink if you hear me, I had said all that day, his eyes frozen in a tearless stare, and we all sat there with him, singing favorite songs, stroking his hands and face and then it happened, and with that last intake of a breath, he blinked.

It was fall, his favorite of all seasons and he had heard everything. He was sixty-four years old and had had a good life. Your daddy was big hearted, people kept saying. Tenderhearted. Good hearted. It was all about the heart, and he had already told us that that's all that there is.

My father once asked me what kind of writer I was. I had written two novels for adults and four novels for young adults. I wrote short stories and essays, and I was starting a memoir. "I just write," I told him. That's what writers do. Joyce Maynard is just that kind of productive, prolific, and successful writer most writers want to be. Her essay here paints the portrait of a close and often difficult relationship with her British-born father, a teacher and a frustrated artist. Joyce also wrote about her mother and father, and her budding career as a writer, in her memoir, At Home in the World. Joyce sent this group photograph of her father standing beside Joyce's now ex-husband. Here, Joyce stands sturdy, smiling, holding her daughter and bracing herself against strong winds.

JOYCE MAYNARD

My Father's Bible

THIRTY YEARS after his death—having now lived longer without my father than I did with him—the images that remain of the man have burned down to a small but powerful few.

I see him standing on the edge of our town pool—the only father, the only person in our whole town most likely, to wear a suit of the old-fashioned style, a relic from his British youth, with a top covering his chest—instructing me in how to swim the crawl. In his fifties when I was born, my father remained a beautiful swimmer.

Saturday mornings we went sketching together—walking side by side through the New Hampshire countryside, each of us brandishing a walking stick. His, he would raise to the sky now and then, a signal to freeze and cease all conversation as he instructed me to study the particular way the light hit a patch of grass, or a cloud formation, or a certain stand of trees.

"Listen, Chum," he whispered, in a manner that commanded reverence. He had detected the song of a warbler. Or a thrush. Possibly (though this was rare) a lark. He knew all their voices, and whistled back to them.

I see him in his attic studio, palette knife in hand, surveying a piece of masonite on which he would be painting—large, bold, beautiful but not remotely representational landscapes, inspired by the places we went on our walks and sketching trips. Making art was not how my father made his living—he worked as a teacher—but the urgency for doing so burned at the center of his life every day. And every night.

He's in our living room, listening to a recording of Mozart Horn Concertos by Dennis Brain, scratched from much playing. He is conducting the music from the chair with wild, passionate gestures. His eyes are moist; Mozart has this effect on him, particularly when combined with vodka.

I have no image of my father drinking, but many of him drunk. Lurching from one half-finished painting to another, moving pieces of construction paper on the board—should it go here, or here, what did I think? My father was a man in love with color, with paint on canvas, lines on paper, forms, and the spaces between forms. His paintings consumed him, but hardly anybody in our town or anyplace else ever saw them besides my mother, my sister and me. Mostly these viewings took place late nights in our attic. Mostly, under the influence of alcohol.

There was a question he would ask of people who came to our house—possibly an old friend but equally likely a random acquaintance—most horrifyingly, to my sixteen-year-old boyfriend, come to pick me up for a night at the movies. My date was not yet through the threshold of our door before I heard my father speak the familiar words.

"Tell me my good man," my father said to the boy I hoped would be my boyfriend, in a voice whose timbre and inflection could have served him well on the stage, "what is the definition of Beauty?"

Silence.

~

There is this one other image I hold of my father, all these long years since the last time I heard his voice. So many years later, in fact, that I am now myself close to the age he must have been when I first registered this picture of him.

It's early morning, possibly not even six o'clock, but he is up and dressed—a heartbreakingly handsome man, who managed to look dapper even though his clothes tended to be a little shabby. He rises before the sun, and because I am his daughter, and I adore him, and I know he believes that when the sun gets up so should I, I am coming down the stairs to start my day with him.

He is sitting at our dining room table, eating his poached egg and toast. There is a book on either side of his plate. One is a heavy, oversized volume called *The Loom of Art*, filled with reproductions of paintings from the Louvre—from before the Italian Renaissance up through the Impressionists. Mornings like these, my father may study a single image for whole minutes. Possibly the entire meal. He is always checking art books out of the library, but this one we own, and because we don't own many, he knows every image as well as he knows my face.

The other book I see before him on the table contains no illustrations. The print on the pages is impossibly small, even for my young eyes, and surely must strain his, except he is sufficiently familiar with the words he barely needs to read them. This book is the Bible—King James version, Old Testament and New. And though it has been decades since my father worshipped at a church, and longer since he would have spoken of himself as a believer—though he is married (problematically) to a Jewish woman—it is this book he values more than any other in our household. More than Milton, Elliot, Spenser, Yeats, or even the poetry of William Blake, though in his deep, melodious voice he recites to me "Little Lamb Who Made Thee?" every night when he puts me to bed. If—in our household filled with books—a fire were to threaten us, and there was only time to retrieve a single volume, it would be his Bible my father would reach for.

Yet it is also the book that represents everything my father tried to leave behind him long ago when he left home—and never could. As much as my father loved the Bible, he despaired of its hold on him. And because I grew up the daughter of a man who was powerfully conflicted in his relationship to that book, I carried my own brand of ambivalence about it.

"You know, Chum," he says to me often on these mornings. "You really need to read the Bible."

"Mmm," I might say before turning back to my Nancy Drew.

My father was the son of British missionaries, born in India, in a little outpost somewhere in the south of that country, where his minister father and fellow Salvation Army follower mother had come, from England, to spread the word of the Lord. His parents had eventually left the Salvation Army because its practices and creed had come to seem too liberal, and joined instead a sect known as the Plymouth Brethren, who believed that a person needed one book and one book only to get through this lifetime on earth.

My father was a naturally curious person, hungry for the world and eager to experience what he called "the life of the senses" that his own stern parents disdained and prohibited. Even as a child, he sought out music and literature and most of all art, and was punished severely when he went against his father's bidding and secretly purchased—with his life savings—a paintbox.

I cannot begin to fathom how it could be that the images an eight-year-old boy made in his sketchbook with a dime store box of paints could be viewed as the devil's work. But I suppose in the world of the Plymouth Brethren any endeavor that took a person away from studying the Bible was an endeavor to avoid. The paints were confiscated.

That story, more than any other of his childhood, captured my imagination during my own growing up years. No fairy tales for my father, or Greek mythology, or Norse fables. But he knew the Bible inside out, and could recite the Psalms and long passages from the Old Testament. He never lost his love of it, though he left the church young—abandoned the teachings of his family and the tight constraints religion had placed on him to become a modern artist. It was a book he studied all his life.

My father didn't simply read his Bible. He remained engaged in a sixty-some year conversation with its authors. And so his copy—the one he took out every morning at breakfast—was not simply well-worn but heavily annotated. I doubt there was a page in that book on which he had not written some comment or observation. Generally many.

Along with that question—"What is Beauty?"—there was a line he delivered to me at least a hundred times over the years of my growing up—two, actually. He told me regularly that I needed to develop a good crawl stroke. He told me with even greater frequency that I needed to read the Bible.

I had better things to do. To a ten, or twelve, or fourteen-year-old girl—or a twenty-one-year-old, or a twenty-five-year-old—studying the Bible was as undesirable an activity as learning to play bridge, or embarking on a course in embalming. Like most young people of my day, I sought out what was entertaining and diverting and popular. There was no place in my life for boils and pestilence, women cast out by their husbands for the failure to conceive offspring, and the sacrificing of goats. I had rock and roll to occupy me. Clothes. Movies. Getting into college and figuring out who I was in the world. I wanted to explore the stuff of real life—not some dusty out-of-date story from long ago.

The year after I left home, my parents' marriage had ended, and my father—now an advanced alcoholic, but still painting daily, and still a man in possession of devastating charm and a kind of wild and raging brilliance—took up with a student of his, forty-five years younger than he. They moved to a house in the country and she became his sketching companion. They moved to England, but things did not go well. They moved back to New Hampshire and they parted, violently.

His life spun more and more out of control after that—with middle-of-the- night phone calls to me when things with her got impossible, when he was desperate. The girlfriend was going crazy. There was no money. His health was failing. The world was a mess. Where, where, where in all of this lay Beauty?

Married now, with children of my own to raise, I saw him only a few times a year after that. He was thinner than me now, with every bone in his skull visible, though he still sported those jaunty ascots of his and took walks with his sketching pad and stick, quoting poetry and noting the songs of birds along the way. And he still painted.

At the age of seventy-three, he moved out to the west coast of Canada and was recognized at last as an artist in a small but significant way by first one gallery there and then others. He was celebrated with a one-man show. He joined AA, where his testimony was, I'm told, an unfailing inspiration to all who struggled for sobriety.

When I was twenty-seven, my father came down with pneumonia. He had been sober for a while but had a relapse, went on a bender, and it did him in. He died a few months shy of his eightieth birthday, leaving stacks of sketchbooks and several hundred beautiful paintings, a few art books, a half dozen natty ascots and fedoras, and drawers full of art supplies.

From three thousand miles away I came for the funeral, and to assist in what is known as putting the affairs in order—though how is a person to put in order a life that never was?

The paintings—after my sister and I made our personal selections—were consigned to a gallery. The clothing was given away. My father had been living those last years in a single room of an old person's residence hotel. He owned almost nothing.

It took no more than a few hours to clean out his room. There was a twelve step manual and an unfamiliar looking Bible. When I asked about his old one—the one I grew up with, in which he'd written all his life—nobody could find it.

"I think he gave it to Susan years ago," one of my father's friends told me. Meaning the girlfriend.

I registered the news with more shock than I would have ever guessed, and more than that, a terrible and crushing sense of loss. All my life my father had urged me to read the Bible. Knowing I had never done this, he had quoted from it as liberally as a lawyer might invoke the Constitution. But in the end, it was not I, his well-loved younger daughter, but this strange interloper who had taken off with his most precious book.

～

Maybe he'd given up on my ever opening it. Maybe he'd given up on the possibility that I'd ever know real wisdom or enlightenment, or even seek it out. Maybe he'd lost all hope somewhere along the line.

I could have purchased my own Bible, of course. It is never difficult to find a copy of the King James edition. There's been one in nearly every hotel room I've ever spent a night. But it wasn't simply the Bible I wanted. It was my father's voice, speaking to me, his only Chum, from those oft-thumbed pages, and offering up his vision of what mattered in this life—as he had all those years when I'd taken his voice so for granted, and, too, often, registered only impatience and annoyance with what he said.

And here I am. Three decades have passed since my father died, but he remains a daily presence, and only in part because the walls of the house I live in are covered with the art he made. In my fifties now, I wonder: Which were the psalms he loved best? Which of the disciples? What were the stories he underlined, and the comments he would have written beside them in the margins in his fine, elegant artist's hand? What pages did he turn to in those most brutal times, for solace and comfort? Where are the words that might offer me guidance now?

It would please my father to know I've developed a reasonable crawl stroke. Not as strong or rhythmic as the stroke he executed, cutting cleanly across the water of our town pool, half a century ago, when I was little, back when he taught me how to swim. Still, if there is a place of worship for me, it is probably the pool where I go, early mornings before the sun comes up, to swim my laps and meditate.

As for my father's other wish for me: I have yet to read the Bible, and though it's a poor excuse to say this is because I do not own the copy that I wish I did, it's the excuse I give, because only reading his copy would I hear his voice speaking to me. As it is, I am left to rent old movies featuring Sir John Gielgud. The closest I can find to someone who sounds like my father, speaking to me.

I hear him often, but only in my head. Sitting in his Mozart chair in our living room as I read outloud to him from some story or essay I've written for school, making notes on three-by-five file cards, of words and phrases I should reconsider. He's sitting on my bed, reciting "The Lady of Shallot" to my eight-year-old self—all twenty stanzas.

Or William Blake. "Tyger, tyger, burning bright." Or Yeats. "I shall arise and go now. And go to Innisfree"...

I hear lake water lapping with low sounds by the shore, he is reciting.

He is telling me to cup my fingers together and I push through the water. He is standing in front of a Van Gogh at the Boston Museum of Fine Arts, where we have traveled two hours by bus to see this show. So moved, he's nearly weeping. My God, he is saying to me. This man ....this man....this man....This man understood.

We are in his small attic studio, and he is standing—palette knife in hand—over a piece of masonite on which he has been painting the image of a road leading into a forest. A stand of trees. The moon. It's midnight, I should be in bed , but I am standing in my nightgown beside my father (I'm eight years old still, or nine maybe) because he wanted my opinion. Should this shape go here, he asks—moving a piece of construction paper to first one spot, then another. Or here?

Cerulean blue, Chum? Or viridian green?

He is holding the telephone receiver, and it is nighttime—an hour (after seven thirty) we always try to grab the phone before he gets to it, but this time we did not succeed, and now he is speaking—not loudly, but with a passionate insistence—to the person on the other end. Could be a friend. Could be a woman fund-raising for a new fire truck.

What is Beauty?, he asks this person. Drunk or sober, my father asked it all his life.

It has only recently occurred to me that I never asked him what he believed the answer to be. Had I asked, I think his response might have had something to do with poetry, and something to do with colors, forms, and light. The natural world might have received mention. As would Mozart. I am thinking his answer would probably have contained the word God.

Phillip Lopate put Melora Wolff in contact with me and I am so glad he did, especially after reading this remarkable essay, which is told in a surprising first person plural. Melora's authoritative voice directs us to ask, "Who were the fathers?" She forces us into a group search for fathers, for surely they are somewhere out there on the upper east side of Manhattan, out in front of the school, or down that long hallway, looking for us, too. Though she never names him in her essay, "Masters in This Hall" is dedicated to her father, Raymond A. "Dutch" Wolff, pictured here as a young man. Emma Dodge Hanson took Melora's recent photograph.

MELORA WOLFF

Masters in This Hall

WHO WERE the fathers? We wanted to see them, to hear them—their coughs and quips, their songs and snorts, their belches and yawns, their whoops and rants—we wanted to hug them, to hug them all the time, to practice daily our hugging of fathers. Maybe we remembered hugging the fathers when we were little girls and they were like trees, and we balanced on the tops of their shoes; maybe we remembered lifting our arms above our heads and waiting for our fathers to lift us up as if we were little ballerinas, into the air where we spun and squealed; maybe we remembered climbing onto the broad backs of the fathers, hanging our tired selves around their shoulders and nodding to sleep, our saliva moistening their shirts while they kept walking through city parks; maybe we remembered lying on the pavement, knees skinned, trying hard not to look at the oozing blood because looking at blood—hadn't our fathers warned us?—would only make us cry. Maybe we had known we would always be alone with our torn knees and brimming tears until the fathers swept us up in their arms and carried us home, toward bandages and mothers' balms. Or maybe we remembered none of this at all. Maybe we wondered instead why we had never felt our fathers hugging us, why they always slipped away whenever we came near them, why they looked so very afraid.

Where were the fathers? They weren't in the lobby of the school. They weren't waiting to escort us beside the East River safely home. That was not the duty of the fathers, but of the unemployed mothers, who walked with us along the boardwalk, or under the school pier past the loiterers, the skateboarders and bikers, or across the busy New York City avenues.

They listened to our descriptions of the day. *We tied our belts together to look like Siamese twins! We flushed all the toilets at the same time! We saw Andy Warhol eating lunch in the cafeteria! We learned to sing Negro spirituals!* Yes, these were the details we told the weary mothers or sometimes the big sisters with their big-sister school bags slung over their shoulders, each bag emblazoned with The Brearley School's initials, "B.S." Some of the girls' mothers and big sisters never waited for them in the lobby after school at all, and those girls had their own chauffeurs waiting for them, groomed and chunky guys the girls shouted out to warmly—"Buddy!", or "Rocky!"—as if their chauffeurs were beagle pups or guppies. But we rarely saw the fathers who had made us. They appeared most often after dinner and just before bedtime, and we knew they would likely vanish again before sunrise. When they arrived home at dusk, they tugged at the ties around their throats; they dropped their overcoats, their brief cases or wallets, their typewriters or instruments with a loud thud in the dining rooms; they asked the mothers for a martini, or an Old Fashioned or a scotch and soda. They sighed and draped their bodies across the furniture, like wide unfolded flags.

Many years ago, the new young fathers had gathered in groups at birthday parties, where they wore golden construction paper crowns on their heads, scooped ice cream and cut the purple cake. They had crawled on their hands and knees through the giant caterpillar slinky, and emerged glorious from the other side, their hands filled with costume jewelry. They had marched us through the halls to the big treasure chest with the padlock they broke open like a band of gruff pirates, and tossed bracelets, bangles, necklaces and chocolate coins into the air for us to gather up in our party skirts. They helped us beat the piñata violently to shreds with tennis rackets, and we had all cheered together. So the fathers were persuaded to show up years later at the Gold and Silver Balls—the cotillions held in the school auditorium—where they leaned silently against the walls as our chaperones. The cotillions were always controlled, proper, and festooned. There was hot tea, a platter of donuts, and Simon and Garfunkel harmonized on the loudspeakers, "I am a rock, I am an island". Peripheral, the fathers slouched in their nostalgia while we danced by them in our patent leather high heels. They appeared lost and sad. Although the cotillions were nothing like the musky dances held at the boys' school on the West Side of the city, we knew that these moping fathers were nevertheless necessary as our witness—to preserve decorum, to defend our girlish decency and to beat back predators as if they were piñatas.

Above the heads of the fathers gathered vigilantly in the auditorium loomed the portraits of the Heads of School for the past century. First were the older portraits of the Masters, beginning of course with the school's founding father, Samuel Brearley. In his portrait, Samuel wore nineteenth-century clothing, and had long curled hair like a girl. Skeptics, who opposed the intellectual and social advancement of young girls, had asked Samuel, Will education remove the blush from the girls' cheeks? "No, it will not!" our founding father Samuel had decreed. He delivered lectures on education for women, he answered questions; he asked for further financial support; everywhere, he promoted and publicized his newly founded girls' school. After Samuel's sudden death from typhoid, another man became Master of the school and when that Master died quickly, as though some supernatural office disapproved of Masters in schools of girls, the Heads that succeeded the two men were women, dour, sturdy, and imposing. The headmistresses posed for their portraits oily and weary in black robes. The fathers stood beneath these portraits, and watched us twirl in our dotted Swiss dresses. The fathers breathed in our Middle School breezes of tea-rose perfume. They glanced at our bodies, spindly and coiffed in the arms of panic stricken boys. The fathers looked proud, embarrassed, violent, tender, fierce, exhausted, indifferent, curious, covetous, competitive, loving, amused and mean. They lowered their eyes as we went past them. They whispered to each other every now and then and burst into very loud laughter. Sometimes, they slapped each other hard on the back or shoulder. Sometimes they held out pale sticks of gum to one another. The fathers chewed gum as if it were pieces of raw flesh, their mouths moist and open.

We launched an enthusiastic campaign, inviting as many fathers as possible to visit our classes and tell us about their jobs—regardless of their line of work—so that we could stare at them. While the fathers described their jobs to us, we were able to study the men themselves, like a new and foreign subject in our classrooms. We could admire their long legs—elegantly and professionally crossed—, the cashmere of their suits, the gleam of their freshly shaven faces, stray locks of their combed hair slipping boyishly across their foreheads as they spoke. Amazing, we thought, that the fathers could look so much like boys; amazing that this was so very appealing, whereas boys never looked at all like fathers and were never appealing. We were also amazed to gain the fathers' intimate insider perspectives on their work. From the obliging fathers, we learned about architecture, screen-writing, white water rafting, neurology, symphony performance, opera, podiatry, campaign management, newspaper journalism, painting, banking, publishing, composing, aircraft control, television production, psychiatry, gynecology, and the Supreme Court. Lena's father demonstrated the candy dispenser he had invented, a plastic stick with a smiling head on the top. If you twisted the head, a pink candy spurted out. Sarah's father, the architect, took us on a tour of Times Square, pointing to all of the buildings he had designed.

"That big tall one over there," he said as we hurried behind him with our teacher Miss Dunn, "I made that one—and that one too. You should see it at night. It lights up. It's something."

We attracted a certain attention that day—the sharp, sleek father and his coterie of girls in matching uniforms, socks and wool jackets with B.S. insignias, marching beneath red neon flashing marquees, and past clusters of older women wearing wigs, heavy make-up and matching outfits of their own. Some of the ladies smiled at us. Others did not.

Miss Dunn said she was feeling dizzy, and so we all headed back to the school without finishing the architectural tour. We didn't mind. We thought the buildings Sarah's father had made all looked exactly the same, completely boring, but we said nothing to him, as he was sweating and seemed exhausted by his abbreviated tour.

In the afternoons, we trained in gym class where we yelled and shoved each other, divided into two furious teams, The Reds and The Whites. When the weather was good, the Reds and Whites trained on the securely wire-fenced pier above the river. We had a fleeting audience of rakish looking men, sailors on the decks of boats gliding by the school. "Hoa, girls!" the sailors shouted and whooped, "Throw that ball over here! Why don't you come away with us?" and they waved their arms as they passed.

Our sport was *Blitzkrieg*, which was actually Dodge Ball, but the lady gym teachers preferred the name "*Blitzkrieg*." Dodge Ball was for losers. *Blitzkrieg* was for leaders. We flung the hard pink balls deliriously at each other with a force that sent many girls crying to the Nurse. The school Nurse had been the inspiration for a classic black and white film made in the nineteen-fifties, a dramatic depiction of her own youthful wedding called *Father of the Bride*. In the film, our school nurse was played by the most beautiful and glamorous of women, Elizabeth Taylor, which we found both impressive and unbelievable, as the nurse bore no resemblance whatsoever to Elizabeth Taylor but was grey haired and wore white orthopedic shoes, a little white cap, horn rimmed glasses, and white knee socks. She had a general aura not of femininity, but of anonymity and resignation. In the film, our nurse's father had been played by Spencer Tracy. When we had all gathered in Heather's living-room to watch a reel to reel film of *Father of the Bride*, we laughed at Spencer Tracy looking robust and peeved as he struggled into his cutaway tuxedo for his daughter's wedding day. "You have a little girl," Tracy faced the camera and lamented to his fellow fathers, "You're her oracle. You're her hero. And then the day comes...." From Tracy we understood that a handsome, flustered father may grieve when his daughter leaves him for another man.

Battered and ambitious, we *Blitzkrieg* soldiers staggered from gym class with our bloody noses to the Hollywood Nurse's clinic, where we lay on her medical cots moaning like the Northern and Southern Civil War soldiers in *Gone with the Wind*. Nurse definitely did not approve of young ladies playing *Blitzkrieg*, but we assured her that bloody injury was our badge of honor. The Whites were winners! The Reds were losers. Nurse adjusted our pony-tails and sent us back into the drama of the battle.

Sometimes we gathered at the boy's school gym, to watch the really fit boys sweat, and to admire their speed, their new muscles and their remarkable knees. The boys' gym stank of their sweat and dank t-shirts. The old heating pipes clanked above the ball court as the boys ran like demons, shoving and shouting. This was not unlike our own gym classes. We applauded the boys, half-heartedly, at their games. We knew that those sweaty boys weren't the real males; they were just the miniatures, many of them with noses that bled suddenly during conversation with girls at the Gaiety Mixers, without any *Blitzkrieg* injury at all. The boys' noses just spontaneously ejaculated blood down their shirt fronts, and they wiped the blood away with the back of their hands and kept trying to talk to us, pretending nothing had happened, pretending their shirts weren't soaked. They looked like they'd been stabbed. Their voices cracked and groaned. They had a rowdy humor that made us shudder. The jocks pounding past us at the basketball games were the same boys that threw each other around for hours on rubber mats after school, a coach screaming in their ears, pound harder! They lost their teeth and didn't mind. They broke their whole faces and didn't mind. They limped and spit. They burped and stretched. They grinned too much, too.

But what would happen after that? After they grew older? Could any one of them ever earn our love and respect, or Spencer Tracy's wrath? We cheered whenever a tall boy dunked the ball through the net with impeccable force and scored, but we didn't really care. Our determined lady teachers—all of them impressive—had taught us girls emphatically: women are essential, men are just inevitable. We were taught never to forget that. Women, they said, would build the world! Men would just live in it. It was 1972.

We all pressured Sue to invite her father to visit the school, because she had told us once, very casually, that her father was an actor and had a role on *The Mod Squad*. But she wouldn't invite him to come to our school so we never believed she was telling the truth about his profession at all, until one afternoon, her mother failed to appear in the lobby and Sue's father was summoned at once by the American History teacher. Girls started gathering in the school lobby at 2:30 p.m. We chatted in little cliques, hoping to see Sue's father when he arrived. Some teachers gathered too, over by the coat check room where they kept a low profile. At 3:05, Mod Squad Dad sauntered into the lobby, his dark glasses perched on the end of his nose, and his jeans slung low on his hips. He lit a cigarette. Who would tell this father that he could not smoke his Marlboros in the lobby of the girls' school? While he waited for Sue to collect her books and gym bag, he read the notices pasted around the elevator, performing, portraying his deep interest in the new Latin Club, in the publicity posters for our all-girl production of *The Importance of Being Earnest* and in the audition announcements for our exciting upcoming co-ed production of *West Side Story*, which we would produce with the boys' school. We had selected *West Side Story* as our co-ed show because Nina's father had composed the music for it and had one day actually played "I Feel Pretty" for us on his own grand piano, and a few chords too of "A boy like that! Who kills your brother!" until we accidentally tipped a giant library ladder over on top of him and smashed his music rack. We were impressed by his good nature about this incident. Our poster for *West Side Story* featured an illustration of boys at the rumble—The Jets and The Sharks—waving big knives, and a fuzzy looking Maria weeping in the background. Mod Squad Dad soon lost interest in our poster board. He unzipped his black leather jacket. He had a sexy gap between his teeth and when Sue arrived, he whistled through the gap like the start of an excellent musical overture. We pretended not to care when Sue kissed his cheek and he lifted her, briefly, off the floor. Enviously, we watched Sue swing out the glass doors of the school with her groovy, crime-busting dad.

In the late autumn, we practiced for the Christmas Assembly. We worked for several months to perfect the program. All of the parents attended the annual Christmas Assembly in Assembly Hall, the mothers seated in the upper balcony as queens might be seated, and the fathers seated in the lower darkness beneath the balcony, like galley slaves. The girls' chorus was disciplined to gather beneath the portraits of the founding father and headmaster Samuel, and of the other masters and headmistresses. The chorus would then lead all of the classes and visiting parents in a medley of carols our music teacher Miss Havey had selected for us—*We Three Kings, God Rest Ye Merry Gentlemen, Good King Wenceslas*—and perform a strange minor-key song Miss Havey called "a lively holiday anomaly," about a Spartan boy who was bitten to death by a fox he kept hidden inside his coat. Why, we wondered, didn't the Spartan boy scream if his fox was biting him to death? Why didn't he keep his fox somewhere else, like in a cage or a box? Katie said this must be a cautionary song about male masturbation. As editor in chief of the girls' school literary magazine, *The Beaver*, Katie was an expert in metaphors, but even she conceded that the lyric was inscrutable. Would Miss Havey pick a male masturbation song for the Christmas Assembly? It seemed unlikely. The chorus of the song went, "So he dropped down dead- a-dead-a-dead all dead but ripe for glory." This sentiment, whatever its meaning, seemed best suited for the beginning of the Christmas program, as a warm up of sorts, before we gathered steam with *Here Comes Santa Claus*.

The bell carriers were to stand in the front of the chorus, poised for the ringing of the Christmas bells. I was the low D bell. We were to hold our bells resting against our shoulders like small babies we were about to burp, and when our note approached, we were to lift the bell gently from our shoulder, and then, at just the right moment, plunge the bell fiercely downward as though we were hurling the baby to the floor with a wrenching thrust of the arm. Christmas would sound as the ancients had intended it to sound when they first filled the air with the echoing of bells, with song and sweet voices raised on high heralding the birth of Jesus, the Holy Son of God, the Blessed Father.

We doubted that any father would impress us as much as Sue's Mod Squad father, until Mimi's father visited our class. Mimi's father was a gynecologist. On the day he visited, he stood confidently at the front of the room in front of the blackboard, his hands on his hips as he faced some thirty of us in our jumpers and doily collared blouses.

Behind him blazed the single word he had written on the blackboard like the opening title of a television detective show, "Spermicide." We waited uneasily for his insights. Our home-room teacher Mademoiselle France also looked uneasy in her place behind the front desk.

"Girls," he said, "I know you're just twelve. But you should all get yourselves diaphragms. So when you have sex you won't get pregnant and ruin your lives. Getting pregnant doesn't automatically ruin your life. That's not my point. But if you're pregnant and you're twelve, well, I don't care what those girls did back on the prairie in the olden days. We aren't on the prairie. We're in New York City. I know some of you are having sex, right?"

Nobody spoke. Was Mimi having sex? Or did he mean someone else? Was he just guessing?

"Well," he went on, "I know some of you are. And I think that's *terrific*. Sex is terrific. You should all know that. It's my job to tell you that." This seemed like an unusual job, but we were intrigued.

"So if you've never seen a diaphragm before," he continued, "it looks like this." He reached over to the teacher's desk and grabbed Mademoiselle France's silver desk bell, which he waved above his head. "A diaphragm looks like this. Except it doesn't have a bell. It doesn't ever ring. And you can fold a diaphragm in half, but this thing is made of metal, so they're different in those ways. A diaphragm isn't made of metal. It's made of latex. Otherwise, they're the same. But don't mess around with this thing"—he dinged the bell—"because Ouch. You get the idea. Do you have any questions?"

Was it possible that anyone had a question? Mademoiselle France looked pale. A hand shot up. It was Madeleine, who we had long suspected yearned for something close to sex during lunch break with the drama teacher, a very young fellow we all called contemptuously by his first name, Eddie.

"Do you like having sex?" Madeleine called loudly to Mimi's father from the back of the room.

We all sank lower in our seats.

Mademoiselle France said, "I'm afraid we're all out of time, but this has been terrific—not *terrific*—but informative and so useful."

"I love having sex!" Mimi's father bellowed. "It's my job to tell you that!"

In Latin class, we had completed our translations of *Julia*, a short book about a little girl who walks by the sea and tries to learn the history of Greece and Rome, just as we all tried to translate *Julia* out of Latin into English, so that her story could become even less interesting. When we had finished translating Julia, we remembered only the opening sentence, "*Iulia puella parva est*"—"Julia is a little girl." We were excited to embark next on a translation of *The Aeneid*. Madame Kostke paced at the front of the room in her black dress and oxford shoes, proclaiming *The Aeneid*'s dramatic opening sentence, "*arma virumque cano!*" and we chanted back, "I sing of arms and the man!" Madame helped us through pages of the hero's battles in the Trojan War, the advance of the Trojan Horse, and of the returning warriors' funeral games. When Heather failed to bring her copy of *The Aeneid* to Latin class, Madame Kostke said fiercely, "Heather, you remind me of the potato fields in Greece!"

Many years ago, Madame Kostke was a little girl—as little as Julia, she emphasized—and lived on a farm with her father and brothers five miles from the fields where men dug potatoes. She begged the men to let her dig potatoes. One dark morning, Madame Kostke reported, her father allowed her to walk the five miles to dig potatoes with the men. But when she arrived at the potato field, she saw she had forgotten to bring her shovel. She walked the long way back alone. "And what is the moral of this story?" Madame Kostka demanded of Heather.

"Don't live on a farm," Heather said.

"If you want to work alongside men," Madame shouted, as though she might melt, "you must be prepared, girls! You must bring your tools! Men will not help you, they will only laugh! You cannot dig potatoes if you do not bring your shovel!"

We nodded. We wrote this moral in our notebooks between "*Iulia puella parva est*" and "*arma virumque cano.*"

Once, a father appeared abruptly in our classroom and removed a daughter by force. He offered no apology. He gave no explanation. The air in the classroom went still, a silence fell, and Mademoiselle France changed the subject quickly as the door slammed after the father and the stumbling girl. She was that girl who never spoke. She wasn't like the rest of us, with our shiny long hair twirled in buns and braids and pony tails. She was the one who wore black eyeliner, kept her gaze on the floor and wore her hair very short. She kept her shoulders rounded, and she had pierced her nose five times. She was a real talent on the guitar, a star. She played her guitar every afternoon out by the lockers at recess, and her lonesome wails echoed. She was a dark wave that rolled through the hallways of the school, drowning everyone in her path. She scared us all.

In our new and progressive psychology class, the peppy Play Therapy teacher with the turquoise earrings and tie dyed skirt who told us all to call her "Miss Julie," asked us all to build "environments" we dreamed of, out of potted plants and blocks and plastic dolls she distributed to us all like blank checks, which we would have preferred.

"Dolls?" the shadow girl snorted.

I shrugged and stripped all my dolls. Slowly, I worked on making a tribal jungle village on the banks of the Amazon River. I arranged some naked natives launching a raft I made out of a short wood ruler, on which I laid a maiden bound by rubber bands. But the shadow girl worked very quickly. She built a massive medieval fortress, fortified with high walls, a blue yarn moat, and a large forest of ivy plants and jade. She placed paper clip catapults along the block walls.

"Why isn't there a drawbridge for the fortress?" Miss Julie asked, "So people can get inside?"

"Because they don't want anyone to get inside," the girl said.

"Who are they keeping out?" There was a slight tremor in Miss Julie's voice. The girl stared at her, and said flatly, "The Army of Fathers."

In history class, Miss Nestle scheduled movies about the Second World War. Several of the fathers had served in one war or other, Miss Nestle said, and although she herself had never seen any of our fathers except at the parent teacher meetings, where they sat silently behind the mothers until money was mentioned, she said they were all heroes. Katie said she thought Hilary's father must still be depressed from the war in Korea. She had glimpsed him during her sleepover visits to Hilary's. He lay curled up in a tight ball on a tiny thread bare loveseat beneath a painting of the sea, not moving. He clutched the pages of news about Viet Nam inside his fists as he slept. He wouldn't get up. He didn't seem to have a job. "Something wasn't right with him", Katie said. "A father shouldn't sleep like a homeless man under newspapers on a tiny loveseat."

We wanted to believe Miss Nestle when she said the fathers were heroes, even though we knew she had certainly never seen the fathers in the kitchen late at night, making peanut butter sandwiches; she had never spied on them spinning the dials around and around on the radio in the dark morning, listening to bursts of music and static; she had never seen them hanging a door poorly on its hinge, or scouring a burned frying pan, or trying to give water to a baby guinea pig with a syringe. She would not have been able to imagine these unlikely acts of heroism, just as we were not able to imagine—never wanted to imagine—the fathers with guns, with grenades, with backpacks and bullets on their belts.

We had seen no photographs of the fathers in Germany, or in Korea. In our dreams, even the fathers' faces remained shaded under helmets so that we could not see their eyes, and their boy-soldier bodies crawled through mud toward some enemy, or dozed restlessly and anonymously in shadows on bedrolls, in the backs of covered trucks, in dirt, or in trenches. Perhaps the fathers had dreamed of their unborn daughters then, just as we dreamed of our fathers now. Or maybe they dreamed they would never have daughters at all, only sons that would beget more sons that would beget more sons. Maybe they prayed to God they would never have children at all.

On a Friday Film Day, Miss Nestle announced that there would be an afternoon screening of *The Twisted Cross* for anyone who was interested. After lunch, we all gathered on blankets on the History classroom floor to watch Hitler rise to power. Miss Jones—the woodshop and pottery teacher—arrived unexpectedly for the screening. Downstairs in the shop, Miss Jones had taught us all how to swing a hammer, how to use a table saw, how to build benches and shellac bookshelves. She had taught us how to heat the massive black kiln and bake our pottery cups and bowls inside, and how to glaze them again to perfection when we removed them from the oven. We wouldn't need a man, she said, to build our houses or put food on our tables! We girls would build the world! We were the future! She strode in to the room on *The Twisted Cross* day covered in sawdust, with her lunch in a paper bag. She pulled up a chair, and joined our audience. She was in a good mood, a fine mood, a movie-going mood. She was ready, she said, to see Hitler again. Miss Jones said, "Girls, you don't know what Hitler meant for us then, for all the Youth. He was so charismatic. He was so handsome, so strong! He was the father some of us had never had."

Our education had not prepared us to consider Hitler as our pottery teacher's father. We simply watched as Miss Nestle hurried to the light-switch. She tripped on a blanket in the dark. She told us the film was broken, our screening of *The Twisted Cross* was cancelled, she apologized. Miss Jones tossed her apple core into the trash can and left. Two days later, the rumors began. The teachers whispered. The big sisters whispered. Discreetly, the fathers had formed a chain of command. They had left their work; they had hurried at dusk in a rainstorm; they had gathered in the lobby of the school, stomped rain from their boots; they had walked together through the halls to the headmistress's office. The fathers spoke their peace, and in a sudden flash, Miss Jones was gone, as though she had never shellacked a shelf or baked a bowl—as though she had never existed. None of us saw her extinguished. Maybe it never happened. Maybe I write to command the army of the fathers.

When Missy's father had completed his Erhard Seminars Training, he allowed a few of us to visit his art studio to see his latest paintings. After his est, he said, he had decided to work on a new series of paintings, each one with a black background, and with a vase of bright flowers depicted at the center of each canvas. So far, he had painted chrysanthemums, roses, sunflowers, irises, baby's breath, pansies, day lilies, and gardenias. He propped each canvas against the wall so that we might study the flowers and the three dimensional effects he had achieved. He said that after he completed his est, flowers meant more to him than they had before— he had discovered a place of silence at the center of his being that was filled with flowers. He had freed himself from his base desires, from his impulses of rage and violence and from his desire to control other human beings. He had discovered Peace. He was in command of Serenity. During his est, he said, everyone had been locked into a large room, and no one was allowed to leave until they had met their inner selves and taken control of their impulses.

"How did you go to the bathroom?" Katie asked Missy's father.

He said, "We didn't go to the bathroom, Katie, we had to stay locked inside the room until we completed our est training. We controlled our bodily needs. We didn't go to the bathroom. We were locked in the large room. We stayed there. We met our inner selves. We made drawings. Look," he said, and he gave each of us a small blank card with a curved line drawn on it, "Do you girls know what this curved line represents? Can you complete this drawing?"

Missy's father waited while we each drew a picture on our index card, incorporating the strange curved line into our own imaginative scenes. I drew a tiny man staring up at a leafy tree. Missy drew a pregnant owl sitting on a branch. She gave the owl a caption balloon, in which she wrote the word "Who?" Her father collected our pictures and nodded.

"Yes" he said, "these drawings reveal your budding sexual natures, just as my flowers reveal my fading sexual nature." He held above his head a large painting of wilted pansies. Secretly we wondered, would Mimi's father think these paintings were terrific?

Another father—my father—had also been in the war, in Germany. I knew for a fact that my father did not sleep on a sofa inside the daily news of Viet Nam, and when I stayed up late one night to tell him we had studied the assassination of Archduke Ferdinand, the Western Front, invasions, concentration camps, and exterminations, he agreed reluctantly to visit our history class. He arrived in khaki trousers, a wool sweater and sneakers. Miss Nestle greeted him warmly and offered him a desk-chair at the front of the room.

"Tell us whatever you remember," Miss Nestle said encouragingly, and added, "Anything. We know you were a very young man, just a little older than the girls are now."

My father folded himself awkwardly into the desk-chair and looked at all our faces without saying anything. The air was tense. I feared my father would fail his classroom visit. Then, he described the beautiful countryside in Germany. He described long roads unwinding like velvet ribbons, and convoys of trucks rolling over the hills in darkness. He described nights without moonlight, an abandoned manor balanced like a jewel on a cliff, and how the men in his unit curled on its marble floor until dawn, breath held and waiting. He described music rising among the trees. He said there were unfamiliar smells wafting over the fields on a wind. He said if we were careful he would show us an object he had discovered in a camp during the last days of the war, after the liberations—a golden knife with a porcelain handle. We passed this knife carefully around the room, and studied the nearly illegible signature engraved on the handle: Adolf Hitler. We sat very still. Miss Nestle returned the knife to my father, and

I saw she did not touch the signature. My father said he still had dreams about the war, and suddenly I knew this for a fact too, because each night, I heard him through the bedroom walls of our city apartment, shouting and moaning like a little boy in his sleep, and I plugged my ears trying not to listen. He told us all his dreams were grey, and that sometimes it was very hard to wake up from his dreams. Many girls exchanged a glance, maybe thinking of Hilary's father still asleep on the threadbare love seat. I stared at my father's sneakers as though I'd never seen them before. His laces were untied.

Our co-ed "Inter-School" production of *West Side Story*, which we would perform in the week preceding the Christmas Assembly, featured more girls than boys, because few boys auditioned and only a few of these boys could pass as gang members. Some resembled Jets, but none of them looked like Sharks. The four boys finally cast as Sharks were all named Dan. There was no explanation for this. Our musical director Miss Rose signaled to us to practice our first act finale. We stood in our knee-socks, blouses and gym shorts and piped in four-part harmony with The Jets and The Dans, "We're going to rock it tonight! We're going to live it up and have us a ball!"

"No girls! You're angry!" Miss Rose shouted at us. "Let me hear Anger! You live on the streets! Your parents don't love you! You're angry West Side misfits!"

We rehearsed the rumble, and the deaths: Bernardo killed Riff, Tony killed Bernardo, and Chino killed Tony. A freckled boy we had never seen before played the sniper Chino. Song and dance and knives and guns made men of all the boys. We watched them spin with a natural grace unavailable to those jocks we had seen pounding each other on rubber mats at the boys' school gymnasium. These agile theater boys threw each other to the floor like pros. They rolled and jumped to the music Nina's father had composed. They lunged. We were pleased to see they dodged. When the boys stepped off stage, they handed each other sticks of gum and slapped each other on the back. In stage make-up, they all looked older. In stage-light, they all looked handsome. We thought the boys smelled familiar, too. Lisa held DJ's sweaty hand, and whispered, like a Capulet,

"Don't tell my father, he'll kill you"; then Mimi kissed Roger; Lee kissed Dan; Sylvia kissed Paul; Katie kissed Dan; Jen kissed Dan; Liz kissed Jack; Katie kissed Bill; Elaine kissed Jay; Missy kissed Jimmy; I kissed Tony. We kissed and kissed, with lyrics in our heads—*Tonight, tonight, won't be just any night!* We sang of love and arms and men. We pictured our fathers beating all these beautiful boys to death with tennis rackets. We pictured our fathers looking sadly into the camera, just like Spencer Tracy.

Our lips still aching, we gathered onstage with the boys around the fallen body of Tony, for the funereal end of the show. The boys hung their heads while the girls pretended to sob. We draped a black veil over the face of the girl who played Maria. Then The Jets and The Dans struggled to lift the body of Tony onto their shoulders and they carried him away beneath the blue lights, past the carefully designed set of wire fences and into the blackness of the wings where they dropped him, and he got back to his feet. Mr. Foote, our piano player, rang the minor chords of the final dirge.

We knew of only one girl among us whose father had actually died. She had been small when it happened. She was a little girl. Clearly, this girl's oracle was nothing like our own, but perpetual, and all powerful in his planetary silence. She was that older girl with the straight brown hair, always brushed, and with the pale brows and solemn eyes. She had a tender glance for each of us, she never looked away. We did not expect such a glance from a girl who had lost her father—as though she worried for us all, or knew she was gazing at us from an isolated galaxy we would someday occupy ourselves. She walked with a straight and dignified posture, her school books balanced on her arm, and when she passed us in the hallways, we stepped aside for her and did not know what to say. There was nothing we could say. We felt awe when we saw her. We felt hot shame. We felt a distant, intimate anguish that made us turn from her and then look back. Her father was gone yet she continued to live. His sudden death was a violation of a natural order. How would she be a daughter without her father? We felt we knew this girl's father, even, perhaps, that we loved him, although we had only heard about him, from our mothers, from our fathers too, and had read about him in archived newspapers and in our American history books. Everyone mourned her father, who had been killed by a sniper on a grey day in Dallas when our lives had barely begun.

Did the fathers weep? Did they close the doors and lower themselves, broken, into chairs? Did they wipe the palm of their hands across their faces, and feel ashamed of their weeping, and frightened by it, and yet surrender to their sobs like boys whose hearts have been permanently broken? Did they try to clear their throats and smooth their hair and adjust their neutral gaze before stepping again into the stoic world of still living fathers? We knew that many of the fathers did cry, quietly, invisibly, in secret locked rooms we would never dare enter. We imagined their shoulders trembling, their arms folded across their stomachs, their bodies torn with an unfathomable pain they kept concealed inside their coats. We imagined those fathers who, in some other catastrophic disruption of the natural order, had survived their own daughters, for a few school girls among us were gone, without any explanation: the girl who fell head first down the slope of ice, her skis and legs tangled; the girl who took a short cut down a dark alley; the girl whose body folded slowly into paralysis; the girl who had a tumor; the girl hit by a car on a quiet street; the girl who leapt and didn't leave a note; the girl who glided like the dead through rooms; and the girls—too many of us girls—who starved for no apparent purpose, like prisoners of a war we could not name, our breasts shrinking, our hair falling out like fairy dust, our hips bending like carved bowls, our twelve ribs piercing our own flesh like blades.

On the day of the Christmas Assembly, we wore our crisply laundered uniforms and marched in perfect rank and file beneath the school flag. We could hear the school orchestra already playing Christmas carols, setting the holiday mood in Assembly Hall. We heard the warbling voices of all the elegant mothers seated in the balcony, anticipating our carefully choreographed arrival. We spotted the School Nurse. She was not wearing her white cap, or a bridal gown, but a fashionable and feminine lace dress and high-heels. She looked elegant. We entered Assembly Hall through the four open arched doorways, and saw the golden light of the Hall, the stage decked with smaller holiday bulbs, the wooden stairs where the chorus would gather, and the large metal rack that held all of the bells we would soon ring in joyful noise. We saw the podium where the headmistress would deliver her Christmas Speech heralding a shifting world, a new world built by the smart young girls gathered before her. We saw too, one after another, the faces of the headmistresses staring blankly at us from their portraits as they had stared through a century of Christmas Assemblies, and the faces of the two fallen headmasters, ending with Samuel, our founding father, who looked approving.

The smallest and youngest girls led us into the Hall beneath Samuel's portrait. The fifth graders were followed by the sixth graders, then by the sevenths, the eighths, and once we girls had all gathered nervously in front of our chairs, we awaited the entrance of the fathers. They would follow behind us, marching to their places beneath the balcony. Then, we would sing.

We could see the fathers standing in the hallway, waiting to march. Every girl tried to glimpse her own father, but they had become one river of blue suits, no man independent of another. They shuffled through the pages of their lyrics, and dropped pages on the floor without noticing. We could hear them coughing, too. They made phlegmy hacking sounds. There were a few short bursts of laughter from the unruly fathers, followed by the shushing sounds of the disciplined fathers. We heard the sound of their dress shoes scraping on the tiled floor. We had never seen so many men's polished dress shoes! Then Mr. Foote began pounding out the chords of the seventeenth-century French carol we had rehearsed. The descending chords of this obscure carol were the fathers' signal to enter the hall.

As the fathers moved forward, we noted with some amazement that they walked very clumsily, as though they did not know how to march and that they strayed from their formation and bumped into one another. A few times they completely stalled, as though they were in traffic. Metal chairs scraped and clattered, and the fathers finally came to a discombobulated halt. Miss Havey stood at the front of the hall facing the fathers, eyeing them grimly. They quieted down. Her expression remained stern and forgiving. She raised her baton to signal the start of the Assembly, the entrance chords reached a crescendo, and in one booming voice that echoed between the walls of portraits, the chorus of fathers sang out,

"Masters in this Hall
Hear ye news today!
Brought from over sea
And ever I you pray!"

There was a ripple of laughter from the girls. We had never heard such a strange sound in our own girls' school Assembly Hall, the sound of one hundred and seventy-five fathers singing together—the impossibly thunderous voices of the fathers who had backed away when we were born, afraid of holding us, afraid of dropping us, afraid of teaching daughters; fathers who had carried us, and knelt beside us, and pressed our first glass of champagne to our lips; heroes who had lifted us onto the carousel and watched us shout and ride our wooden horses in such harmless cavalry; fathers who knew everything and nothing about us, who loved us too little and loved us too much; oracles who became rocks, and islands, and ghosts; fathers who closed their doors or flew into the clouds or looked into the camera or looked away; men who had all, so far, survived themselves.

"This is Christ the Lord,
Masters be ye glad!
Christmas is come in,
And no folk should be sad!
Nowell! Nowell! Nowell!
Nowell sing we clear!
Holpen are all folk on earth,
Born is God's Son so dear!"

We knew in our bones this was a sound—like the rumbles of a shifting earth—we would never hear again. In our strongest voice, we sang with our fathers

After reading Jessica Woodruff's remarkable and honest student essays about growing up in brutal foster homes, I asked if she had a story about her biological father. Jessica responded with this essay about a road trip that reads more like an adventure story. There is an archival quality to Jessica's work. The experience, the essay, is an artifact now, not just a bad memory. In his Confessions, St. Augustine said that cogo (collect) was related to cogito (re-collect, cogitate, reflect). To remember is to re-collect, to sort, and to understand. Jessica is no longer the young girl in the pages of this essay. She is an artist looking at her life story, meditating on what it all might mean. Jessica is pictured here with the man she now calls dad, Glenn Soucy. Glenn and his wife adopted Jessica a year ago.

Crossing State Lines

WHEN I WAS growing up, my father was a long-haul trucker. It seemed like he was always on the road, and sometimes he was gone for a week or more. Father always wore his company hat—a dark gray mesh cap that hid his balding, red hair. He looked as if he hadn't showered, shaved, or changed clothes since the day he had left for the road, and he smelled like gasoline, tar, and Marlboro cigarettes.

When my five siblings and I went into foster care, we didn't see our parents much, because, when I was four, they were arrested for child abuse and neglect, their legal rights were terminated, and they divorced. My siblings and I were allowed to see our parents, but their visits had to be supervised. Our mother didn't visit with us as often as our father did—she was in and out of jail for making and selling drugs.

Sometimes when my father visited, we went to the park near his apartment. If he had money, he packed us a picnic: bologna and cheese sandwiches or hotdogs, a bag of chips or pretzels, and soda cans of Big Red. Sometimes he took us to see his parents.

We usually went fishing at a park before seeing our grandparents— our grandmother usually fixed goulash and cornbread whenever we came. Sometimes he visited with us at our foster house. On these visits, he didn't stay for very long, leaving not long after he got there, but when he did stay, he usually ate lunch or dinner with us.

Once, when I was a Brownie in Girl Scouts, he came to our father-daughter dance on Valentine's Day. The dance was held in my elementary school's cafeteria. I wore a sparkling purple, long-sleeved dress. He bought me a corsage, and he wore a light pink buttoned-up shirt tucked inside dark kakis. He even wore a tie; it was navy blue. I'd never seen Father wear a tie before, except for in my parents' wedding pictures. When he married my mother, he wore a white suit and tie.

For a while, Father visited us almost every weekend. And one Friday in March, when I was nine, he even drove his semi to our house. He parked his truck on the side of the street—up the hill of our driveway, a half-mile walk from our house. When he told us he drove his truck, we begged our foster mother to let us see it. On visits, he sometimes showed us where he had parked his truck, but we could only see what the outside of his bobtail looked like: black, white, and silver with dual smoke stacks—one on each side of the truck. But, I'd never seen the inside of his truck before. My little brothers and I chased each other up the gravel hill to see who got to the truck first. He told us not to push any buttons or touch anything on the dash.

"Don't touch the gear shift or the wheel," he shouted as we climbed over each other and piled inside the passenger side.

He had a picture of each of us kids taped onto his dashboard. The pictures were old, though, because the picture he had of me was from Kindergarten. I wore a pink dress with a white lace collar, holding a light brown teddy bear on my lap.

"What's this?" I asked, pointing at what looked like a cable above the driver door. "Pull it," he said.

I hesitated because he told us not to touch anything. "Go ahead. It won't hurt cha," he assured.

I pulled the cable and jumped, my brothers screamed, my ears buzzed.

"And that's...the horn," he said, smiling.

"It's so loud," I said.

"Go on, look in the back." He motioned for me to look behind the black curtain that separated the cab from the sleeper. He climbed inside the truck and sat sideways in the driver seat.

He had a mini-closet with a few empty wire hangers, a TV strapped inside a cubby, a radio, several storage cabinets, and a bed. He kept his food—an empty box of Twinkies—in the cabinet above his TV. He kept a twelve-pack of Big Red in a cabinet behind the passenger seat.

"They're bunk beds," he said when we sat down on his bed. "Get up. Watch." He pulled a handle and a small bed flipped open above the bottom bed. After a few minutes, we got out of his truck because it was hot.

While we were walking down the driveway, he asked, "Wanna go for a ride?"

"Really?" I asked, excited.

"Yeah. Just you. The boys are too little. C'mon, let's go," he said, tugging my arm.

"I'll go ask," I said, running off and into the house. "He wants to take me for a ride. Can I go? Please?"

My foster mother was at the kitchen sink peeling potatoes for dinner and humming a church hymn. "What? Slow down. Who?" she asked.

"Daddy, in his semi. Can I go, please?"

"I'm not sure. I'll need to talk to him first."

He was standing in the doorway between the kitchen and the foyer when he said, "She just wants to see what it's like riding in the truck. That's all."

"Pretty please, can I go?" I begged.

"It'll only be to the highway and back," he said.

My foster mother stood by the stove, leaning over the trashcan to empty the potato peelings. She hesitated, and then said, "All right, you can go. But make it quick. Supper's almost ready."

"We won't be gone long," he said.

"Thank you," I shouted and ran out the door.

"Buckle up," he said when he started his truck. The engine sounded loud. My body felt tingly and numb from everything rattling in the cab. It sounded like the truck was going to fall apart. It took a few minutes before we took off down the country road and got onto the highway. He told me the truck had to warm up.

When we waited at the stoplight at the end of the country road, he asked, "Whataya think?"

"I can't really see," I said, trying to push my body up so I could see over the dash. "Here," he said, leaning over and touching a button on the side of the passenger seat. "Unbuckle and push this."

"Woah," I said when the seat rose higher.

"Pretty cool, huh? Didja hear that noise it made? There's air in it. If you push it again, the seat'll go down."

"It kinda feels like a roller coaster. It's bouncy."

"Yeah, it'll feel even more like one when we go down a hill."

We drove down the highway and through the main street in town. But when we waited in a line of traffic to pay the toll between Indiana and Illinois, I asked, "Where're we going?"

"I gotta pick up a trailer."

"OK," I said as we crossed the blue bridge over the Wabash River, crossing the Illinois state line.

When the sun started setting, I said, "Daddy, it's getting dark out." I was worried because I was supposed to be home for dinner.

"Don't worry, honey. I'll getcha back."

"But I gotta be home. I'll get in trouble."

"You won't get in no trouble. You're with me. It'll be OK."

"But I'm hungry."

"Hey now, dontcha start crying. We'll get some food in a little bit. OK? Wanna do me a favor? See that little green sign on the side of the road?"

"The one with the number?"

"Yeah, that's the yardstick, the mile marker. Will you write it down? Look under your seat. There should be some paper and a pen somewhere."

I wrote down the number. "OK, now what?" I asked.

"Every time you see one of those green signs, add that number to the other."

"How come I gotta add these numbers?"

"'Cause that's how I get paid. Gotta keep track of all the miles I make. I'll even give you some of the money for helping."

When it started getting late, I got tired and kept dozing off. "Are you asleep?" he asked.

"No, I'm awake. I'm adding the numbers," I said, waking myself up.

He laughed. "Why dontcha go in the back...lay down for a while. It's all right. Go on. I'll wake you when we stop."

I climbed in the back and lay on Father's bed. His bed was unmade, and he didn't have any sheets on the mattress. His blanket smelled like the rest of his truck, like gasoline, tar, and cigarettes. Crushed Big Red cans lay on the carpet behind his seat. I was tired, but I couldn't fall asleep, at first. All the noises I heard kept me up: the cars passing by, the rough pavement and potholes, the men's voices over the CB radio, the engine rattling. But soon, all these sounds turned into white noise and I fell asleep.

"Hey, get up. It's time to eat," he said when we stopped.

"Where are we?" I asked. I looked out the window. It was nighttime. There were trucks parked all around us in a large parking lot.

"At a truck stop."

I don't remember what our waitress looked like. Father ordered coffee and catfish. I don't remember what I ordered. When we were finished eating, Father showed me around the truck stop. There were showers, pay phones, an arcade room with pool tables and video game machines, and a TV room. Father told me to stay in the TV room while he went to the restroom. There were a few truckers watching a movie. As I stood by the pay phones, two men wearing cowboy hats walked inside the TV room and stood next to me. They asked me how I was doing. I mumbled "fine" and slowly moved closer to the door.

"Where ya goin', pretty lady," they said and whistled at me as I left the TV room. I sat in a chair outside the restrooms and waited for Father. When he was finished, he took his leftover catfish and a to-go cup of coffee, and we went to the truck. "Time to hit the road. Boogity, boogity, boogity," he said. I didn't say much after we left the truck stop. I was tired, bored, and I missed home.

Father told me that truckers use code words to warn each other about cops on the road or other dangers. "It's how we talk to each other," he said. Father told me a lot of the lingo truckers use to communicate: "Smokey Bear" is a cop, a "camera" is a police radar gun, "green stamps" are money, "cash registers" are toll booths, "chicken coops" are weigh stations, a "one-eyed monster" is a TV, a "pickle park" is a rest area, a "skater" is a car.

I had fallen asleep in the seat again, but when I awoke, it was Saturday morning and Father was yelling at me.

"Get up! Get in the back," he yelled.

"What? Why?" I asked.

"Just go. Now," he shouted.

When I climbed in the sleeper, he told me to hide under the blankets. "Don't move or say a word until I say so," he said when he pulled the black curtain shut. I heard talking, but I couldn't recognize where the voice came from. I couldn't hear if the voice was a man or a woman. I heard Father mumble, but I couldn't make out what he said. It was hot under the blankets and it smelled like dirty feet. After a few minutes, Father pushed aside the black curtain and told me it was safe to come out.

"What's goin' on?" I asked.

"A chicken coop," he said.

"But why did I have to hide?" I asked.

"'Cause you ain't supposed to be riding in my truck."

"How come?"

"'Cause you ain't old enough, that's why. Next time, when I say get up and move, don't ask questions...just do what I say, OK?"

"OK."

"Sorry for yelling."

After a few minutes I asked, "Where are we?"

"We're outside the Big D. Dallas, Texas," he said, smiling. "If you're hungry, there's leftover catfish in the food cabinet. I saved half for you."

"Thanks," I said and tore off pieces of catfish with my fingers. The catfish was cold and tasted nasty, but I ate just enough of it to stop the hunger pangs.

While in Texas, we made a stop at a warehouse in the middle of nowhere and Father picked up a trailer. It took a while for the trailer to be ready. "They have to fill it up," he said. We took a nap while we waited. He slept on his bed. I slept on the top bunk. I saw his truck driver's manual, a first-aid kit, and a fire extinguisher in the top storage cabinet behind his seat.

I woke up to loud banging noises. I looked under the bunk to see if Father was awake, but he wasn't in the truck. I was scared because I didn't know where he was. I sat back in the seat and waited for him. When he came back, I asked him where he had gone. He told me he had to hook up the trailer.

A gas station was a few miles down the road from the warehouse. There weren't many buildings around this gas station, except for a small diner and an antique shop. There were a few semis parked alongside the gas tanks. When Father got out of his truck to pump gas, I got out and stood next to his driver door. I watched Father unlatch the hood. It wasn't like popping the hood of a car, where the hood pops back. The hood of a semi tilts forward. Father had to climb on top of the front left fender to see the engine. Father said he couldn't show me because the engine was hot. When he was finished looking, he closed the hood, latched it, and washed the front windshield. His hands were black with oil. When he was finished, he said it was time to go home.

On the road that day, going back to Indiana from Texas, Father and I asked each other a lot of questions. When he asked about school, he asked what my favorite subject was, how many friends I had, and what I did at recess. I answered, "Science," "one: Tiffany," and "play tetherball or collect bugs." When I asked him the same questions about when he was in school, he answered, "work shop," "my best friend was Mark," and "play football." When I asked him how he and my mother met, he said, "At a bar a few years after I moved from Chicago." When I asked why he didn't try to keep us, he said, "I tried, but I couldn't. I couldn't raise all of you by myself and work too." I asked him if he missed my mother. He said, "Yeah, most of the time." He asked if I did too. I said, "Yeah, all the time." He asked if I missed him too. I didn't know how to answer him. I missed him, but not like I missed Mother. I'm not sure why I didn't miss him as much as I did her. Maybe it's because I felt like I barely knew him. It seemed like he was always on the road, even when I lived with my parents, before foster care. Sometimes it seemed like he loved the road more than he loved us. But I couldn't tell him this, so I nodded.

"What was Chicago like?" I asked. "I've never been there."

"You've been there. We lived there for a little bit. You just don't remember 'cause your mom was pregnant with you. We moved before you were born."

"But what was it like when you were little? Didja like it?"

"I did, for the most part. It got better when I got older, though."

"How come? Was it bad when you were little or somethin'?"

"Kinda. Just some bad stuff happened."

After a few minutes passed, he said, "Remember when I found out about your Girl Scout leader's husband hurting you and your sister... when I saw the story in the paper?"

I nodded.

"I had a guy hurt me like that too when I was little."

"Oh. What happened?" I asked, and then, he told me the story.

When he had lived in Chicago, Father and his three older siblings stayed at their uncle's house after school or during the summers until their mother got home from work—their uncle didn't live but a mile or two down the road from where they lived near Norwood Park, Illinois. One year, when Father was a small boy, there was some construction going on in a neighborhood in between their uncle's house and their house. When he was younger, Father always loved tractors and trucks, which is one reason why he became a trucker—the other reason was because his father was a trucker. Nearly every day, Father stood outside the fence and watched the tractors work while his siblings hurried home, leaving him behind.

Once, a man had noticed Father watching the construction and asked him if he wanted to see inside of his tractor. My Father went with the man. While inside the tractor, Father told me that the man said he had more tractors at his house and he could take my father there to show him. Father then said this man "touched" him "in his private area." He said the man stopped touching him when his older brother came to the construction site looking for my father that afternoon. At home, Father told his mother he had seen the tractors, but he didn't say anything about the man touching him. He said he didn't tell because the man had asked him not to. Father said he didn't remember how old he was. He said he might have been my age. Later, Father saw the picture of this man on the news and asked his mother what the man had done. His mother said, "He's going away for a long time because he hurt little boys." Father learned that this man was John Wayne Gacy.

"He showed me the tractor," he said. But he didn't tell his mother what had happened inside the tractor.

After Father finished telling me this story, he told me he had never told anyone before. I'm not sure why he told me what John Wayne Gacy had done to him. Maybe he wanted me to understand that he and I shared more in common than we both thought. Maybe he wanted me to understand that I could trust him because he could keep a secret, like he had kept the secret about what Gacy had done. Or, maybe he had some other reason for telling me. I didn't know what to say to Father after he told me what had happened to him, but I asked him if he was happy the man was locked up.

"He's more than just locked up," he said. "He's dead. He was killed… executed seven years ago. But, yeah, I'm pretty damn happy."

We didn't make many stops on our way back to Indiana. Sometimes we stopped for gas or for a restroom break. I remember sleeping a lot on the way home, and when I awoke, it was Sunday morning and Father was yelling at me again.

"Hey, get up," he shouted. "Hurry now. Stay quiet." I did as he said and stayed as quiet as I could.

I heard a voice over the CB say, "Gotcha ears on, driver? I gotta eyeball on Smokey Bear…blue light special…front door of the cash register."

"10-4," Father said into his radio.

"Looks like a bear trap, Ace. Smokey gots his gumball machine a-goin'."

"Roger. Preeshaydit, Bubba."

When we crossed the blue bridge over the Wabash River, crossing the Indiana state line, about five cop cars were parked along the toll road, and they squatted outside their cars with their guns pointing to the truck.

"Hold tight," Father said, slamming on his breaks. When he braked, it sounded like air was being released and his tires squealed. I thought we were going to crash into the cop cars surrounding the toll booth, but I felt safe when he reached his arm across the passenger seat to protect me.

"Daddy, I'm scared."

"Don't be, honey. Everything's fine."

"Then why're we stopping? How come we can't go through?"

"I don't know. I need you to be quiet now."

Then, a voice came over the radio and told Father to shut off his engine and put his hands on the wheel. "We're sending an officer to get the girl," the cop said.

"Go," Father said.

"But Daddy?"

"Just go. Get out," he shouted.

I opened the door. Outside smelled like burnt rubber, tar, and gasoline. I grabbed the two hand-holds—one on the inside of the door panel and the other on the exterior of the cab frame—and climbed down the two metal steps. I looked back at my father. His face looked scruffy. Red stubble covered his cheeks and chin. He looked back at me.

His green eyes welled with tears. Then he looked ahead, staring at the blue and red flashing lights, the cops standing outside their cars with their guns aimed at his truck. "Go," he said. "Please."

When I stepped in front of the semi, a police officer grabbed me by the arm and pulled me behind a cop car. He asked me if I was OK and if my father had hurt me.

"No, he didn't hurt me," I said. Then, I watched my father slowly climb out of his semi with his hands on top of his head. Two police men ran toward the truck with their guns pointing at him.

"Daddy," I shouted, watching my father lay on the pavement with his hands behind his back as the cops arrested him. "He didn't do anything wrong. We were just going for a ride."

That Sunday morning in March, Father was arrested for kidnapping. Back then, I thought Father was arrested because he had let me ride in his truck, even though I wasn't old enough to ride in a semi. I didn't know that our road trip to Texas meant he had kidnapped me. I thought since he was my father, it was OK to be with him on the road. But because I was in foster care and his rights were terminated, he legally wasn't my father and it was illegal for him to take me across state lines.

Riding with my father in his semi from Indiana to Texas and back happened so fast that, sometimes, it feels like I dreamed that entire weekend. But when I think about that trip, I don't think about my father kidnapping me. Instead, I think about the trucker lingo he taught me, the truck stops we went to, the stories he told about school and my mother, and his secret I will never forget about John Wayne Gacy, the serial killer who had lived in Chicago, who molested and killed over thirty teenage boys, and who was executed in 1994.

I loved telling my father about what my former students were doing with their lives after they graduated, when they became colleagues and friends. One of these students is Jane Friedman. Jane never wrote or spoke to me about her father, though I met her charming mother on several occasions, as we are practically neighbors. I came to know Jane's family story only after I read this moving essay about coming to terms with two polar opposite versions of a difficult-to-understand man. The author makes a bold move and decides how she would like to remember him, making their narrative her own. Here they are pictured together perfectly, on a merry-go-round at a local park in Indiana.

JANE FRIEDMAN

The Memory I Choose

THERE ARE TWO versions of my dad: the one I experienced until the age of twelve, when he died, and the one my mother insists is true. I've spent my life trying to reconcile these two versions.

The facts are these: My father was the youngest of seven children, born of Russian Jewish immigrants. He grew up in Brooklyn, served in the Second World War on a medical ship, and lived in New York most of his life. At some point after his first marriage ended, he moved to San Antonio, Texas, to start his own business. He mainly worked as a typographer and practiced calligraphy on the side.

I don't recall asking my father how he met my mother, nor did he tell me stories about his life before I was born. I've only heard details from my mother, and her conclusion is that he was a con artist. He lived in debt, made enemies of his family, and manipulated others into supporting him.

My mother's relationship with him began as a business correspondence. She was living in rural Indiana with five teenage children, and looking for a new life after her divorce. In the Yellow Pages a relative had sent from Texas, my mother found information about my father's design firm and wrote to him inquiring about a job. My father responded himself, and after exchanging a few letters, they started talking on the phone.

During their first weekend together in Texas (he paid for her flight), my mother discovered the design firm consisted only of my father and his studio apartment. They spent their time visiting art galleries and museums, since they both had a love of art. My father kept calling after she returned to Indiana, pressuring her to get married as soon as possible. My mother brushed off his advances, but he didn't take "no" for an answer. She says he began shipping things to her house, including his electric organ.

When he himself arrived in southern Indiana (unannounced, as the story goes), they went to a Justice of the Peace to get married. About that time, my mom realized my father had been lying about his age. He was fifty-five, not fifty. (She was forty.) Two of my mother's sisters went as witnesses to the marriage. They hated my father. Actually, as my mom tells it, everyone who met him hated him—except her, in the beginning.

When they married, my father demanded that my mother's five children move out of the home. Their ages at the time ranged from thirteen to nineteen. I don't know how long it took, how hard it was, or if it was in process before he arrived, but they all did leave, except for the youngest (though he eventually did, too, not long after I was born).

My mother claims temporary insanity during that time. I wonder how difficult it was to see her kids leave, and how much she was blinded by the relationship. In a home movie that my father took before I was born, he and my mother drive around town, drink, and blow kisses at each other. They can only be described one way: in love.

Whether it was love or insanity, my mother didn't plan on what happened next: becoming pregnant at age forty-one. My half-siblings were mortified.

I don't talk about my father with my half-siblings. I don't ask them to set the record straight on what my father did or did not do. Their silence on the matter says everything I need to know. They did not attend his memorial service when he died, and they rarely tell stories about him.

Nonetheless, whatever their feelings, every Thanksgiving and Christmas, all my half-siblings returned home to celebrate, along with their spouses. And there was nothing my father loved more than a celebration. He had a Super 8 movie camera and captured every holiday event, from arrival to departure. Throughout the year, he spent a great deal of time shooting photos, processing film, and curating albums and clips—though my mother would be quick to point out, these memories were focused primarily on me. But if my father didn't like my half-siblings, I saw no evidence of it as a child. No one argued. Everyone seemed happy. Thanksgiving and Christmas became my favorite times of the year.

My dad's home movies were largely forgotten after he died, until I had the film digitized. I created a DVD of the hours of footage he took, and categorized it all by year and holiday. Then, as a Christmas gift, I gave copies to my family, expecting it might become a part of our holiday tradition again.

We never watch it.

~

My dad was one of the most recognizable characters in Oakland City, Indiana, where I grew up. This was partly because he was Jewish, a New Yorker, and not shy. But also he loved long walks. He'd go out in his bell-bottom jeans, smoke cigars, and stroll all over town. I don't know where he went, but everyone knew who Mr. Friedman was, even if they had never spoken to him. Whenever the boys in my class spotted him, they would yell a greeting and ask for a puff of his cigar. Many mistakenly thought he was my grandfather since he was in his sixties. Recently, a childhood acquaintance said he vividly remembers the news of my father's death, even though they didn't have a personal relationship, and even though such events rarely marked the time for a twelve year old. But he remembered, he says, because my dad always brought a smile wherever he went.

After my parents divorced, sightings of my father increased at school. He would walk over during recess or lunch to spend time with me and my friends. When I mentioned this to my mother, and said that having Dad around was sometimes embarrassing (I was in the sixth grade, when simply having parents is an embarrassment), she demanded that I call him right away and tell him to stop visiting. I refused. I knew it would hurt his feelings. But my mother commanded it. So I did. I was crying as I spoke into the phone, and he asked if this was something my mother was telling me to do. I can't remember how I answered, but he quietly said he would not visit me at school any longer. We never spoke of it again.

~

My mother was likely resentful that my father fought her for custody of me. During one of our weekend visits, as divorce proceedings started, he took me to his lawyer's office, where I was questioned about whom I preferred to live with, as my father stood right there. I was paralyzed. It seemed right that I should live with my mother.

Even at age ten, I knew she was better at running a household and taking care of me. On the other hand, my father was the fun-loving parent, the one who made me smile. He was the one who woke me up in the mornings. Even as a child, I was not a morning person, but he made it the happiest occasion possible, announcing that the world was waiting for me. Once he'd gotten me out of bed, he'd give me a hug, sing a cheerful nonsense song while scratching my back, and direct me to the kitchen. He'd make buttery cinnamon toast and let me choose what cereal I wanted to eat. I walked to and from school by myself, and in the afternoons, he'd often meet me on the walk home, smoking a cigar.

We never had enough money as a family to go on vacations, but my dad took me on day trips—to the community lake, and to museums and libraries. He took me to see action movies that I was too young for, and he called me inside from playing to watch TV shows like *Knight Rider* and *A-Team*, or to watch one of his old movies, usually James Cagney (the one I liked best was *Yankee Doodle Dandy*), or my favorite black-and-white film he owned, Frank Capra's *Lost Horizon*.

I didn't want to choose between living with my dad or my mom. So I just told the lawyer that it didn't matter to me.

My mother was furious when she heard what had happened (and at my noncommittal answer), and said my father had no interest in taking care of me—that he only wanted to make things difficult for her.

Of course, my mother won the custody battle.

I wonder if my father, after losing that fight, considered moving somewhere else. Maybe it was too much trouble to leave and he didn't have the money. Maybe the peace and quiet of rural Indiana suited him in his retirement. Maybe he enjoyed being eccentric and vibrant in that small town. And maybe he wanted to stay near me, and my mother.

When I think and write about my father, it feels as though my mother is as much the subject. Her words infiltrate and shape how I know him, even reshape my own memories. The narrative that she has long been developing, to make sense of what happened for herself, presses down hard. While it might be an exaggeration to say she wants to convince me not to fondly remember my father, she has never held back on framing his presence in both our lives as negative.

I don't know what my father would say in his own defense, but in my presence, he didn't speak ill of my mother. Until the end, I believe he loved her, and wanted to be close to her.

For a brief moment, he got his wish. Not long after he was diagnosed with terminal cancer, I came home from school to find him sleeping on the couch, looking thinner than ever. He woke up and warmly greeted me, as he always did. Later, on the front porch, he drank iced coffee over an amicable conversation with my mother. It was the dream every child has for their divorced parents: a happy reunion.

Maybe the two of them did make peace, but my mom couldn't take care of him as he declined, and he died several months later in a nursing home. My mother and I visited him once, together. He was confined to a wheelchair and incoherent, probably drugged. As my mother talked to a friend of his, he begged me to help him escape. Later on, in the nursing room courtyard, I helped him light a cigar, which felt like one of the last pleasures afforded him.

During my last outing with my father—right before he could no longer take care of himself—he served as a parent chaperone on my seventh grade school trip to Marengo Caves in Indiana. He was sixty-nine years old. I didn't know about his cancer diagnosis then, but during the mile-long trek underground, he became disoriented and fell down. The two tour guides had to leave my class alone in the caves while they escorted him back to the entrance. I reacted as I did to most things those days: I remained silent, even as some of the other students imitated him falling down.

When the class finished the tour, and we re-emerged above ground, no one could tell me where he had gone. After searching on my own, I found him strolling the park grounds and smoking a cigar as if nothing had happened, unflappable as usual. Later, he had the teacher feel the bump on his head like it was a battle scar. After we finished lunch and sat together alone, I stared at the insects crawling along the ledge we sat on, still feeling awkward and unsure about what had happened. He stared at the insects, too, and commented on the fragility and smallness of life. I didn't know he was dying, and he didn't tell me. Maybe he thought he could beat it—he was ever the optimist. My mom always said my father thought he'd live to be a hundred, and was enthusiastic about the future and living in it. He carefully looked after his health, ate mostly vegetarian meals, and hung a poster up in the kitchen that illustrated the healthiest food choices.

In any case, I was left to piece together the hard truth that he was dying. One day, I asked my mother when my father would be well enough to leave the nursing home, and she said, half-shocked, "Well, never. He's not coming back." We were in the car when she said it, and I still remember the stretch of road when I heard it. I looked out the window, and tried hard not to have a visible emotional reaction.

My parents had a terrible fight not long before they divorced, when I was about nine or ten years old. My mother was drinking, and maybe my father was, too. My mom says he drank a lot, though I never recall him being drunk.

Whatever sparked the fight, the disagreement took on a slow burn through the evening, until it exploded into violence. I remember only images, not a chain of events: asking my father for an ice cream cone in the kitchen, as my mother admonished me (how could I ask that man for an ice cream cone?); my father calling my mother a lush; my father and I sitting in lawn chairs in the backyard, as my mother came out of the house carrying my father's framed calligraphy, and smashing it on the sidewalk; my mother, in her nightgown spotted with blood, carrying a sledgehammer through the house.

When my parents decided to split, it was my father who told me. He didn't make an emotional show of it; he stated things simply and directly: that he and my mother were separating, and I'd have to decide whom I wanted to live with. Of course, it wasn't up to me, but that's how he often framed things—as if I were an independent person rather than a child.

After his death, my mother and I went to his rental house to sort through his belongings. I took a couple T-shirts (one said "Calligraphy" in his own hand), some VHS tapes, and his typecase, which he used to store mementoes.

My mother was not sentimental and was primarily looking for anything valuable that could be sold. We were completely broke by that point and for a while lived on food stamps. I remember she took his old records (some did turn out to be worth something) and calligraphy supplies, but little else. I don't know if she thought to take his artwork hanging on the wall, but to this day, I still ache thinking of how we left it all there. I have none of my father's calligraphy.

There is a chance that my father's two children from his first marriage have some of his work. At least one of them visited his house after his death, though they did not attend his memorial service. More important, they have insight into the kind of man my father was if anyone does. They knew him as adults. They knew him as a grandfather to their children. Do they know his values? Did my father con his own family? Did he abandon them? What were his weaknesses and sins in their eyes?

I'm not sure I want to hear their stories. My father was a loving father—to me. His joyful affection was abundant, and I lost that from my life when he died. He made me believe that I could do and be anything, and that he'd support it. If I ever become a parent, that will be my benchmark for success.

It's at this point in the story that I can hear my mother insisting in the distance: But he stole money from your childhood savings account; he was selfish and didn't save anything for your future; he didn't care about you. My mother has misjudged me on a number of occasions, usually because she only has part of the story. It doesn't seem so hard to believe she might've misjudged my father too. I remember a man who taught me to be true to myself, and to live life on my own terms, the rest of the world be damned. But the paradox is that he always treated me well and with consistency, despite what was happening around us, and acted as if what he did made a difference in my life. As a result, his actions speak far louder to me—even twenty years after his passing—than the words of a mother still alive.

I knew Barbara Shoup would have an essay, because whenever I saw her, we would talk about our families, our mothers, and our fathers. Barbara and I met at an Associated Writing Programs conference, and to this day, whenever I visit with Barbara, it feels like there isn't enough time because we have so much left to say to each other. In "Waiting for My Father," Barbara reflects about events that really happened and about what did not happen, as she tries to figure out her father, her mother, their marriage, and how to move beyond them both. Barbara is a writer forever intrigued by the search. She is the author of eight novels, including the recent Looking for Jack Kerouac.

Waiting for My Father

Wʜᴀᴛ ɪꜰ?

My father was nearly thirty when he enlisted in the Army, after Pearl Harbor. He was stationed at an air base in England, a master sergeant in charge of supplies, which, unofficially, included the kick of supplying his fellow recruits with black market goods. He was a handsome, witty, good-time guy who loved jazz and looked great in his uniform.

My mother, from the East End of London, ten years younger, had escaped the confines of a strict household to join the Women's Royal Air Force. Attractive, slim, vivacious, a ballroom dancer, she was proud to be a part of the war effort and having the time of her life.

They met one night at the Golden Lion Pub. They fell in love.

They married when the war was over: my dad in a sharp double-breasted suit and silk tie, my mother in a stylish dress and fabulous hat.

I was their first child, born on their first wedding anniversary, a god-send for my homesick mother, a marvel to my father, who holds me, feeds me, bends over my crib, takes my small hand in photographs from my early childhood, pure delight reflected in his face.

What if they had stayed in England after the war?

What if they'd settled in an American city new to both of them, instead of settling in my father's hometown?

What if I'd been their only child? What if I'd been their second—or third or fourth child?

What if I hadn't loved to read, so never knew there was a different way to be?

What if my father's drinking hadn't been a secret?
What if he'd stopped drinking earlier?
What if he'd never had a drinking problem at all?

Life, like a story, sets its own course. In time the "what if's" of your childhood fall away, the bits and pieces that brought you to the beginning of your adult life, combust, and begin to move toward an ending you can't imagine but becomes clearer, inevitable, the farther you go.

Still, you can't help thinking what might have happened if the bits and pieces had sorted themselves out differently. If you had been able to maneuver them into the story you meant your life to be. If they'd been completely different bits and pieces, and any story you might have made of them would be one that the person you are now can't even imagine?

BEGINNING

I'm four years old, waiting at the back door for my father to come home from work. My mother is busy in the kitchen; my little brother is busy playing. But I wait. I want to be the first one he sees. My heart lifts when I see him turn the corner from the bus stop and start down the alley: young, handsome, smiling. Mine.

This was before we were a family with four stair-stepped children. Before there was never enough money to pay the bills and buy everything we needed. Before we moved to a horrid little prefab house in the suburbs in Hessville, Indiana. Before my father started drinking too much—so much, in fact, that by the time I was in high school he'd come home from work every day, collapse on the couch, and sleep until my mother called him for dinner. He'd get up, eat, then return to the couch and sleep through the evening.

He'd surface now and then, muttering.

If someone changed the TV channel and he didn't like the program.

If the phone rang.

If we kids were bickering.

My mother would sit, knitting, on the little space left at the end of the sofa. Sometimes he'd prod her with his foot because, he said, the clicking of her knitting needles drove him crazy.

Around eleven, he'd get up; go find his car keys.

"I've got to mail a letter," he'd say, closing the door behind him.

"A drinking problem," that's what people called it then—and even that was whispered, for adults' ears only. "Alcoholic" was a word we knew, but to say it was tacitly forbidden. "Codependent" and "Enabler," hadn't been invented yet. Children of alcoholics were pitied. But while it was easy to see how a parent's drinking could make them angry and cause them to behave badly, it never occurred to anyone that children who were perfectionists, super-responsible, obsessive achievers might be acting out in a different way. "Therapy" was "psychoanalysis," and it happened in places like New York. In our working class world, there was nothing between being fine and having a "nervous breakdown," the very idea of which scared people to death—and for good reason. You could end up in an insane asylum, a nuthouse, a funny farm, where they could give you shock treatment if they felt like it and even cut out part of your brain if that didn't calm you down enough, turning you into some kind of zombie.

If you were a drinker, you promised yourself and your loved ones that you'd quit—and you'd try. You'd refuse a drink at a cocktail party and endure the jokes about "being on the wagon." Maybe you'd even submit to the humiliation of Alcoholics Anonymous, where you'd have to sit in a circle with a bunch of other drunks and say "I am an alcoholic" out loud. But it wouldn't last.

If you were the spouse or child of a drinker, you'd ignore, beg, wheedle, threaten, pray. But you'd keep the secret, even from each other. You'd tell yourself that some people believed drinking too much was a disease and there was nothing you could do about it. You'd hope this was true because, if it was, that spouse or parent wasn't wrecking your life on purpose.

I was a nosy child, an intrepid eavesdropper, determined to hear what I wasn't supposed to hear, to find out what I wasn't supposed to know. But I never heard a whole conversation, rarely saw a scene play all the way out. And my father was a quiet, desperate drinker, who drank in taverns, or alone; he was never abusive or out of control. So all I had were bits and pieces to puzzle out what was happening in my family—not so different, I realize now, from the odd collection of images and ideas and snippets of dialogue that tumble out of your head and nag, nag, nag until you figure out how to glue them into a story.

I remember sitting on a heat register, a book open on my lap, pretending to get warm, but really listening to the adults talk about my father's new job.

"Let's hope it will do him good to be outdoors," one of them said.

What did that mean? And why did he have to get a new job, anyway? I liked his old one, at the pawnshop. Sometimes we'd take the bus downtown to visit him there and he'd take jewelry from the glass case and let us touch the diamonds and I'd get to play on the typewriter for a little while. Then he'd take us to lunch at Roth's Tavern and Mrs. Roth would come out, wiping her hands on her apron, beaming at the sight of us.

"Why can't he just keep working there?" I wanted to ask. But I kept quiet.

If I spoke, my mother would notice me.

I remember the Christmas my father played Santa Claus for the neighborhood kids. My brother and I were old enough to know that Santa wasn't real, and we were in on the secret. But my little sisters still believed in him, so we played along, whipping them into a frenzy. They ran around, screaming. They drew pictures on the frosty picture window with their fingers, rubbed circles and pressed their faces against the glass to look for him.

Finally, the knock on the door. The "Ho! Ho! Ho!"

My father was a skinny guy and looked ridiculous in the Santa suit. He also looked, well, like my father. But my sisters didn't notice.

"Have you kids been good this year?" he asked. "Yes!" they cried.

He looked at me, grinning. "And you, little girl?" I giggled wildly.

He gave us all some candy, wished us "Merry Christmas!"

Afterward we waited and waited for him to come home so we could go to the family Christmas party at our aunt's.

My sisters got cranky. My brother and I started spinning on the green spinning chairs my dad had bought my mom for Christmas last year and which she hated. We got going so fast that the chairs crashed against the wall and made black marks on it and my mother yelled at us to stop, all of us, settle down! If we kept at it and kept at it and messed up our good clothes, we wouldn't be able to go to the party at all.

She picked up the phone, dialed. "Wanda," she said in a fake-cheerful voice, "Has Santa been to your house yet? Oh, yes, he's been here, too. Do you have any idea—what?" She listened. "Those darn Daugherty boys." She set the receiver on the end table and went to the window, rubbed her own circle on the glass, and peered outside. She picked up the receiver again and said, "No. I don't see a thing. Let me know if you hear anything, will you? Sure. I'll do the same."

She hung up, dialed again. "Ruth?" she said in the same fake voice. "Listen. Dick's not home from work yet, so we're running a little late. Yes, we're coming. We'll be there as soon as we can."

Eventually he appeared, a can of Schlitz in his hand. He was wearing his regular clothes, but they were rumpled. His hair was every-which-way. Our across-the-street neighbor was with him, both of them half-leaning against each other, laughing.

"Goddamn Daugherty boys," the neighbor said, leaning against the door frame. "They took after him and he had to hide in the Ramsey's shed. That's why we're so late. They took after Santa," he clarified, glancing at my sisters. "I'll tell you what. It's a darn a good thing your dad and I saw those boys, so we could save him!"

I was furious with the Daugherty boys. Juvenile delinquents, everyone in the neighborhood called them. They were always up to something bad: burning snakes in their garbage can, soaping windows—and now they'd tried to wreck Christmas Eve.

My mother was furious with my father, which I thought was totally unfair. What else could he have done when they started chasing him?

I remember, years later, coming upon a small glass bottle when I was looking for something under the front seat of the car. I opened it, smelled it: whiskey. Oh, I thought—something plunging inside me. Then closed it and put it back right where I'd found it.

I was a teenager before I put these and countless other pieces together and finally understood that my father had a serious drinking problem. The knowledge sat heavily inside me, worse for the fact that I didn't dare let it out. I rarely brought friends to our house for fear of finding him, passed out, on the sofa. On the few occasions he drove us someplace in the car, I rolled down my window, afraid they'd smell the whiskey on his breath. I dreaded big family gatherings: the looks that sometimes passed among my aunts and uncles at the sight of the shuffling, disheveled person he'd become.

I loved school: the order, the sense of belonging, how it was so obvious what you had to do to make things turn out right. I loved reading, I loved the worlds it opened up to me. Any time I wasn't at school—evenings, weekends, holidays, all through long, boring summers—I lost myself in novels about happy, popular girls in happy, normal families that I checked out over and over from the library.

MIDDLE

"It is worth mentioning, for future reference, that the creative power which bubbles so pleasantly in beginning a new book quiets down after a time, and one goes on more steadily. Doubts creep in. Then one becomes resigned. Determination not to give in, and the sense of an impending shape keep one at it more than anything," Virginia Woolf wrote in her diary.

I've read—needed—this quote many times in the process of working my way through the inevitable confusion and disarray the middle of any piece of writing presents. I need it right now, in the middle of this essay, my subconscious scrambling, looking for the key that will unlock some box in my head that holds the words to say what I feel.

Somewhere in the middle of his story, my father lost his way.

When you get to the middle of a story you're writing and you can't make it work, you can put it away for a while and come back to it when you figure out how to fix it. If your life isn't working, you can't hit "pause" and wait until you know what to do. It goes right on, taking you with it, for better or worse—and your family, too, especially if they can't or won't acknowledge what is happening. Every time you try to pull yourself together, a nasty little voice whispers, "Quit. You know you can't do this, anyway." Like my father, you fall into depression, another thing we didn't name or talk about or understand.

I was caught in the freefall of his life. I see, now, that I was depressed, too. I hated the tacky house we lived in, so deep in the endless suburbs cropping up in the wake of World War Two that it took half an hour just to walk to the bus stop. I hated never having any privacy. I really, really hated being poor.

I also see now that, drinking his way home from work, collapsing on the sofa every night, my father must have felt exactly the same way.

We all slogged through his middle with him. He quit playing golf, which he loved. Half the time he slept in his clothes. His old friends avoided him. Eventually, his drinking became so bad that it was impossible to ignore. Once, drunk, smoking in a bathroom stall, he dropped his cigarette into the cuff of his pants, set them on fire, and ended up in the hospital.

My brother disappeared when he could. Why stay around and listen to tirades about his long hair, bad attitude, and no-good friends? My mother and sisters became a triumvirate, making the best of things—though one of my sisters did take to emptying my father's liquor bottles when she found them and even occasionally marching into the Bluebird Tap to demand that he come home. Humor helped. They'd laugh at the crazy things he muttered in his sleep. He bathed infrequently and, as a result, his hair was greasy and lay on his head in flat strands. "Slippery Dick," they started calling him. Or just "Slip," which became their affectionate nickname for him in the next part of his story—but which hurt me and made me sad every single time I heard it.

Meanwhile, my own bits and pieces had gathered and launched me into my own story. I was married by then, with a family, a life. I visited only when I absolutely had to—and then it was mostly because of my children. Despite the ways my parents had failed at making a secure life for me, they were wonderful grandparents to my daughters. My mother let them make cupcakes or finger paint, no matter the mess. She'd be the customer in their endless games of "Waitress," always coming up with something new to order and thanking them profusely for their good service. My father treated them the way I remembered him treating me when I was a very little girl, like short adults, in cahoots with him against the rules.

His drinking worried me, but I told myself he'd never, ever risk hurting them—and, besides, my mother would be there to make sure they were all right. Once, though, we were all in the car together, my father driving—and he rolled through a stop sign, without looking to see if there was a car coming.

"Stop at the fucking stop signs," I said, shocking myself and everyone else.

I felt horrible. I'd never said that word in the presence of my parents, never ordered either one of them to do anything. I should have apologized. Instead, all the rage and helplessness I'd suppressed for years spewed out in a rant that ended with my saying, "I can't do this anymore. I mean it. I can't let them be with you if you don't stop drinking. I won't."

I don't remember how either of them responded, just that when we got back to the house I looked up the number for Al-Anon, called, and arranged for someone to pick up my mother for a meeting the next week. "I know you can't stop Dad from drinking," I said to her. "But you have to at least try to deal with it in a better way than you're dealing with it now."

She didn't want to go, but she went—and, finally, the long middle came to a close.

ENDING

There is a happy ending to my father's story.

Maybe my meltdown scared him.

Maybe Al-Anon made my mother change in some way that made a difference.

Maybe, as he told my husband, he nearly hit a child with his car when he was drunk, and made up his mind that he'd stop drinking then and there, no matter what it took.

Maybe he just looked at himself in the mirror one day and said, "Enough."

Maybe it was all of the above.

In any case, he quit drinking—and was sober for the last twelve years of his life. He and my mother put together enough money to buy a little condo in Florida. She worked as the hostess at a country club, a role that suited her perfectly. He worked as a courier for a construction company and spent his days driving around to various sites, delivering whatever needed to be delivered, and chatting with the friends he'd made along the way.

They put their bad times behind them. They fell back into love. They were happy.

I was stuck in the middle of my own story by then, a bundle of neuroses, only beginning to understand the full effect of my father's drinking on my life. I was a classic Child of an Alcoholic, it turned out: a textbook case. Zero self-confidence, angry, controlling, paralyzed with guilt. Struggling for some kind of balance in my life, grieving for the childhood I might have had. The bad times still seemed all too real to me. But the few times I tried to talk to either of my parents in an effort to make sense of what had happened to our family, it upset them so much that I felt it would be cruel to continue.

I forgave my father. I understood he never meant to hurt us. I was proud of him for what he'd done, grateful that he and my mother had been able to begin again. But that other time lived like a ghost between us, and the relationship I had with him was superficial, strained.

Only now, nearing the end of this essay, do I see that the grief and confusion of my childhood were only part of why I failed at developing a close relationship with the new, sober incarnation of my father: the child still inside me wanted her real father back. All those years, I'd harbored the subconscious delusion that if my father ever stopped drinking, the young, handsome, smiling person he had been would magically reappear and I would take my rightful place as the first, only, beloved daughter.

Stories, good ones, offer resolution; each thread pulled through to a satisfying conclusion. Lives come to an end with threads dangling; characters, ideas, mysteries, intentions, subplots have been lost along the way. Near the end, if you can bear it, you can look back and see exactly how and why things happened the way they did. There are no rewrites, though, no way to make them come out differently.

Maybe my father felt that my part in his story was happily resolved. I hope he did. But he is a dangling thread in mine. He's gone now. Our relationship was what it was. Still, I try to find him, rescue what we might have been in the stories I write, half-believing my imagination can somehow reassemble the bits and pieces and bring my real father back, set him walking down the alley toward where I wait for him on the porch.

Maxine Hong Kingston *created a worldwide sensation with her first book,* The Woman Warrior: Memoirs of a Girlhood among the Ghosts, *which won the National Book Critics Circle Award for nonfiction in 1976.* China Men *followed in 1980 and won the American Book Award. In this excerpt from* China Men, *we read about MaMa and BaBa and growing up in a younger, scrappier San Francisco, surrounded by "white people." We cannot help but fall for Maxine's hard-working BaBa, and empathize with his remarkable rise and fall and rise again. Unfortunately, Maxine could not send a picture of her father. In the 1990s, her home in California burned to the ground, and in the process destroyed the novel she was writing along with photographs of her family, including those of her father.*

MAXINE HONG KINGSTON

The American Father

IN 1903 MY father was born in San Francisco, where my grandmother had come disguised as a man. Or, Chinese women once magical, she gave birth at a distance, she in China, my grandfather and father in San Francisco. She was good at sending. Or the men of those days had the power to have babies. If my grandparents did no such wonders, my father nevertheless turned up in San Francisco an American citizen.

He was also married at a distance. My mother and a few farm women went out into the chicken yard, and said words over a rooster, a fierce rooster, red of comb and feathers; then she went back inside, married, a wife. She laughs telling this wedding story; he doesn't say one way or the other.

When I asked MaMa why she speaks different from Baba, she says their parents lived across the river from one another. Maybe his village was America, the river an ocean, his accent American. My father's magic was also different from my mother's. He pulled the two ends of a chalk stub or a cigarette butt, and between his fingers a new stick of chalk or a fresh cigarette grew long and white. Coins appeared around his knuckles, and number cards turned into face cards. He did not have a patter but was a silent magician. I would learn these tricks when I became a grown-up and never need for cigarettes, money, face cards, or chalk.

He also had the power of going places where nobody else went, and making places belong to him. I could smell his presence. He owned special places the way he owned special things like his copper ashtray from the 1939 World's Fair and his Parker 51. When I explored his closet and desk, I thought, This is a father place; a father belongs here.

One of his places was the dirt cellar. That was under the house where owls bounced against the screens. Rats as big as cats sunned in the garden, fat dust balls among the greens. The rats ran up on the table where the rice or the grapes or the beans were drying and ate with their hands, then took extra in their teeth and leapt off the table like a circus, one rat after another. My mother swung her broom at them, the straw swooping through the air in yellow arcs. That was the house where the bunny lived in a hole in the kitchen. My mother had carried it home from the fields in her apron. Whenever it was hopping noiselessly on the linoleum, and I was there to see it, I felt the honor and blessing of it.

When I asked why the cellar door was kept locked, MaMa said there was a "well" down there. "I don't want you children to fall in the well," she said. Bottomless.

I ran around a corner one day and found the cellar door open. BaBa's white-shirted back moved in the dark. I had been following him, spying on him. I went into the cellar and hid behind some boxes. He lifted the lid that covered the bottomless well. Before he could stop me, I burst out of hiding and saw it—a hole full of shining, bulging, black water, alive, alive, like an eye, deep and alive. BaBa shouted, "Get away." "Let me look. Let me look," I said. "Be careful," he said as I stood on the brink of a well, the end and edge of the ground, the opening to the inside of the world. "What's it called?" I asked to hear him say it. "A well." I wanted to hear him say it again, to tell me again, "Well." My mother had poured rust water from old nails into my ears to improve them.

"What's a well?"

"Water comes out of it," BaBa said. "People draw water out of wells."

"Do they drink it? Where does the water come from?"

"It comes from the earth. I don't think we should drink it without boiling it for at least twenty minutes. Germs."

Poison water.

The well was like a wobble of black jello. I saw silver stars in it. It sparked. It was the black sparkling eye of the planet. The well must lead to the other side of the world. If I fall in, I will come out in China. After a long, long fall, I would appear feet first out of the ground, out of another well, and the Chinese would laugh to see me do that. The way to arrive in

China less obtrusively was to dive in head first. The trick would be not to get scared during the long time in the middle of the world. The journey would be worse than the mines.

My father pulled the wooden cover, which was the round lid of a barrel, back over the well. I stepped on the boards, stood in the middle of them, and thought about the bottomless black well beneath my feet, my very feet. What if the cover skidded aside?

My father finished with what he was doing; we walked out of the cellar, and he locked the door behind us.

Another father place was the attic of our new house. Once I had seen his foot break through the ceiling. He was in the attic, and suddenly his foot broke through the plaster overhead.

I watched for the day when he left a ladder under the open trap door. I climbed the ladder through the kitchen ceiling. The attic air was hot, too thick, smelling like pigeons, their hot feathers. Rafters and floor beams extended in parallels to a faraway wall, where slats of light slanted from shutters. I did not know we owned such an extravagance of empty space. I raised myself up on my forearms like a prairie dog, then balanced sure-footed on the beams, careful not to step between them and fall through. I climbed down before he returned.

The best of the father places I did not have to win by cunning; he showed me it himself. I had been young enough to hold his hand, which felt splintery with calluses "caused by physical labor," according to MaMa. As we walked, he pointed out sights; he named the plants, told time on the clocks, explained a neon sign in the shape of an owl, which shut one eye in daylight. "It will wink at night," he said. He read signs, and I learned the recurring words: Company, Association, Hui, Tong. He greeted the old men with a finger to the hat. At the candy-and-tobacco store, Baba bought Lucky Strikes and beef jerky, and the old men gave me plum wafers. The tobacconist gave me a cigar box and a candy box. The secret place was not on the busiest Chinatown street but the street across from the park. A pedestrian would look into the barrels and cans in front of the store next door, then walk on to the herbalist's with the school supplies and saucers of herbs in the window, examine the dead flies and larvae, and overlook the secret place completely. (The herbs inside the hun-

dred drawers did not have flies.) BaBa stepped between the grocery store
and the herb shop into the kind of sheltered doorway where skid-row
men pee and sleep and leave liquor bottles. The place seemed out of business; no one would rent it because it was not eyecatching. It might have
been a family association office. On the window were dull gold Chinese
words and the number the same as our house number. And delightful,
delightful, a big old orange cat sat dozing in the window; it had pushed
the shut venetian blinds aside, and its fur was flat against the glass. An
iron grillwork with many hinges protected the glass. I tapped on it to see
whether the cat was asleep or dead; it blinked.

BaBa found the keys on his chain and unlocked the grating, then
the door. Inside was an immense room like a bank or a post office. Suddenly no city street, no noise, no people, no sun. Here was horizontal
and vertical order, counters and tables in cool gray twilight. It was safe in
here. The cat ran across the cement floor. The place smelled like cat piss
or eucalyptus berries. Brass and porcelain spittoons squatted in corners.
Another cat, a gray one, walked into the open, and I tried following it,
but it ran off. I walked under the tables, which had thick legs.

BaBa filled a bucket with sawdust and water. He and I scattered
handfuls of the mixture on the floors, and the place smelled like a carnival. With our pushbrooms leaving wet streaks, we swept the sawdust
together, which turned gray as it picked up the dirt. BaBa threw his cigarette butts in it. The cat shit got picked up too. He scooped everything
into the dustpan he had made out of an oil can.

We put away our brooms, and I followed him to the wall where
sheaves of paper hung by their corners, diamond shaped. "Pigeon lottery,"
he called them. "Pigeon lottery tickets." Yes, in the wind of the paddle
fan the soft thick sheaves ruffled like feathers and wings. He gave me
some used sheets. Gamblers had circled green and blue words in pink
ink. They had bet on those words. You had to be a poet to win, finding
lucky ways words go together. My father showed me the winning words
from last night's games: "white jade that grows in water," "red jade that
grows in earth," or—not so many words in Chinese—"white waterjade,"
"redearthjade," "firedragon," "waterdragon." He gave me pen and ink, and I
linked words of my own: "rivercloud," "riverfire," the many combinations

with horse, cloud, and bird. The lines and loops connecting the words, which were in squares, a word to a square, made designs too. So this was where my father worked and what he did for a living, keeping track of the gamblers' schemes of words.

We were getting the gambling house ready. Tonight the gamblers would come here from the towns and the fields; they would sail from San Francisco all the way up the river through the Delta to Stockton, which had more gambling than any city on the coast. It would be a party tonight. The gamblers would eat free food and drink free whiskey, and if times were bad, only tea. They'd laugh and exclaim over the poems they made, which were plain and very beautiful: "Shiny water, bright moon." They'd cheer when they won. BaBa let me crank the drum that spun words. It had a little door on top to reach in for the winning words and looked like the cradle that the Forty-niner ancestors had used to sift for gold, and like the drum for the lottery at the Stockton Chinese Community Fourth of July Picnic.

He also let me play with the hole puncher, which was a heavy instrument with a wrought-iron handle that took some strength to raise. I played gambler punching words to win—"cloudswallow," "riverswallow," "river forking," "swallow forking." I also punched perfect round holes in the corners so that I could hang the papers like diamonds and like pigeons. I collected round and crescent confetti in my cigar box.

While I worked on the floor under the tables, BaBa sat behind a counter on his tall stool. With black elastic armbands around his shirtsleeves and an eyeshade on his forehead, he clicked the abacus fast and steadily, stopping to write the numbers down in ledgers. He melted red wax in candle flame and made seals. He checked the pigeon papers, and set out fresh stacks of them. Then we twirled the dials of the safe, wound the grandfather clock, which had a long brass pendulum, meowed at the cats, and locked up. We bought crackly pork on the way home.

According to MaMa, the gambling house belonged to the most powerful Chinese American in Stockton. He paid my father to manage it and to pretend to be the owner. BaBa took the blame for the real owner. When the cop on the beat walked in, BaBa gave him a plate of food, a carton of cigarettes, and a bottle of whiskey. Once a month, the police raided with a paddy wagon, and it was also part of my father's job to be arrested. He never got a record, however, because he thought up a new name for himself every time. Sometimes it came to him while the city sped past the barred windows; sometimes just when the white demon at the desk asked him for it, a name came to him, a new name befitting the situation. They never found out his real names or that he had an American name at all. "I got away with aliases," he said, "because the white demons can't tell one Chinese name from another or one face from another." He had the power of naming. He had a hundred dollars ready in an envelope with which he bribed the demon in charge. It may have been a fine, not a bribe, but BaBa saw him pocket the hundred dollars. After that, the police let him walk out the door. He either walked home or back to the empty gambling house to straighten out the books.

Two of the first white people we children met were customers at the gambling house, one small and skinny man, one fat and jolly. They lived in a little house on the edge of the slough across the street from our house. Their arms were covered with orange and yellow hair. The round one's name was Johnson, but what everyone called him was Water Shining, and his partner was White Cloud. They had once won big on those words. Also *Johnson* resembles *Water Shining*, which also has *o*, *s*, and *n* sounds. Like two old China Men, they lived together lonely with no families. They sat in front of stores; they sat on their porch. They fenced a part of the slough for their vegetable patch, which had a wooden sign declaring the names of the vegetables and who they belonged to. They also had a wooden sign over their front door: TRANQUILITY, a wish or blessing or the name of their house. They gave us nickels and quarters; they made dimes come out of noses, ears, and elbows and waved coins in and out between their knuckles. They were white men, but they lived like China Men.

When we came home from school and a wino or hobo was trying the doors and windows, Water Shining came out of his little house. "There's a wino breaking into our house," we told him. It did occur to me that he might be offended at our calling his fellow white man a wino. "It's not just a poor man taking a drink from the hose or picking some fruit and going on his way," I explained.

"What? What? Where? Let's take a look-see," he said, and walked with us to our house, saving our house without a fight.

The old men disappeared one by one before I noticed their going. White Cloud told the gamblers that Water Shining was killed in a farming accident, run over by a tractor. His body had been churned and plowed. White Cloud lived alone until the railroad tracks were leveled, the slough drained, the blackbirds flown, and his house torn down.

My father found a name for me too at the gambling house. "He named you," said MaMa, "after a blonde gambler who always won. He gave you her lucky American name." My blonde namesake must have talked with a cigarette out of the side of her mouth and left red lip prints. She wore a low-cut red or green gambling dress, or she dressed cowgirl in white boots with baton-twirler tassels and spurs; a Stetson hung at her back. When she threw down her aces, the leather fringe danced along her arm. And there was applause and buying of presents when she won. "Your father likes blondes," MaMa said. "Look how beautiful," they both exclaimed when a blonde walked by.

But my mother keeps saying those were dismal years. "He worked twelve hours a day, no holidays," she said. "Even on New Year's, no day off. He couldn't come home until two in the morning. He stood on his feet gambling twelve hours straight."

"I saw a tall stool," I said.

"He only got to sit when there were no customers," she said. "He got paid almost nothing. He was a slave; I was a slave." She is angry recalling those days.

After my father's partners stole his New York laundry, the owner of the gambling house, a fellow ex-villager, paid my parents' fares to Stockton, where the brick buildings reminded them of New York. The way my mother repaid him—only the money is repayable—was to be a servant to his, the owner's, family. She ironed for twelve people and bathed ten children. Bitterly, she kept their house. When my father came home from work at two in the morning, she told him how badly the owner's family had treated her, but he told her to stop exaggerating. "He's a generous man," he said.

The owner also had a black servant, whose name was Harry. The rumor was that Harry was half-man/ half-woman, a half-and-half. Two servants could not keep that house clean, where children drew on the wallpaper and dug holes in the plaster. I listened to Harry sing "Sioux City Sue." "Lay down my rag with a hoo hoo hoo," he sang. He squeezed his rag out in the bucket and led the children singing the chorus. Though my father was also as foolishly happy over his job, my mother was not deceived.

When my mother was pregnant, the owner's wife bought her a dozen baby chicks, not a gift; my mother would owe her the money. MaMa would be allowed to raise the chicks in the owner's yard if she also tended his chickens. When the baby was born, she would have chicken to give for birth announcements. Upon his coming home from work one night, the owner's wife lied to him, "The aunt forgot to feed her chickens. Will you do it?" Grumbling about my lazy mother, the owner went out in the rain and slipped in the mud, which was mixed with chicken shit. He hurt his legs and lay there yelling that my mother had almost killed him. "And she makes our whole yard stink with chicken shit," he accused. When the baby was born, the owner's wife picked out the scrawny old roosters and said they were my mother's twelve.

Ironing for the children, who changed clothes several times a day, MaMa had been standing for hours while pregnant when the veins in her legs rippled and burst. After that she had to wear support stockings and to wrap her legs in bandages.

The owner gave BaBa a hundred-and-twenty-dollar bonus when the baby was born. His wife found out and scolded him for "giving charity."

"You deserve that money," MaMa said to BaBa. "He takes all your time. You're never home. The babies could die, and you wouldn't know it."

When their free time coincided, my parents sat with us on apple and orange crates at the tiny table, our knees touching under it. We ate rice and salted fish, which is what peasants in China eat. Everything was nice except what MaMa was saying, "We've turned into slaves. We're the slaves of these villagers who were nothing when they were in China. I've turned into the servant of a woman who can't read. Maybe we should go back to China. I'm tired of being Wah Q," that is, a Sojourner from Wah.

My father said, "No." Angry. He did not like her female intrigues about the chickens and the ironing and the half-man/ half-woman.

They saved his pay and the bonuses, and decided to buy a house, the very house they were renting. This was the two-story house around the corner from the owner's house, convenient for my mother to walk to her servant job and my father to the gambling house. We could rent out the bottom floor and make a profit. BaBa had five thousand dollars. Would the owner, who spoke English, negotiate the cash sale? Days and weeks passed, and when he asked the owner what was happening, the owner said, "I decided to buy it myself. I'll let you rent from me. It'll save you money, especially since you're saving to go back to China. You're going back to China anyway." But BaBa had indeed decided to buy a house on the Gold Mountain. And this was before Pearl Harbor and before the Chinese Revolution. He found another house farther away, not as new or big. He again asked the owner to buy it from him. You would think we could trust him, our fellow villager with the same surname, almost a relative, but the owner bought up this house too—the one with the well in the cellar—and became our landlord again.

My parents secretly looked for another house. They told everyone, "We're saving our money to go back to China when the war is over." But what they really did was to buy the house across from the railroad tracks. It was exactly like the owner's house, the same size, the same floor plan and gingerbread. BaBa paid six thousand dollars cash for it, not a check but dollar bills, and he signed the papers himself. It was the biggest but most run-down of the houses; it had been a boarding house for old China Men. Rose bushes with thorns grew around it, wooden lace hung broken from the porch eaves, the top step was missing like a moat. The owner's wife accused her husband of giving us the money, but she was lying. We made our escape from them. "You don't have to be afraid of the owner any more," MaMa keeps telling us.

Sometimes we waited up until BaBa came home from work. In addition to a table and crates, we had for furniture an ironing board and an army cot, which MaMa unfolded next to the gas stove in the wintertime. While she ironed our clothes, she sang and talked story, and I sat on the cot holding one or two of the babies. When BaBa came home, he and MaMa got into the cot and pretended they were refugees under a blanket tent. He brought out his hardbound brown book with the gray and white photographs of white men standing before a flag, sitting in rows of chairs, shaking hands in the street, hand-signaling from car windows. A teacher with a suit stood at a blackboard and pointed out things with a stick. There were no children or women or animals in this book. "Before you came to New York," he told my mother, "I went to school to study English. The classroom looked like this, and every student came from another country." He read words to my mother and told her what they meant. He also wrote them on the black board, it and the daruma, the doll which always rights itself when knocked down, the only toys we owned at that time. The little *h*'s looked like chairs, the *e*'s like lidded eyes, but those words were not *chair* and *eye*. "'Do you speak English?'" He read and translated. "'Yes, I am learning to speak English better.' 'I speak English a little.'" "'How are you?' 'I am fine, and you?'" My mother forgot what she learned from one reading to the next. The words had no crags, windows, or hooks to grasp. No pictures. The same *a*, *b*, *c*'s for everything. She couldn't make out ducks, cats, and mice in American cartoons either.

During World War Two, a gang of police demons charged into the gambling house with drawn guns. They handcuffed the gamblers and assigned them to paddy wagons and patrol cars, which lined the street. The wagons were so full, people had to stand with their hands up on the ceiling to keep their balance. My father was not jailed or deported, but neither he nor the owner worked in gambling again. They went straight. Stockton became a clean town. From the outside the gambling house looks the same closed down as when it flourished.

My father brought his abacus, the hole punch, and extra tickets home, but those were the last presents for a while. A dismal time began for him.

He became a disheartened man. He was always home. He sat in his chair and stared, or he sat on the floor and stared. He stopped showing the boys the few kung fu moves he knew. He suddenly turned angry and quiet. For a few days he walked up and down on the sidewalk in front of businesses and did not bring himself to enter. He walked right past them in his beautiful clothes and acted very busy, as if having an important other place to go for a job interview. "You're nothing but a gambler," MaMa scolded. "You're spoiled and won't go looking for a job." "The only thing you're trained for is writing poems," she said. "I know you," she said.

(I hated her sentences that started with "I know you.") "You poet. You scholar. You gambler. What use is any of that?" "It's a wife's job to scold her husband into working," she explained to us.

My father sat. "You're so scared," MaMa accused. "You're shy. You're lazy." "Do something. You never do anything." "You let your so-called friends steal your laundry. You let your brothers and the Communists take your land. You have no head for business." She nagged him and pampered him. MaMa and we kids scraped his back with a porcelain spoon. We did not know whether it was the spoon or the porcelain or the massage that was supposed to be efficacious. "Quit being so shy," she advised.

"Take a walk through Chinatown and see if any of the uncles has heard of a job. Just ask. You don't even need to apply. Go find out the gossip." "He's shy," she explained him to us, but she was not one to understand shyness, being entirely bold herself. "Why are you so shy? People invite you and go out of their way for you, and you act like a snob or a king. It's only him to reciprocate." "You act like a piece of liver. Who do you think you are? A piece of liver?" She did not understand how some of us run down and stop. Some of us use up all our life force getting out of bed in the morning, and it's a wonder we can get to a chair and sit in it. "You piece of liver. You poet. You scholar. What's the use of a poet and a scholar on the Gold Mountain? You're so skinny. You're not supposed to be so skinny in this country. You have to be tough. You lost the New York laundry. You lost the house with the upstairs. You lost the house with the back porch." She summarized, "No loyal friends or brothers. Savings draining away like time. Can't speak English. Now you've lost the gambling job and the land in China."

Somebody—a Chinese, it had to be a Chinese—dug up our loquat tree, which BaBa had planted in front of the house. He or she had come in the middle of the night and left a big hole. MaMa blamed BaBa for that too, that he didn't go track down the tree and bring it back. In fact, a new loquat tree had appeared in the yard of a house around the corner. He ignored her, stopped shaving, and sat in his T-shirt from morning to night.

He seemed to have lost his feelings. His own mother wrote him asking for money, and he asked for proof that she was still alive before he would send it. He did not say, "I miss her." Maybe she was dead. And the Communists maintained a bureau of grandmother letter writers in order to get our money. That we kids no longer received the sweet taste of invisible candy was no proof that she had stopped sending it; we had outgrown it. For proof, the aunts sent a new photograph of Ah Po. She looked like the same woman, all right, like the pictures we already had but aged. She was ninety-nine years old. She was lying on her side on a lounge chair, alone, her head pillowed on her arm, the other arm along her side, no green tints at her earlobes, fingers, and wrists. She still had little feet and a curved-down mouth. "Maybe she's dead and propped up," we kids conjectured.

BaBa sat drinking whiskey. He no longer bought new clothes. Nor did he go to the dentist and come back telling us the compliments on his perfect teeth, how the dentist said that only one person in a thousand had teeth with no fillings. He no longer advised us that to have perfect teeth, it's good to clamp them together, especially when having a bowel movement.

MaMa assured us that what he was looking forward to was when each child came home with gold. Then he or she (the pronoun is neutral in the spoken language) was to ask the father, "BaBa, what kind of a suit do you want? A silk gown? Or a suit from the West? An Eastern suit or a Western suit? What kind of a Western suit do you want?" She suggested that we ask him right now. Go-out-on-the-road. Make our fortunes. Buy a Western suit for Father.

I went to his closet and studied his suits. He owned gray suits, dark blue ones, and a light pinstripe, expensive, successful suits to wear on the best occasions. Power suits. Money suits. Two-hundred-dollars-apiece New York suits. Businessmen-in-the-movies suits. Boss suits. Suits from before we were born. At the foot of the closet arranged in order, order his habit, were his leather shoes blocked on shoe trees. How could I make money like that? I looked in stores at suits and at the prices. I could never learn to sew this evenly, each suit perfect and similar to the next.

MaMa worked in the fields and the canneries. She showed us how to use her new tools, the pitters and curved knives. We tried on her cap pinned with union buttons and her rubber gloves that smelled like rubber tomatoes. She emptied her buckets, thermoses, shopping bags, lunch pail, apron, and scarf; she bought home every kind of vegetable and fruit grown in San Joaquin County. She said she was tired after work but kept moving, busy, banged doors, drawers, pots and cleaver, turned faucets off and on with kachunks in the pipes. Her cleaver banged on the chopping block for an hour straight as she minced pork and steak into patties. Her energy slammed BaBa back into his chair. She took care of everything; he did not have a reason to get up. He stared at his toes and fingers. "You've lost your sense of emergency," she said; she kept up his sense of emergency every moment.

He dozed and woke with a jerk or a scream. MaMa medicated him with a pill that came in a purple cube lined with red silk quilting, which cushioned a tiny black jar; inside the jar was a black dot made out of ground pearls, ox horn, and ox blood. She dropped this pill in a bantam broth that had steamed all day in a little porcelain crock on metal legs. He drank this soup, also a thick beef broth with gold coins in the bottom, beef teas, squab soup, and still he sat. He sat on. It seemed to me that he was getting skinnier. "You're getting skinny again," MaMa kept saying. "Eat. Eat. You're less than a hundred pounds."

I cut a Charles Atlas coupon out of a comic book. I read all the small print. Charles Atlas promised to send some free information. "Ninety-seven-pound weakling," the cartoon man called himself. "I'll gamble a stamp," he said. Charles Atlas did not say anything about building fat, which was what my father needed. He already had muscles. But he was ninety-seven pounds like the weakling, maybe ninety pounds. Also he kicked over chairs like in the middle panel. I filled in the coupon and forged his signature. I did not dare ask him how old he was, so I guessed maybe he was half as old as his weight: age forty-five, weight ninety. If Charles Atlas saw that he was even skinner than the weakling, maybe he would hurry up answering. I took the envelope and stamp from BaBa's desk.

Charles Atlas sent pamphlets with more coupons. From the hints of information, I gathered that my father needed lessons, which cost money. The lesson had to be done vigorously, not just read. There seemed to be no preliminary lesson on how to get up.

The one event of the day that made him get up out of his easy chair was the newspaper. He looked forward to it. He opened the front door and looked for it hours before the mailman was due. *The Gold Mountain News* (or *The Chinese Times*, according to the English logo) came from San Francisco in a paper sleeve on which his name and address were neatly typed. He put on his gold-rimmed glasses and readied his smoking equipment: the 1939 World's Fair ashtray, Lucky Strikes, matches, coffee. He killed several hours reading the paper, scrupulously reading everything, the date on each page, the page numbers, the want ads. Events went on; the world kept moving. The hands on the clocks kept moving. This sitting ought to have felt as good as sitting in his chair on a day off. He was not sick. He checked his limbs, the crooks of his arms. Everything was normal, quite comfortable, his easy chair fitting under him, the room temperature right.

MaMa said a man can be like a rat and bite through wood, bite through glass and rock. "What's wrong?" she asked.

"I'm tired," he said, and she gave him the cure for tiredness, which is to hit the inside joints of elbows and knees until red and black dots—the tiredness—appear on the skin.

He screamed in his sleep. "Night sweats," MaMa diagnosed. "Fear sweats." What he dreamed must have been ax murders. The family man kills his entire family. He throws slain bodies in heaps out the front door. He leaves no family member alive; he or she would suffer too much being the last one. About to swing the ax, screaming in horror of killing, he is also the last little child who runs into the night and hides behind a fence. Someone chops at the bushes beside him. He covers his ears and shuts his mouth tight, but the scream comes out.

I invented a plan to test my theory that males feel no pain; males don't feel. At school, I stood under the trees where the girls played house and watched a strip of cement near the gate. There were two places where boys and girls mixed; one was the kindergarten playground, where we didn't go any more, and the other was this bit of sidewalk. I had a list of boys to kick: the boy who burned spiders, the boy who had grabbed me by my coat lapels like in a gangster movie, the boy who told dirty pregnancy jokes. I would get them one at a time with my heavy shoes, on which I had nailed toe taps and horseshoe taps. I saw my boy, a friendly one for a start. I ran fast, crunching gravel. He was kneeling; I grabbed him by the arm and kicked him sprawling into the circle of marbles. I ran through the girls' playground and playroom to our lavatory, where I looked out the window. Sure enough, he was not crying. "See?" I told the girls. "Boys have no feelings. It's some kind of immunity." It was the same with Chinese boys, black boys, white boys, and Mexican and Filipino boys. Girls and women of all races cried and had feelings. We had to toughen up. We had to be as tough as boys, tougher because we only pretended not to feel pain.

One of my girl friends had a brother who cried, but he had been raised as a girl. Their mother was a German American and their father a Chinese American. This family didn't belong to our Benevolent Association nor did they go to our parties. The youngest boy wore girls' dresses with ruffles and bows, and brown-blondish ringlets grew long to his waist. When this thin, pale boy was almost seven, he had to go to school; it was already two years past the time when most people started school. "Come and see something strange," his sister said on Labor Day. I stood in their yard and watched their Mother cut off his hair. The hair lay like tails around his feet. Mother cried, and son cried. He was so delicate, he had feelings in his hair; it hurt him to have his hair cut. I did not pick on him.

There was a war between the boys and the girls; we sisters and brothers were evenly matched three against three. The sister next to me, who was like my twin, pushed our oldest brother off the porch railing. He landed on his face and broke two front teeth on the sidewalk. They fought with knives, the cleaver and a boning knife; they circled the dining room table and sliced one another's arms. I did try to stop that fight—they were cutting bloody slits, an earnest fight to death. The telephone rang. Thinking it was MaMa, I shouted, "Help. Help. We're having a knife fight. They'll kill each other." "Well, do try to stop them." It was the owner's wife; she'd gossip to everybody that our parents had lost control of us, such bad parents who couldn't get respectable jobs, mother gone all day, and kids turned into killers. "That was Big Aunt on the phone," I said, "and she's going to tell the whole town about us," and they quit after a while. Our youngest sister snuck up on our middle brother, who was digging in the ground. She was about to drop a boulder on his head when somebody shouted, "Look out." She only hit his shoulder. I told my girl friends at school that I had a stepfather and three wicked stepbrothers. Among my stepfather's many aliases was the name of my real father, who was gone.

The white girls at school said, "I got a spanking." I said we never got spanked. "My parents don't believe in it," I said, which was true. They didn't know about spanking, which is orderly. My mother swung wooden hangers, the thick kind, and brooms. We got trapped behind a door or under a bed and got hit anywhere (except the head). When the other kids said, "They kissed me good night," I also felt left out; not that I cared about kissing but to be normal.

We children became so wild that we broke BaBa loose from his chair. We goaded him, irked him—gikked him—and the gravity suddenly let him go. He chased my sister, who locked herself in a bedroom. "Come out," he shouted. But, of course, she wouldn't, he having a coat hanger in hand and angry. I watched him kick the door; the round mirror fell off the wall and crashed. The door broke open, and he beat her. Only, my sister remembers that it was she who watched my father's shoe against the door and the mirror outside fall, and I who was beaten. But I know I saw the mirror in crazy pieces; I was standing by the table with the blue linoleum top, which was outside the door. I saw his brown shoe against the door and his knee flex and the other brothers and sisters watching from the outside of the door, and heard MaMa saying, "Seven years bad luck." My sister claims that same memory. Neither of us has the recollection of curling up inside that room, whether behind the pounding door or under the bed or in the closet.

A white girl friend, whose jobless and drunk father picked up a sofa and dropped it on her, said, "My mother saw him pushing *me* down the stairs, and *she* was watching from the landing. And I remember him pushing *her*, and I was at the landing. Both of us remember looking up and seeing the other rolling down the stairs."

He did not return to sitting. He shaved, put on some good clothes, and went out. He found a friend who had opened a new laundry on El Dorado Street. He went inside and chatted, asked if he could help out. The friend said he had changed his mind about owning the laundry, which he had named New Port Laundry. My father bought it and had a Grand

Opening. We were proud and quiet as he wrote in gold and black on big red ribbons. The Chinese community brought flowers, mirrors, and pictures of flowers and one of Guan Goong. BaBa's liveliness returned. It came from nowhere, like my new idea that males have feelings. I had no proof for this idea but took my brothers' word for it.

BaBa made a new special place. There was a trap door on the floor inside the laundry, and BaBa looked like a trap-door spider when he pulled it over his head or lifted it, emerging. The basement light shone through the door's cracks. Stored on the steps, which were also shelves, were some rolled-up flags that belonged to a previous owner, gold eagles gleamed on the pole tips.

We children waited until we were left in charge of the laundry. Then some of us kept a lookout while the rest, hanging on to the edge of the hole, stepped down between the supplies. The stairs were steep against the backs of our legs.

The floor under the building was gray soil, a fine powder. Nothing had even grown in it; it was sunless, rainless city soil. Beyond the light from one bulb the blackness began, the inside of the earth, the insides of the city. We had our flashlights ready. We chose a tunnel and walked side by side into the dark. There are breezes inside the earth. They blow cool and dry. Blackness absorbed our lights. The people who lived and worked in the four stories above us didn't know how incomplete civilization is, the street only a crust. Down here under the sidewalks and the streets and the cars, the builders had left mounds of loose dirt, piles of dumped cement, rough patches of concrete tamping down and holding back some of the dirt. The posts were unpainted and not square on their pilings. We followed the tunnels to places that had no man-made materials, wild areas, then turned around and headed for the lighted section under the laundry. We never found the ends of some tunnels. We did not find elevators or ramps or the undersides of the buckling metal doors one sees on sidewalks. "Now we know the secret of cities," we told one another. On the shelves built against the dirt walls, BaBa had stacked boxes of notebooks and laundry tickets, rubber stamps, pencils, new brushes, blue bands for the shirts, rolls of wrapping paper, cones of new string, bottles of ink, bottles of distilled water in case of air raids. Here was where we would hide when war came and we went underground for gorilla warfare. We stepped carefully; he had set copper and wood rat traps. I opened boxes until it was time to come up and give someone else a chance to explore.

So my father at last owned his house and his business in America. He bought chicks and squabs, built a chicken run, a pigeon coop, and a turkey pen; he dug a duck pond, set the baby bathtub inside for the lining, and won ducklings and goldfish and turtles at carnivals and county fairs. He bought rabbits and bantams and did not refuse dogs, puppies, cats, and kittens. He told a funny story about a friend of his who kept his sweater on while visiting another friend on a hot day; when the visitor was walking out the gate, the host said, "Well, Uncle, and what are those chicken feet wiggling out of your sweater?" One morning we found a stack of new coloring books and follow-the-dot books on the floor next to our beds. "BaBa left them," we said. He buried wine bottles upside down in the garden; their bottoms made a path of sea-color circles. He gave me a picture from the newspaper of redwoods in Yosemite, and said, "This is beautiful." He talked about a Los Angeles Massacre, but I wished that he had not, and pretended he had not. He told an ancient story about two feuding poets: one killed the other's plant by watering it with hot water. He sang "The Song of the Man of the Green Hill," the end of which goes like this: "The disheveled poet beheads the great whale. He shoots an arrow and hits a suspended flea. He sees well through rhinoceros-horn lenses." This was a song by Kao Chi, who had been executed for his politics; he is famous for poems to his wife and daughter written upon leaving for the capital; he owned a small piece of land where he grew enough to eat without working too hard so he could write poems. BaBa's luffa and grapevines climbed up ropes to the roof of the house. He planted many kinds of gourds, peas, beans, melons, and cabbages—and perennials—tangerines, oranges, grapefruit, almonds, pomegranates, apples, black figs, and white figs—and from seed pits, another loquat, peaches, apricots, plums of many varieties—trees that take years to fruit.

Presences

I have followed Ann Hood's career ever since I read her moving novel Somewhere off the Coast of Maine, and grieved along with so many of her other readers when I read her painfully honest memoir, Comfort: A Journey Through Grief, which recounts her daughter's untimely death. Ann responded immediately when I approached her for an essay, and, within days, I was reading about her father and his own health challenges. This is a no-nonsense essay about a family's struggles with the messy and often soul-crushing details of end-of-life care, what to do, how to do it, how to decide, and who will decide. This should be required reading for anyone in the medical field. Catherine Sebastian photographed Ann.

Life Saver

Daddy," I say, looking into my father's big blue eyes, "the doctors are saying that you're dying."

Those baby blues grow bigger. "What?" he asks me in disbelief. The fever has turned his cheeks pink. The cancer has made him gaunt. "That's ridiculous."

When he came to the hospital in respiratory failure two months earlier, we had been told the same thing. Huddled in a hallway outside the room where my father lay struggling to breathe, a doctor had prepared us for the worst. That time, miraculously, he survived. But he hasn't left the hospital yet, plagued by pneumonia on top of pneumonia and weakened from chemotherapy. We've been on a path through this hospital, from the ICU to a cheery room with a non-stop flow of therapists—physical, respiratory, occupational—back to the ICU and finally here, on a regular ward that seems to be filled with the terminally ill. Every day I pass another empty bed, another family clutching each other in the hall, another stone faced doctor heading somewhere with bad news.

"Look, Poops," my father says to me, "tell them I'm not ready to die. Tell them to do everything to keep me alive." He levels his gaze straight at me. "Everything. You got that?"

I nod, unable to tell him that the doctor tells me daily to give up, that there is no hope. Just this morning he told me that if he stopped the antibiotics, the pneumonia would finish things off. The doctor had looked away from me when he said this. But my father does not look away.

"I promise," I tell him.

At the end of the hall, in the family room, my cousin Gina and my niece Melissa are working on a jigsaw puzzle. Every day—no, every hour, they vacillate. Let go, one of them says. Then later: Fight. But I am the daughter. The only child since my brother Skip died fifteen years earlier. My mother is in a state of denial, ordering my father to watch the news to keep his mind active and going off to shop at the mall or play cards with her friends. Somehow the burden of whether my father lives or dies has fallen on me, the person who perhaps wants him to live more than anyone.

Before I can make it into the family room, the doctor intercepts. "Well?" he says anxiously, as if he just wants to get this over with. "Give him antibiotics," I say. "Give him everything to keep him alive."

I swear, the doctor rolls his eyes. "You seem like an intelligent person," he says in frustration. "What don't you understand here?"

In that moment, time stops. I am no longer standing in a hospital hallway negotiating my father's life. No. I am standing in a harbor watching a ship come in. And as that ship gets closer, I see that it is full of men in white sailor suits, and I search those men's faces for my father's. I am so young that I have to crane my neck to do this. My mother has dressed my brother and me up in our Easter outfits, even though it is long past Easter. She has on a hat adorned with tiny white flowers, a fancy suit, high heels and lipstick. Finally the ship docks and the sailors begin to walk off it, toward us. Finally, one of them is familiar, walking faster and faster, until he reaches us and in one movement seems to have all three of us in his arms. I smell Old Spice and Vitalis and salty sea air.

These are the smells that will always be my father's to me. Maybe that began in that moment, that hug.

And then I am slightly older and we are living in an apartment building in Arlington, Virginia, because my father is working at the Pentagon for Admiral Rickover. The job is important. I understand this. In his dress uniform, my father goes to dinners at the White House and meets President Kennedy. He goes to parties with senators. But he also takes my broken Chatty Kathy doll to the doll hospital and brings her home good as new. When I have the measles, he pulls the draperies shut tight, and hands me tiny sunglasses to wear, and holds me all night.

My father is tall, six-foot-three, like a movie star, and blond like a hero in the Greek myths I like him to read me. He has a Southern accent. He puts elbow macaroni under his chili, cheddar cheese on apple pie, salt on watermelon, and he cooks corn on the cob in milk. He won't eat chestnuts or mangos because he thinks they might be poisonous; he can't stand the fuzz on a peach. I watch everything he does, his every move. I note his eccentricities, which make him even more special. He has lived in China and San Francisco. He ran away from home when he was seventeen. He has a tattoo of an eagle in front of a rising sun on his left forearm. This I trace over and over, as if by memorizing it, I am also memorizing him.

It is my father who rushes me to the hospital when Skip jumps on the bed I am hiding beneath after I scratched his new 45 of Chubby Checker's "The Twist." It is my father who holds the facecloth to my chin as he drives, his hand growing wet with my blood. He stands at my side while the doctor stitches me up, never flinching, though years later he confessed that afterward he threw up.

Then I am back in Rhode Island with my mother and Skip, living at my grandmother's while my father is stationed at Guantanamo Bay in Cuba. I wait for letters, struggling to read his messy handwriting. I count the days until he'll return, so many days. But life without him is off-kilter. We get a silver Christmas tree that year instead of a real one. Somehow my father manages to send us two baby alligators that my mother kills by leaving them outside in the frigid winter night. He is bit by a mongoose in Cuba, and has to undergo a grueling series of rabies shots. I begin to read the dictionary: mongoose, rabies, Cuba.

Finally, finally, he is home again. There is a real Christmas tree and a purple bike under it for me. My father teaches me to ride that bike, holding the back of it to keep me steady, running along with me as I pedal. In an instant, I realize he has let go and I am flying down the street on my own. In another instant, he is teaching me to drive our oversized green Chevy Impala. In between, he sits and listens to all the stories and poems I write, blushing with pride. He takes me to the library every Tuesday after supper. And every Friday he takes me to the post office where I mail my newest novel—twelve handwritten pages on lined notebook paper— to Bennett Cerf. Every time I get a rejection letter back, my father says that if I keep trying one day I will get an acceptance letter.

My father is full of sayings. Charlie Hood didn't raise no fool. And: Fool me once, shame on you. Fool me twice, shame on me. And: Don't become what you hate. He disperses advice all the time, and I take it. My father is the smartest person I know. Even when I go off to college, he calls me every morning to say hello. I call him to see which class he thinks I should take, how to break up with a boy, and for travel advice as I begin to make my way in the world. He never missed a school play, an awards ceremony, a graduation. My father is always there, grinning back at me, as I walk across stages and disappear into jetways and reappear at Customs or train station exits.

After college I tell him I want to see the world and that to do this I want to become a flight attendant. So he drives me to Logan Airport, from terminal to terminal, while I gather applications. Back at home, he helps me fill them out, my first important forms. Then he is beaming at me as I deplane in my TWA uniform, he is coming with me on flights to Paris and Amsterdam, we are vacationing in San Francisco and Brussels.

In 1982, when Skip died suddenly, my father holds me up. We sit together that endless hot summer and drink beer and shake our heads and wonder how such a thing can happen. We go together to Pittsburgh to my brother's house and to the coroner's, my mother too devastated to come along. The next summer we begin a ritual of renting beach houses, to get away for that anniversary. My father and I begin to cook together, creating bumbleberry pie and our own barbecue sauce.

Every time I move, my father comes to help me. He lines my shelves and hangs my pictures. He puts my glasses in neat rows and makes my bed with hospital corners. My father tells me to call off my first wedding and it is the first time I don't take his advice. A few years later, I'm divorced and my father is once again helping me move. He never reminds me that he told me so. He just takes a level, holds it against the wall, and hangs my pictures straight and even.

And then I am a parent myself, and my father is washing baby clothes and changing diapers and holding my son Sam in the palm of his hand, grinning. And he is sitting on my bed the night I bring my daughter Grace home from the hospital. Grace is asleep in my arms, Sam is sprawled beside me. "You have everything you need here," my father tells me. "No! I need you too!" I say. The next day he is diagnosed with terminal lung cancer.

And now I am standing in a hospital hallway and a doctor is rolling his eyes at me, and asking what it is I don't understand.

"What don't you understand?" I ask the doctor. I open my arms, wide. Then I am turning and running back to him, to my father.

"Daddy," I call. "Daddy!"

He is sitting up in bed, watching the news as my mother has instructed. The nurse has started the IV antibiotics and already the flush of fever has left his cheeks. My father turns at the sound of my voice, and he smiles at me. No. He beams.

"These people," he says, pointing to the TV, "they all put on running shoes and killed themselves, thinking they can live on some comet."

I sit beside him on the bed, glancing at the television where a picture of a comet streaking across the sky fills the screen.

My father takes my hand in his big one. In just two weeks, he will die despite everything I do to save him. But I do not know that yet. For this moment, I just sit with my father. I listen to each precious breath he takes.

My father was a huge fan of Alexandra's father, William Styron, a writer who confronted the South, history, and morality head-on in Lie Down in Darkness, The Confessions of Nat Turner, Sophie's Choice, and Darkness Visible. In this honest account, which appears as a chapter in her memoir Reading My Father, Alexandra writes about growing up with a famous father, who was widely praised and often recognized wherever they went, a father who, in fact, focused so much on his work, he often forgot he was supposed to be looking after his daughter. Alexandra shares this adorable family photo, in which she sits in the yard with her father.

ALEXANDRA STYRON

Reading My Father

USED TO THINK my father looked like Desi
Arnaz. Anyone who ever met Bill Styron, or
has seen a picture of him, knows this is crazy. My father looked about as
much like Desi as he looked like Lucy. His complexion was Scotch-Irish
fair, his thin lips were peaked by a faint cupid's bow, and his expressive
eyes lay tucked behind sloping, hooded lids that lent him a permanent
look of world-weariness. As for the way Daddy put himself together, he
didn't. He wore the same clothes day after day, shambled about in whatever worn and homely shoes would accommodate his troublesome feet,
and let his hair take the attitude it struck when he awoke that day. As
Mike Nichols said of him at his memorial service, "Bill had a great sense
of style. He never had any idea what he was wearing." My father's resemblance, then, to the slick Cuban crooner with full mouth and limpid gaze
began and ended with the color—brown—of his eyes and hair.

I thought he looked like Desi Arnaz because I watched a lot of television. Most American kids growing up in the seventies and eighties
watched too much TV. I watched more. Returning home at the end of
the day, I could run through the kitchen, drop my book bag, and twist the
knob on our Zenith in less time than it took whoever had picked me up
that day to shut the car door I'd probably left open. And there I would sit,
like some doped-up zombie, till it was time for bed. My brother watched,
too. Racing me to the TV room, he'd grab the best seat, then tee up a
butch menu—"Emergency!," "Adam-12," "Mission: Impossible"—that I endured like any kid sister, glad enough to be allowed to breathe the same
air. Eventually Tommy wandered off, on to girls and Bob Dylan and dab-

173

bling in the silver market, and I had the joint to myself. I ate my dinner in front of the TV. I did my homework (or didn't) in the same spot, with the television on. And on weekends I feel asleep there, to the laugh track of "The Carol Burnett Show" (or the famous theme to "The Twilight Zone," if I was sugared up enough to last that long). Between kindergarten and tenth grade, I suppose I saw every episode of every popular television show broadcast between 4:30 and 9:00 p.m. Eastern Standard Time. "I Love Lucy," on nightly in reruns, inveigled its way into my spongy mind.

Most of the time, no one bothered me about my despicable habit. My father was oblivious. And Mum, a great believer in the value of fun, would have let me set my hair on fire if I told her that I wanted to. Also, they were busy. In addition to the house on the Vineyard, my parents kept a small apartment in Manhattan, a two-hour drive away.

My mother, in particular, spent a lot of time there. In the early seventies, she took up the cause of human rights, which, along with her poetry and love of travel, absorbed her more and more over the years. Sometimes several times a week, she went "into town" for work as well as pleasure. There were board meetings and benefits, marches and symposiums, early-morning flights to Eastern Bloc countries, and dinners that went too late to make the long drive home. Sometimes, she came in the door just in time to see me off to school. With the old name tag still on her jacket, she'd be gone again by afternoon.

When they were home together, my parents ate at nine or so, European-style, after the house had calmed down and the children were out of their hair. As often as not, this didn't go so well. Mum would get on the phone and forget about the stove. Smoke drifted into the TV room like some cartoon cloud, oozing down the hallway, where it would soon deliver the bad news to my father: dinner was ruined. Mum chatted, the steak burned. I pulled up tight on the couch and waited for the ax to fall. Rose! Jesus fucking Christ!...I'm sorry, sweetheart, I just turned my back a second...Well, look, it's totally ruined!...No, no, I can fix it. Look... Just forget it! I'm not hungry! On better nights, usually just as I was getting ready for bed, Daddy would call to me. "Albert! You want to get us some wine?" Screwing up my courage, I'd head for the basement. I had no memory of my infamous tumble. But beneath the kitchen was a dark and musty netherworld, mysterious holes in rock foundation tunneling back into oblivion, and it terrified me. Still, I took my job seriously and did it with pride. Scurrying back upstairs with a nice bottle of cabernet, I'd hoist myself up on the counter, where I could get some leverage on the corkscrew, and tug till I got the clean pop. "Thank you," Daddy would say, reaching out for the handoff. Then I'd beat a hasty retreat, while Mum ran things back and forth to the table. My father was already plunging into his meal.

Occasionally, they drove to the city together. A book party, an opening, or an event at which my father was being honored would coax him out of Wallabees and into a blue blazer. While he paced back and forth through the TV room, periodically shouting up the stairs, Goddamn it, Rose! We've got to leave NOW!, I'd pry myself off the couch and reach up to dust the dandruff from his lapels. "How do I look?" he might say. "Groovy," I might reply ironically, returning to my spot like a dog to her bed. I'd listen over the laugh track to the clatter clatter of shoes down the stairs and Just one more thing and Well, I'm going out to the car! I'm going without you! And I'm coming, darling, and then they were gone.

~

I wasn't usually alone. Help of every description came and went at our house. Ethel and James Terry, a couple whom my parents had hired when my sisters were small, were for years the rock foundation of our family. Ettie, as we called her, was a big woman with the wide-planed face of her Native American people. She cooked, did laundry, and babysat. Terry (always just "Terry"), about the only black man in Litchfield County, was a handyman, gardener, and driver. He was also Tommy's godfather and, along with Lillian Hellman, the dedicatee of *The Confessions of Nat Turner*. They lived in New Milford, a short drive away. When they weren't at our house, Terry ran a little car repair outfit from the back of his house, for which Ettie (Terry could not read or write) tended the books. Early in the morning, they would drive over the hill to Roxbury in time to get us ready for school.

"You had a good home, but you wouldn't stay there!" Terry would holler, standing over my bed. Years after he'd moved north, his South Carolina drawl remained thick as mud. I sometimes had no idea what he was talking about; phrases picked up on the cotton farm where he was raised, and from his years in the Army, studded his conversation. But I couldn't miss the intent. If his voice didn't roust you, you'd get a cold washcloth. After that, it was a glass of water.

"Come on, Toolum!" he'd roar as the cold splash hit my face. "We gots to get going! There's more snow out there than Cotta [Cotter? Carter?] got oats!"

Sometimes, when Ettie made me turn the TV off, I'd hitch a ride around the lawn on Terry's mower. Or I'd sit with him in the converted chicken coop that was his toolshed and all-around clubhouse. The place reeked of gasoline, Newport cigarettes, and the charred embers of the wood-burning stove. Along with the feel of his flannel shirt against my cheek, the aroma of Terry's shed was the essence of comfort and permanence.

When I was still small, diabetes began to slow Ettie down. After I was about seven, we saw little of her. Terry continued on at my parents' house for a couple of years after that, but his hours got shorter as he grew dotty and less reliable. In his final years, after Ettie had died, Terry's mind collapsed on him completely. One day when I was about twelve and on a visit, I walked into his living room. All around his sectional couch, he'd opened and propped magazines. The faces of my parents' many famous friends—Ted Kennedy, Frank Sinatra, Joan Baez, people Terry had met and many times served—stared out from each one.

"The Kennedy's, they've been here for days," he said, his eyes tired and anxious. "I've been taking care of them, but they won't leave."

My parents placed Terry in a minimum-care assisted living facility—more like a bed-and-breakfast for the aged—but he kept wandering off. One day, his sister, a craven woman who'd never before shown much interest in her brother, came up from Washington and took Terry, and his savings, away. Tommy went to D.C. a couple of times to visit; seeing Terry in the grim environs of his sister's apartment was awful.

None of the rest of us ever saw him again.

In between, after, and all along the way, dozens of other faces peopled the landscape. Mavis was my baby nurse, and she stayed till I was two. Marjorie lived with us when I was four and five. So did Nicky, the daughter of one of Daddy's old girlfriends, until her bizarre behavior—coming in at 3:00 a.m. and running full speed, Mrs. Rochester-like, up to the attic; hiding out in the laundry room eating dog bones—made her a liability. Local girls like Katie, Stacey, and Sandy from the dairy farm down the hill picked me up at school, made me dinner, and went home. Bertha Jackson cleaned the house. Larry Schmidtheimie, who chewed a stub of a fat cigar and looked not unlike Santa Claus, maintained the yard after Terry left (he also drove me to my first day of college and moved me into my dorm; my parents were, I think, on the Vineyard). Eventually Daphne Lewis arrived, though everyone, including Daphne herself, has a different opinion about when. Shuttling back and forth from her nurse's aide job in Toronto, Daphne lived with us for a few months at a stretch, cooking for my parents and watching after me. She helped look after my grandfather in his final years, and my father in his.

Under the feet of this human parade was a smaller but no less constant stream of animals. Newfoundlands and Labradors; domestic cats and mangy strays; lovebirds, until they were eaten by the cats; mice, until they were fed to the snakes; hamsters, squirrels, guinea pigs, lizards. We had a goat named Feather, who wore out her welcome when she got in bed with my father one morning. And a pony named Gino, kept down in Carl Carlson's pasture, who liked to turn back to the barn at a full gallop, then throw me headfirst through the doorway.

My parents also had a huge circle of friends. Philip Roth, Dick and Jean Widmark, Arthur Miller and Inge Morath, Mike and Anabelle Nichols, Lewis and Jay Allen, Francine and Cleve Gray. When my parents arrived in 1954, Litchfield County was still a remote and relatively untrammeled corner of Connecticut. But, over the years, dozens of urban refugees arrived, drawn by the tranquil beauty of the area and the proximity to New York. By the time I was born, it was all rather Chekhovian, with its countrified intellectuals, rambling dachas, and loops of important conversation unfolding on walks through the green, birch-studded hills. Thanks to Daddy's star power and Mum's charm, my parents were very much at the center of this world. People came from great distances for an evening at the Styrons'. Their dinners were magical, the candlelit table groaning with food, great, running rivers of alcohol, and guest lists that were rarely less than Olympian. Our Christmas party was not to be missed—Leonard Bernstein on the piano, presents for everyone—and even the flimsier holidays got a goosing from my mother until they erupt-ed into crowded, merry festivals. By the ends of these galas, my father was usually in a mellow mood. Kicked back in his favorite yellow chair, with a Scotch and cigar, he would amiably steer the conversation around the tent poles of his desiring—politics, literature, money, high-end gossip. Urgent voices responded in kind, swelled by laughter, profanity, complex movements of thought. The music of a great night rose and fell in our living room, and no one wanted to leave. All of this delighted my mother, for whom a house full of people was the greatest pleasure, a re-ward for all the dark days she endured in between.

~

When I was born, my father was poised on one of his life's great preci-pices. He was forty-one years old. Fifteen years had passed since *Lie Down in Darkness* heralded him as a wunderkind, and six since the publication of *Set This House on Fire*. Having set a punishing schedule for himself, he spent the intervening years transforming exhaustive research into a stir-ring 200,000-word narrative that was about to become *The Confessions of Nat Turner*. As always, his work was at the center of our family's existence, playing like a constant drumbeat under everything we did—whether we were strictly conscious of it or not. On the evening of January 22, 1967, Daddy walked down the hill from his study to find his family assembled in the kitchen. Mum was at the stove; Susanna, Polly, and Tommy were all sitting down waiting for dinner. Eleven weeks old, I was in a bouncy seat on top of the kitchen table, working my pacifier.

"Well, I've finished," Daddy said, weary but triumphant.

On cue, before anyone else had made a sound, I popped the pacifier out of my mouth like a cork from a bottle of champagne.

And so the late sixties were marked in our family by twin births, Nat and me, each making our own noise. The novel arrived in bookstores in October '67. The week of my first birthday, Daddy was on the cover of *Newsweek*. With a few exceptions, *The Confessions of Nat Turner* drew rave reviews. Philip Rahv, in *The New York Review of Books*, called it "a first-rate novel, the best William Styron has ever written and the best by an American writer that has appeared in some years." "A new peak in the literature of the South," said *Time* magazine; "a dazzling shaft of light...a triumph," said *The New York Times*. In November, my father received an honorary degree from Wilberforce University, America's oldest private all-black university, in Wilberforce, Ohio. It was an immensely gratifying experience for him. The risk he'd taken—fictively embodying a rebel slave, a black icon, in order to produce what he called a "meditation on history"—not only had paid off but was being embraced by the people whose acceptance he wished most to gain. In a 1992 essay for *American Heritage*, my father described the event. "There was much applause," he wrote. "George Shirley, a Wilberforce alumnus who was the leading tenor with the Metropolitan Opera, gave a spine-chilling rendition of the "Battle Hymn of the Republic," in which the audience joined together, singing with great emotion. Standing in that auditorium, I was moved by a feeling of oneness with these people. I felt gratitude at their acceptance of me...as if my literary labors and my plunge into history had helped dissolve many of the preconceptions about race that had been my birthright as a Southerner and allowed me to better understand the forces that had shaped our common destiny. For me it was a moment of intense warmth and brotherhood."

It was also a moment that wouldn't last. My father, like many first-rate artists, had a cunning sense of history. He knew there is a time, of urgency and relevance, for certain books, and that hitting that moment right can transform one's words from a pretty bit of business into a profound testament to humanity with a history-enhancing power all its own. Indeed, with a touch of Icarus about him, my father seemed interested almost exclusively in this kind of luminous flight. It was no coincidence that *Nat Turner* came to life in the crucible of the civil rights movement. Likewise, I doubt my father could have been surprised that a high-profile novel about race would provoke some of the same convulsive and polarizing feelings that characterized the era. Many years later, in a documentary about Daddy, the eminent African American scholar (and friend to my father) Henry Louis Gates, Jr., talked about the firestorm of controversy that ultimately erupted around the book. In the era of Huey Newton and the Black Panther culture, he said, my father's decision to conceive of Nat as a man who not only lusts after white women but also has homosexual feelings was bound to provoke outrage. My father's Nat Turner "was at odds with the kind of black man necessary for the times," he said. Daddy "had to know he was setting himself up as a sacrificial lamb," said Gates, adding with a sympathetic chuckle, "as we like to say, 'Nigga please.'"

~

And yet, my father was deeply upset by the controversy. In 1968 our household began to resemble a roiling little microcosm of the drama unfolding all across America. Scathing attacks on *Nat Turner* appeared in *The New Republic*, *The Yale Review*, *The Kenyon Review*, and *The Journal of Negro History*, to name a few. The Marxist historian Herbert Aptheker excoriated my father in *The Nation*, a situation Daddy inflamed when he took the bait and responded in a subsequent issue. Soon the Aptheker-Styron feud was national news. A planned film adaptation of the book was derailed by an organization calling itself the Black Anti-Defamation Association, created by Ossie Davis and Ruby Dee with the express purpose of shutting down the film project. And during two conferences my father participated in, at Harvard and at the Southern Historical Association, he was hectored by the same man, dressed in a dashiki and intent on proving he was a "liar."

In May 1968, just weeks after Martin Luther King's assassination, *The Confessions of Nat Turner* was awarded the Pulitzer Prize. In June, my father served as an honorary pallbearer at Bobby Kennedy's funeral. Two months later, while Daddy was at the Democratic convention in Chicago witnessing firsthand a nation on the brink of anarchy, Beacon Press published *William Styron's Nat Turner: Ten Black Writers Respond*. A compendium of essays edited by a history teacher named John Henrik Clarke, the book is a roundhouse assault on *Nat Turner*, deriding my father's "vile racist imagination," accusing him of "destroying [Nat] as a man and a leader," and, by extension, implicating him in losses more recent and raw. "Black Brothers and Sisters," urged John Oliver Killens in his essay "The Confessions of Willie Styron," "be not deceived by the obscene weeping and gnashing of teeth by white America over the assassination of our great black brother and Messiah, Martin Luther King. They loved him not… they understood him not. Our Martin was a revolutionary, and they did not dig him; therefore they destroyed him."

All through this period, my father was receiving reams of mail, both positive and negative. Some of the letters, from blacks and whites alike, were truly menacing. They unnerved him with increasing frequency. One afternoon while Mum was spending the night in New York and Daddy couldn't reach her, he completely panicked. Jumping in the car without a belt or socks on, he drove to New York and frantically called around the city from my mother's empty hotel room. When she at last turned up—she'd been collaborating with some Russian poets on translations of their work and hadn't thought to call—Daddy was beside himself. For a long while after this incident, he would require my mother to check in with him at regular intervals.

Bumbling along in the pre-memory phase of life, I don't have any concrete recollections of the *Nat Turner* years. What remains is a feeling of foreboding that, in my unformed mind, emanated entirely from the building we called the "little house." A converted barn, the two-bedroom cottage lay just twenty yards up our hill, separated from the main house by a stone walkway covered with a tangled arbor of grape. When my parents first came to Connecticut, they lived in the little house. Two years later, after renovating the main house, they moved down the hill. The little house became my father's study. Cool and dark, with a high-ceilinged living room anchored by an enormous stone fireplace, the little house was, to me, eternally spooky. I always feared someone, or something, would reach out for me from the shadows. Every movement set off a chorus of dust dancing in the scant sunlight. And, though small, the house had dozens of fathomless corners. Next to the chimney there hung a large pen-and-ink print that must have been a tie-in to the publication of *Nat Turner*. About the size of a movie poster, it depicted a wild-eyed "negro" in tattered garments gesturing to two other shabby-looking black men, who are crouched but attentive to the ravings of the man beside them. In the background are the squalid effects of what one assumes are slave quarters. The picture, along with the unpainted wallboards, the gloomy downstairs bedroom, and the squirrels gamboling in the rafters, gave the whole place a thoroughly haunted vibe.

Sometimes there were guests in the little house. It was they, perhaps more than the décor, who account for the confusing ideas I possessed before I had much of a grasp on logic. In 1961, just as Daddy was beginning *Nat Turner*, he and my mother invited James Baldwin to live in the little house. Jimmy was short on funds and trying to finish a novel he was calling *Another Country*. Though he stayed for only a few months, my father took a great deal away from the arrangement; the friendship the two men developed and their many long, late-night conversations had a deep impact on my father's novel. Inevitably, and especially during the most tumultuous time in the book's reception, Jimmy became part of the narrative of *Nat Turner*'s rise and fall. He alone among prominent black writers came to my father's defense. The paperback version of the book still bears Jimmy's oft-cited quotation about my father: "He has begun the common history—ours."

Somehow, in my dim little mind, I conflated the talk of Jimmy Baldwin, Daddy's black friend, and Nat Turner, the raving madman. Matters were tangled further with the arrival of a music teacher, who lived one season in the little house in exchange for teaching my siblings the piano. For a time, I possessed the bizarre idea that some unhinged friend of my father's was going to come over and either teach my sisters scales or murder me with an ax. I lived in a state of constant suspense and hid whenever the piano cover was lifted.

For years this strange memory lay at the farthest reaches of my mind. I left it there like a furry carcass you've seen in the corner of the garage, one you'd rather ignore for a bit than get up close and inspect. Then, a decade ago, the mystery unraveled. One day, when I was living on the Upper West Side of Manhattan, I took my Labrador for her daily trek through Riverside Park. While Wally was being cheerfully harassed by an animated terrier, I struck up a conversation with the dog's owner. A nattily dressed older man, he revealed a few benign details about his life, and I responded with a few of my own. Charles Turner was the man's name. And what was mine?

"Styron?" he replied, surprised. "You're not Bill Styron's daughter, are you? I lived in your family's little house one year." Turner, I thought. Duh. Turner. "I taught you, or perhaps it was your sisters, the piano."

~

The house in Connecticut was, once upon a time, part of a gentleman's farm. The half dozen acres purchased by my mother and father include a traditional nineteenth-century colonial, the little house cottage, and several smaller buildings, all set into a gentle slope in the state's western hills. The improvements they made to the big house included the addition of what we still call the "new" or "big living room" (to distinguish it from the "old living room" near the front door). Built from reclaimed wood and surfaced with rough stucco, the high-ceilinged room is light filled and rustically elegant.

A series of glass doors runs along one wall. An oversize fireplace is flanked by bookshelves, and a built-in bar, made of soft pine, dominates one corner. The big living room was Daddy's domain. Here he read, watched the news, clinked the ice around in his Scotch glass, and hid from the rest of us. During the day, he wrote in his study in the little house. But when evening came, he'd set his manuscript pages up at the bar and pace the gold shag carpet, making revisions to the day's work with Mozart blaring on the hi-fi.

Around the corner, the TV room was a passageway of sorts. Littered with toys and pet hair, it connected, via an elbowed hallway, to the kitchen. Most days, I saw little of Daddy. Before school, I was careful not to wake him. Nor would I have dreamt of disturbing him in the afternoon. So it was sometimes not until he came out to prepare dinner or sharpen his pencils that I ever got a glimpse of him. First came the tinny click of the living room door latch, which let me know he was coming. Then a multipart glottal clearing (my father's chronic ear, nose, and throat problems caused him habitual congestion; the noises he made to clear them were grotesque, and constant). Finally, his profile, hoving into view just about parallel to the television.

"Albert," he'd say, if he was in the mood to linger for a moment, "have you heard about the Man?"

This was one of Daddy's stories. He didn't really talk to me much, like a regular person might. But he had a few stories, and he liked to watch my reaction when he told them. The Man, according to Daddy, was some sort of homicidal maniac. He roamed New York City, killing innocent people—parents, children, the occasional fluffy dog—and then he chopped them up, stuffing their parts into big green garbage bags. With sacks on his back, he made the ninety-mile trip to Roxbury, Connecticut, on foot. Then he stored his victims' remains in the attic of our house. "It's true," Daddy would say, passing back the other way while I tried, aggressively, to ignore him. "They're looking for him. I just saw it on the news."

It wasn't clear to me why the Man chose Lone Spruce Farm, as our place was once called, as his boneyard. Maybe the Man was related to the Farmer's Son. Maybe they were just friends, drawn together by their horrible fetishes. The Farmer's Son, another stone-cold killer my father knew all about, had grown up in our house. Evil to his marrow, the boy (and in my mind he remained a boy) liked to torture animals. Squirrels, cats, chickens, small things you'd find on a place like ours. After they were dead, he too kept and stored his quarry. But the Farmer's Son didn't use the attic, which could be reached only by a set of stairs that began just outside my bedroom door.

Instead, he favored the dreaded basement. Naturally, my big brother liked to get in on this act. He was always convincing me I needed to go down to the bowels of the house, where we had an extra fridge and an old Ping-Pong table our mother used to wrap presents on. Mum left you a toy. That thing you really wanted. I swear! Tommy would say. Then he'd slam the door and turn the lights off, just to listen to me scream.

Beyond our house, the countryside pulsed with plenty of other dangers. Not five miles away, in a bedlam that filled my worst dreams, lived hundreds of residents of the Southbury Training School, a state institution for the mentally retarded. I'd never actually been inside. And I'd only ever seen a few of the inhabitants. But their asymmetrical faces and helter-skelter movements gave me some particular ideas about life inside the big brick buildings up on the hill. When we drove by the rolling campus, I gripped the door handle, or pushed myself back into the car seat. "Some of the really dangerous ones," Daddy liked to tell me, "they escape and do vile things." I watched the men and women ("retards," we cheerfully called them) crossing the campus's green lawn, scattering the geese that hung around near the pond at the edge of the road. "They can't help it," my father continued, a trace of a smile forming around the edges of his mouth. "They're imbeciles. Deranged."

I didn't really believe in the Man. And the Farmer's Son seemed like a bit of a stretch, too. But I couldn't be sure. Uneasiness was the name of the game, especially when my mother was away. Daddy's stories had a way of taking root then, fed by everything else that was not right, till my fears had grown into jungle weed. In my bed at night, I lay paralyzed, listening. The banging shut of the storm door below me. The screeching of the little house door up the hill. The rumble and click of a dying car engine drifted in from the road, followed by a smart closing of a car door and footfalls. The Man and his carnage menaced, then receded, replaced by a truer sound. A Woman, her voice captured in the cold, still air, and my father's whiskey-tongued welcome. With a pillow over my head, I squeezed my eyes shut, the week's rages—I can't stand it anymore. Oh, Bill, please don't be that way. Fuck you! I'm leaving. No, please don't—filling the void of sound. Lifting my head and sucking air, I searched the cerulean underside of my canopy bed for a spot to drift into, a place to take me away. The hours ground on until the car on the road pulled away in the dawn.

~

Like lots of girls, I had a passion for horses. No amount of bucking and tossing from Gino, the pony I inherited from Polly, could dampen my enthusiasm. When I was about seven, Gino was moved from the pasture at the bottom of our hill to a proper horse farm, and I was dropped there after school, on weekends, and nearly every day during vacations. As I got older, I took the sport to another level. Honing my skills with one trainer and then another, I spent the weekends competing, kept an eye on my ranking, and hung my ribbons in row after row around my room. I loved horses, plain and simple. I loved hanging around their stalls, talking to them as I brushed the burrs from their fuzzy coats, loved nuzzling my face into their chests, braiding their manes, and picking the dirt from their hooves. I loved riding bareback down to the river and easing in for a cold swim; loved trail rides, and picnics, and sitting on the fence watching the horses kick up their heels when you let them loose after a night in the barn. I loved the lessons, the sweat, the competition, even the fear. But most of all, I loved life at the barn. The places I rode weren't fancy. Our corner of Connecticut was, back then, a simple place. It was rural and largely middle class; the farms were not manicured, nor had they yet been sold off to slake the coming craving for McMansions. My best friend, Laura, was also a rider. Together, we'd exercise our horses, then exercise a half dozen others. We mucked out stalls, groomed and swept, cleaned our tack and hauled down hay bales, shared our lunch with the dogs, and played practical jokes on our teachers. Everything I longed for—camaraderie and ease, rituals, simplicity—came together on long days at the barn. Going home was a crapshoot. I never knew what I'd find.

My father didn't like horses much. And he really didn't like his children riding them. My mother always said this was why he didn't come to my horse shows more often—it frightened him to watch me flying over huge fences on the back of an eight-hundred-pound animal. It was also why, she said, he wouldn't buy me a better horse, though the problem with the one I had was his tendency to try to kill me. The logic here was not something Daddy was interested in. And his distaste for the whole enterprise might have sown the seed for the story of his I remember best. I was eight. Daddy called me into the kitchen. We were alone in the house, and, having just made himself a late lunch, he sat with his burger and beer, reading *The New York Times*.

"Al," he said, head still in the paper. "Do you know who Ella Grasso is?" "Yes," I replied, standing at attention, a little blossom of pride blooming within me. "She's the new governor." Daddy nodded thoughtfully.

"Well, I've just read something terrible. It seems that Governor Grasso has banned horses in the state of Connecticut."

The beat the followed was long enough for him to silently recheck the facts of the article. He put the paper down and tendered a look of paternal sympathy. "I'm afraid we're going to have to sell your pony to the glue factory."

I remember a tingling around my lips. My legs wobbled. I waited for him to laugh.

"Come on, Daddy," I blurted. "That's not true." "Yes, it most certainly is," he replied.

"That's so stupid," I pushed on, grinning dumbly. "Well, I'm sorry, Al, but that's how it is."

Playful and bold, I grabbed for the newspaper. "Lemme see." "No," he growled, "Now cut it out. Get out of here."

I went back to the TV room, curled up on the couch, and looked at the screen. Later, when Daddy passed through, I tried one more time to draw out a retraction from him. There might have been humor in his eyes, but I couldn't be sure, and I didn't press it. I knew only that the game, or whatever it was, was over.

~

When I got older, Daddy's stories became my own. I took the Man and the Farmer's Son and Ella Grasso's injunction against horses and made them into little set pieces. And I dined out on them frequently. In dorm rooms, at dinner parties, on dates, this ghoulish scenario seemed to satisfy the question *So what was it like having William Styron for a father?*, which often hovered when I got to know new people. The Great Man at home, then, was eccentric, dark, and cruelly funny. His transgressive behavior and his wicked imagination shocked people. But they also stoked a romantic idea about the private lives of famous writers in general, and Bill Styron in particular.

The last time I told my father's ghost stories was at his memorial service, February 2, 2007. His death, when it happened, had been a long time coming; I'm not ashamed to say that when he breathed his last, it was a relief. Still, I was surprised by how shaken I was, at the graveyard, watching my brother lower the box of ashes into its small, deep hole. And I sobbed while that soldier played taps. But, within days, our family had begun to plan a celebration of Daddy's life, a party to which my mother could at last invite everyone. I knew without a doubt that I wanted to write something. It seemed natural, since writing is what I do. It would be an opportunity for closure, as they say in griefspeak. And then I would be really, seriously free from this whole freaking deal.

~

On a messy, sleet-drenched day, more than eight hundred people filed into St. Bartholomew's Church in Manhattan. President Clinton, Senator Kennedy, Mike Nichols, Carlos Fuentes, and Bob Loomis would be offering remembrances. Daddy's best friend, Peter Matthiessen, was delivering the eulogy. Meryl Streep and Mia Farrow were among the readers of Daddy's work, and my siblings had chosen works by Rumi, Faulkner, and Mary Oliver. I'd spent a week or so fussing over my words, but through all the revisions my first line remained the same.

"My father used to scare the crap out of me," I declared. The lurid stories I chose that day were selective (omitting a couple that my husband, Ed, thought were actually too awful to get a laugh). And after I told them, I wondered aloud why he had done it. Why would a grown man scare his children so completely? (He had told similar tales to each of my siblings, and every one of them had a different twist.) Was it catharsis? Was he blowing off steam after a day grappling with all those barbarous slavers and Nazis who inhabited his books—real-life maniacs on the loose inside his head? Or was it a ham- fisted attempt at fatherhood? Was he just a dad with a faulty radar trying to make a connection? The answer that I settled on reflected what I believed was a deeper truth. Whether he meant to or not, Daddy taught us the lesson—a lesson which tested him hard at the end of his days—that life requires courage, and a sense of humor.

Now that he was gone, I had to wonder not why my father told those stories but why I told them. Why was this narrative—as hokey as a 'fifties TV show—the one that I was stuck on? There was something disingenuous about it. These hoaxes, and the way I described them, implied that a certain lightheartedness ruled the day in our house. That it was a Roald Dahl sort of place, and that Daddy, curmudgeonly and outrageous, was still at the core a comic figure. Which really couldn't have been further from the truth.

Even before *Darkness Visible* opened a window onto my father's personal history, I encountered people who appeared to know more. Strangers often seemed hip to some broad and unsavory secret, though they never said it outright. It must have been hard, they would say vaguely, putting a physical ellipsis to the conversation by rhythmically, knowingly nodding their heads. It must have been hard dot dot dot. Or they would laugh a little too loudly and maybe touch my shoulder, smile, and shake their heads. Sympathetic gestures all, but they often hit quite wide of the mark. Retelling Daddy's stories was, I guess, my way of managing that false intimacy by providing satisfying tidbits. They kept me from heading into territory I didn't want to explore. And they preserved a myth I was obviously as invested in as anyone.

I introduced my dad to Nancy McCabe when he visited me in Fayetteville, Arkansas, while I attended the MFA program at the university. My dad loved meeting my friends, all young authors, whose work he had read in Harper's or The Atlantic. Whenever my father came to town, I threw a party in my tiny apartment, and we all talked literature. Back then Nancy and I both began to dabble in creative nonfiction, a fact which annoyed our mentor, Jim Whitehead, and which inevitably made nonfiction, the forbidden fruit, all the more delightful. In "Gifts," Nancy unravels the evolving relationship with her dad, their difficulty finding common ground, personally and politically. He is the practical, upstanding father working on top secrets at Boeing Military Aircraft Company. She is the bookish daughter who doesn't like baseball or any other sport. Together Nancy and her dad find unlikely growth in a garden. They are pictured here together at Nancy's wedding.

NANCY McCABE

Gifts

IN LATE MAY, the peonies have begun to swell, yellow and pink just starting to edge the petals. My dad squats in the garden, cutting flowers. He spreads them out on the dining room table, snipping off the ends and dipping them in paraffin. Stray ants that were attracted to the sticky nectar fall off onto the table. My dad wraps the flowers in plastic to store in the refrigerator downstairs. It gives me the creeps that for two days that refrigerator is filled with flowers meant for dead people. And maybe there are some leftover ants in there as well.

Early in the morning on Memorial Day, my dad carries armloads of cold flowers, closed up tight and sticky to the touch, a little wilted, not very promising, up to the dining room. He slices the cold, waxy stems and fills jars with water, then arranges the flowers in them and whisks them off to the car. By the time he's done, the trunk is crowded with tightly fisted buds, packed in too closely to jostle during our journey.

Three hours later, at Mt. Olive Cemetery in Pittsburg, Kansas, my dad lifts the lid. The trunk has been overtaken by a profusion of flowers in full bloom, crowded together so thick I can't see the jars or the floor of the trunk, only flowers, flowers, flowers, big, heavy heads of red and pink and yellow, purple and white, petals all unfurled, layers and layers of petals. The air is thick with the smell of peonies that can become cloying in warm weather, but right now it is sweet and fresh, a little like citrus, a little like honeysuckle, a little like roses. I am awed by this magic trick my dad performs year after year, turning tiny buds into this extravagant miracle of wall-to-wall flowers.

191

My parents begin the long process of delivering jars to each family grave. When I am young, all of the names on the stones blend together. My dad's mother died long before I was born, and I think of her only as a polished white gravestone like a marble pillow or enormous communion wafer. In my dad's stories, his mother was a shining ray of light. I never hear anything about a stubborn streak or short fuse or moments of rebellion, no feisty sayings or bawdy jokes or embarrassing secrets. Death has whitewashed her to a bland saintliness that I will never live up to. I don't think to ask my dad what it was like, losing his mother so young. And I come to understand, when I am older, that even if I'd asked, he probably wouldn't have known how to answer.

~

In high school, I briefly become obsessed with genetics, with how traits are passed down from one generation to another, and I conclude that my dad and I can't possibly be related. We look a little alike, with the same gray-blue eyes and annoying cowlick, but the similarities stop there. We have nothing in common. He has brown hair and mine is blond. He loves math and science and I much prefer English and psychology. He is happiest outdoors and I hate getting all bitten up and sunburned. He is adept at growing things and the plants in my room wilt and turn brown, leaves crumbling onto my carpet.

My dad is a farmer at heart, each spring fighting the rototiller into lines and cultivating a garden that takes up half of our yard. Each summer he cans corn and beans, carrots and beets. He grows me strawberries and peas that I eat straight from the pod, raw and sweet. He plants grapes and roses just for me, but neither ever quite takes off. They're hard to grow, he says. Instead, each year we have huge crops of small, round, sour gooseberries and long stalks of red rhubarb. He makes pies, smacking his lips, while my brothers and I raise our eyebrows. The pies go to the basement freezer. He's the only one who will eat them.

My dad grew up with three brothers, then married and had two sons. Two sons and me. He doesn't know quite what to do with a daughter, at least not the kind of daughter I am. I'm not interested in gardens, or airplanes, or photography, or pigeons, the things that matter to him.

I don't really even know what he does for a living, his job, its title. He works at the Boeing Military Aircraft Company, but his job is so highly classified, he won't tell me what it's called. He just says, "It's top secret." When I get older I know that he's an electrical engineer, sort of, although he insists that actually he's not an engineer because his degree is in math and physics, not engineering. I'm even more confused. I figure he wires flight-attendant call buttons and bathroom lights. I'm wrong. I will be a little startled when he retires and receives several government citations for his work with electronic warfare.

My dad and brothers go to baseball games together. Sometimes they discuss photography, apertures and lenses, angles and chemicals. My dad and I don't seem to connect at all. Sometimes he gets enthusiastic about helping me with my algebra. But then pretty soon he's calling one of my uncles and they're on the phone forever discussing the theories and implications of some problem, and finally I wander off and read a book because I'm bored.

"Your nose is always in a book," my dad grumbles. He doesn't get it. He likes books, but he thinks that I read excessively, and he's puzzled at the way I sit around writing stories for hours. He also thinks my long phone conversations with my friends, mostly about people we know and why they do the things they do, are base, mere gossip sessions that tie up the phone line unnecessarily. In my family, curiosity about other people is taboo, not just a lowly pursuit but a violation of privacy, but that's what I'm interested in, people and language.

As a teenager, I'm obsessed with what lies underneath surfaces. I want to be able to detect a subtle shift of tone in a poem, to understand what people don't say between the lines of dialogue in a story, to follow how an image can accrue five different meanings so that they all echo off of each other. I want to make sense of why people say and do the things they say and do. I want to be able to decode foreign languages and distinguish the four different voices of a fugue or the faint ding on a triangle before the woodwinds come in.

My dad is interested in more practical things. He spends hours reading dull-looking magazines called things like *American Pigeon Journal* and tending a flock of faded and musty birds with tiny twitching heads, sometimes battering each other in frenzies of wings. These are the kinds of birds ex-terminated as pests in big cities, but my dad has built a cage for them in the yard, with chickenwire and a little door into the metal shed so they can escape from the cold. Every day, twice a day, he goes outside to fill trays with a corn and sunflower seed mixture. It doesn't make any sense to me, but these pigeons, and his hours in the garden, are like meditation for him. They calm and steady him, the same thing that books do for me.

At gatherings with my uncles and their families, I sneak off into cor-ners to read. In my grandpa's kitchen, my mother and aunts and step-grandma cook and chat on one side of the counter and the kids eavesdrop while my dad and his brothers and their dad sit at the table, all of them silent, dignified men. None of them ever hugs hello or good-bye. They don't drink alcohol. They aren't given to compliments or personal reflec-tions. My dad is the oldest and most cerebral brother. Everyone defers to his quiet authority and is intimidated by his intelligent, thoughtful man-ner. He speaks in measured tones, weighing each word carefully.

I'm bored by the men's conversations. They talk about boating and camping and fishing. What part of which lakes they prefer, what kind of bait they use. I lower my book when they start telling stories, loosening up. One of my brothers says that when he was little, he wondered why a fly inside a moving car didn't get squished against the back window. My younger brother and male cousins agree that they were puzzled by this, too. The question has never occurred to me. "Did you think about that when you were a kid?" I ask my dad.

"We didn't have a back window," he says. "And the floorboard kept falling out. We'd get splashed by mud and have to run back for Mom's purse." That starts the brothers reminiscing about that car, with the back door held on by a horseshoe.

I think that I have all the time in the world to hear these stories, so I go back to reading.

When my dad goes on business trips, he brings back gifts, seemingly heartbreaking, painstaking gifts with the intent of fixing me permanent-ly as a little girl: a round charm from Spokane, embossed with the words *Lilac City*; a seashell bracelet from Galveston; a sparkly cable car pin from San Francisco; a charm shaped like the state of Massachusetts; a bracelet with a miniature Brooklyn Bridge, Statue of Liberty, and Empire State Building dangling from it; a New Mexico bracelet alternating totem poles with fake turquoise rocks.

I never actually wear jewelry, and all of these things seem to represent the sweet yellow-haired girl my dad wants me to be. As a teenager I'm filled with sorrow and guilt and embarrassment at how he misses the point, and then, immediately, I'm overcome by a fierce need to protect him from the ungrateful daughter that I am. It will be a few years before I realize that these gifts were not as carefully selected, not quite as loaded with meaning as I once thought, that, in fact, he always brought us the same things, probably chosen in harassed moments between flights. Before the invention of rolling luggage, carrying a suit bag folded over one arm, lugging a hard-sided briefcase in the other hand, he'd likely often just snatched from store shelves entries in each of the appropriate categories: wife, sons, daughter. Souvenir spoons for Mom, key chains for my brothers, jewelry for me—things easy to find in airport gift shops.

But when I'm young, I see these gifts as evidence of how little he understands me. At my grandpa's, I listen to my uncles say things like, "She may have gone to college, but she has no common sense." I hear this often throughout my childhood, and then endlessly in my young adulthood, especially after attaining graduate degrees. There will also be many jokes about my career as a professional student. From a young age, it is clear to me that education and common sense must be mutually exclusive. But my fear of being unable to survive in what my family calls the "real world" doesn't stop me from reading my book in the corner while my brothers and male cousins talk fishing and guy stuff with the men, and my female cousins flirt with Grandpa and then sequester themselves to talk about boys.

I'm comfortable with my status as the family weirdo. "A woman's worth is measured by how many friends she has," one of my aunts likes to say, and I just mentally shrug, more interested in a few close friends than making strained conversation with people with whom I have little in common, including many of my cousins. My older cousins keep forgetting that I'm younger than they are because I'm tall and I read a lot and I'm quiet, which they translate into being more mature. I gain a reputation for being smart, even if what I'm reading off in my corner is *Beany and the Beckoning Road* or *Betsy in Spite of Herself* or *Anne's House of Dreams*, not *War and Peace* or Derrida.

Once or twice as a teenager I argue with dad's youngest brother, a say-what-you-mean-mean-what-you-say kind of guy who has some very firm ideas on education, particularly when it comes to studying literature. He resented having to "interpret" literature in school, as if stories were a secret code that you have to crack. "English teachers have nothing better to do than torture kids with hidden meanings that aren't there," he says, and I feel a bit uneasy, because I suspect I might end up being one of those English teachers. "They just do it so they can feel smarter than everyone else," he says, and scornfully quotes his former teachers. "What did the writer mean to say?" He shakes his head. "The writer meant to say what he said. Why should I read meanings into it?"

I'm with him to a point. I don't like that question, "What did the writer mean to say," which sounds like writers don't really know what they're doing or are purposely obscuring their points just to feel smart. But I can't explain to him that for me, it's not about reading meaning into anything. It's about listening closely, watching carefully, finding the meanings and patterns that are already there, the things people often skim over and ignore. It's an impulse as old and ordinary as my dog's instinct to plow her nose through snow, sniffing for the interesting story of earth and grass and trash and other dogs that have passed through.

When another of my uncles was a little boy, he could sit on the front porch and listen to cars and trucks far away on the highway, and he would announce the make and model and year of the oncoming vehicle just from the sound of its engine, and he was always right. I'm awed by this, the kind of ability that I aspire to, the ability to really listen, to hear something beyond the perception of the untrained ear. I want to have, with words, the equivalent of my uncle's ability, the equivalent of my dad's talent with math and physics and photography and gardening.

One day when I'm sixteen, I tell my dad that I've decided that I'm a pacifist. I'm eating a snack at the kitchen table. My dad stiffens. He puts down his newspaper. "You don't know what you're talking about," he says in a strangled voice.

"But Jesus was a pacifist," I say. My dad is a deacon at church and a leader in a national Bible Study organization. We never miss a church service. And the Christian position on war seems to me obvious and irrefutable, turn the other cheek and all that.

"That's a simplistic interpretation," my dad says insistently. "You don't have enough life experience to have an informed opinion." And then he goes on talking in his slow, patient voice that seems to mask intense agitation. He talks about his years in the Navy and gives me a historical overview of the reasons for the Second World War and the conflict in Korea and the Vietnam War. He doesn't mention his lifelong career with a military aircraft company, a career that I won't know till much later is centered on electronic warfare. I respond feebly. My dad provides a thorough, well-reasoned argument each time I speak. Finally I give up, falling into silence. I feel tears roll down my face as he goes on lecturing me. I understand that I am completely, hopelessly wrong. But deep down, I'm pretty sure I'm still a pacifist.

I vow that someday I will have the skills to win a fight with him.

~

As a senior in high school, I enter a Wichita city-wide essay contest on the theme "Man and his Environment." This is quite an undertaking, since my knowledge of environmental issues is pretty much confined to the slogan, "Don't be a litterbug!" I consult my psychology textbook and write all about "Man's" "inner environment." It's the sort of vague, imprecise essay to which I will never, as a teacher, give an A. But it wins me a $500 scholarship and is published in an advertising circular that goes to every household in the area. My mother tells me that my relatives don't know what to make of my essay. I'm surprised and embarrassed that some of them see it as intimidatingly intellectual. I take after my dad, they say, but I know that if I did, I wouldn't have written a lame piece about psychology. Instead I would have made powerful, convincing arguments about man's connection to the earth.

During college and graduate school, I fully embrace being the family misfit, the outsider, the one who doesn't belong. My dad is most fully himself when he's outside, surrounded by gardens and flowers and pigeons. I've found my own ways of being most fully myself: lost in books, writing stories, conversing with friends who read and write, wandering through libraries, bookstores, and office supply stores.

I think of my dad when I first encounter Theodore Roethke's poem "Root Cellar," with its description of bulbs and shoots and roots that somehow survive without sunlight. I think of the roots that anchor his plants to the soil. I remember when he assigned me the chore of pulling weeds, how they stuck stubbornly in the dirt as I yanked and yanked. How they cut my hands and left dirt under my nails, how the sweat ran down my face as I crab-walked down a garden row in the hot sun. One by one, each weed would suddenly come loose, making me reel backward, dirt raining down.

Now, my brothers remain stubbornly planted into his soil, still living with my parents for years after I have moved away. I read a news story about a girl whose kite was snagged by an airplane, and somehow I identify with her. She flew a hundred feet before she thought to let go. I see myself as skimming the earth, never quite planting my feet on it firmly, and I imagine how exhilarating that flight must have been, and how scary.

In graduate school, I read Willa Cather's O Pioneers!, and I wish I could get my dad to read it, too, because I think he will relate, because this book makes me feel like I understand him better. I imagine that he won't be able to help but love literature the way I do when he reads about Alexandra's connection to the land: "She had never known before how much the country meant to her. The chirping of the insects down in the long grass had been like the sweetest music. She had felt as if her heart were hiding down there, somewhere, with the quail and the plover and all the little wild things that crooned or buzzed in the sun. Under the long shaggy ridges, she felt the future stirring."

I give my dad books, but he doesn't read them. I give him copies of my stories sometimes, but I'm pretty sure he doesn't read them either.

～

On a Memorial Day gathering when I'm in my twenties, my cousins and I play Rummikub for the first time. My cousin John keeps referring to it as "rummy-cub," like "bear cub."

His sister Melinda corrects him. "It's rummy-cube," she says. She points out the pronunciation guide on the back of the box.

"Well, how were you supposed to know that they were violating the laws of phonetics?" I say to John.

The whole room goes silent, conversation halting among my parents and aunts and uncles sitting in their chairs and on the couch.

"Oh, phonetics! Big words!" taunts one of my aunts, and everybody laughs.

My dad never defends me. He just looks pained if I complain about my discomfort at these events. He looks pained when I come home and my mom and I spend a day catching up on family news, gossiping, he thinks. And even worse, I am now firmly a democrat. I am in favor of abortion rights and against the death penalty. I argue with all of my dad's views. He can't plow over me now. Unlike that day when I was sixteen, I now have the confidence and vocabulary and real-life examples to ride roughshod over all of his points. I know he doesn't know what to make of me. I know he disapproves of who I have become.

The women in his life, his mother, my mother, never debated, protested, took themselves so seriously or insisted on being taken seriously. They certainly didn't live messy lives full of mistakes. Unlike me, they didn't get married too young and then leave their husbands, or move from state to state in pursuit of degrees and jobs. They supported their husbands. They were peacemakers. They sacrificed for others' comfort. And here I am, prickly and ambitious, complaining if my parents expect me to sleep on the couch so that my brothers can have the beds. "He doesn't like me," I tell my mom, and I stop attending extended family gatherings. "He's not interested in anything I do."

She writes to me that I am wrong. She tells me things I never knew. That he carries copies of my stories in his briefcase. That he has, on his desk at work, a framed copy of a poem I once wrote.

And then, soon after, in the mail, with no card, no note, only my dad's return address, I receive a package. I open it, mystified. Inside is a music box, round and made of clear plastic, with pink flowers and vines swirling around the words, "Daughters are special people."

My mom always insists that actions are more important than words, that my dad doesn't have to say that he loves us because he shows it by making a living, by offering us the bounty from his garden, by being loyal and steadfast. I understand what a big step this was for him, finding this music box advertised in a Sunday magazine, ordering it for me. He could explain to me how it works, how pins rotate on a cylinder, plucking the teeth of a steel comb, tines ringing as they slip off the pins. He could explain all of that, he could argue with me articulately about almost any subject, but when it comes to talking about feelings, he doesn't have any words of his own.

I put the music box with all of the jewelry he bought me, stuff I would never wear but have still kept all these years.

My daughter is nearly a year old when I adopt her from China. My dad spends almost two months with her, and they develop their own communication, their own language of jingling keys and peek-a-boo games that make her laugh and laugh. I love the tender, sweet person he becomes with all of his grandchildren. And sometimes, now, he approves of me, too, because I have, after all, brought him this beautiful baby. This is the real reason people have children, I think. Not just to pass on genes or wisdom to the next generation, not just to replace ourselves in the world, but because of the strange and miraculous way that the mere presence of children can heal lifelong fractures. We laugh a lot more. We don't take ourselves so seriously.

At first my dad takes lots of pictures and videos of my daughter, but then he gets sick, unimaginably, unexpectedly diagnosed with cancer. During several frantic weeks when he is mostly incapacitated, I take pictures for him, take wobbly videos of all of his grandchildren, buy him books, not the kind I like but the spy thrillers I know he prefers. While I am in Missouri over the Fourth of July, trying to help out, the air conditioner at my parents' house breaks. It's 90 degrees upstairs. My mom has taken him to Springfield for treatment, and I call her and beg her not to bring him home, it's too hot. She is in a daze of exhaustion and grief.

I call every air conditioner repair service within a sixty-mile radius, begging them to come out on a holiday weekend, pleading with them, explaining that my father is dying. No one can come, the part is not available. My mom brings my dad home, and I try to talk her into moving him downstairs, into the basement, which is cooler.

His face gets that old pained look, and my mom quickly says, "If you're uncomfortable, you can put fans down there."

Once when I was a kid, a wayward ball from a neighborhood game slammed me smack in the nose. At first there was nothing but spinning, lights, bewilderment, then pain that vibrated the cartilage of my nose, so my hand flew up to cup it, to contain the pain. I opened my eyes and I was still standing there, it was still daytime, the game went on around me.

Mom's words hit like that, a shock and then a diffuse pain. Unlike a wallop to the nose or a punch to the gut, the pain doesn't shrink to be contained finally by one area: it expands. My parents think I'm concerned for my own comfort, not his. This is how they are determined to see me.

After sleeping in the heat, my dad develops an infection and ends up in the hospital again. If I had just been able to find a way to keep him comfortable, I think, I could have saved him.

It turns out that no one can save him. He dies only a few weeks later.

~

My daughter will grow up knowing him only through the videos and photographs he leaves behind. He's not in any of them, but we look through his eyes at the baby who wads paper on a blanket on the floor, bangs on her xylophone with a plastic hammer, and shakes her plastic keys till she hits herself in the head. Sometimes we hear his voice in the background.

When she is older, my daughter appropriates the music box he gave me. She peels off the paper cover so she can peer right into those complicated gears to the source of the music. Although not related to him genetically, somehow my daughter reminds me of him. She has an instinct for how things work. She is skilled at fashioning roses out of Tootsie rolls, cutting intricate ladders into the sides of her T-shirts, and boiling marbles until the insides shatter, their broken bits sparkling. Then she makes jewelry.

She is twelve when we go back to Kansas and walk around properties that still belong to our family but have long been neglected, like the house out in the country where my grandpa raised his boys. My brother tells me to wear jeans and hiking boots. We drive down a highway near Pittsburg, Kansas, past white mansions with majestic circle driveways, to a thick growth of trees and weeds. If we look hard enough, my brother says, we can see a glimpse of the ruin of the farmhouse through the jungle. I do see a flash of white, but I can't make out what it is. None of the neighbors consider this place an eyesore, my brother says. After all, the fruit trees still produce, attracting deer, creating a neighborhood hunting ground.

My brother pulls over. It's almost 100 degrees. He's staying in the car.

My daughter and I wade into the tall weeds, into a buzzing, humming forest where twigs cover the ground and broken limbs lay askew. Weeds flog our legs and make us itch. They leave little sticky flecks on our socks. Patches of stickers like tiny porcupines wait with their spiky teeth. Our shirt sleeves are snagged by branches and thorny vines.

We walk through spiderwebs stretched from tree to tree, thin filaments we feel before we see them, soft and sticky against our faces, wafting against our skin, tickly against our arms, tangling in our hair, so hard to detect visually that they begin to seem like tactile hallucinations, like ghostly barriers that we break with each step. We brush them off, brush obsessively, trying to rid our skin of the feel of them. Sometimes the vegetation is so dense it feels like we're inside a lightproof box, and yet, as with Roethke's root cellar, nothing sleeps here. Even the dirt seems to breathe.

In this primeval forest of majestic trees, of brambles and gnats and mosquitoes and chiggers that we slap away, my daughter recoils. She wants to go back. This is gross. A gross is 144, my dad would say to her if he were alive today, just as he always said to me. It used to infuriate me how he'd refuse to acknowledge that a word could have more than one meaning.

I remember once when I was about eleven that I forgot to weed the garden because I was so busy writing a story. And then my dad burst into the room in a fit of rage and seized my papers from me, tearing them into pieces. I watched my words flutter to the floor like confetti. And I remember my anger, out in the garden, as I grabbed randomly, ripping off weed-tops, bending and breaking stalks, leaving roots implanted. Haphazard, arguing with my dad in my head, I seized and pulled blindly until a tomato plant loosened from the dirt and came up, snaky roots and all. A ripe tomato plopped onto the ground. He had destroyed my work. I would destroy his.

Two hours later, when I went into my room, I stopped short at the papers lying in a neat if lumpy pile on my bed. They had been patched together unevenly like a strange puzzle, and I couldn't imagine how much work that had been, the laborious matching and taping of all of those shaggy pieces. My words glistened beneath tape, slightly askew, tears jigsawing across them. I stood, frozen in place, horrified by this meticulous reconstruction. It was a silly story, anyway, not worth all of this effort. It was a silly story that I would never have let anyone read, and I didn't know whether to feel touched or violated by all of this meticulous effort.

Now, my daughter and I push on through the high weeds to the old farmhouse, sagging there like a creepy horror movie set or a setting from a Gothic novel, gradually, inexorably falling into ruin. We peer inside. There's a decaying couch still in the living room, holes in the upholstery, springs showing. Wildlife scrambles above our heads. Something black flits along the edge of my vision. The floors are rotted, the walls full of holes. The diamond wallpaper and elegant arch of doorway remain intact. Somewhere here, maybe when his mother was dying of cancer, my dad planted his first gardens and built his first pigeon pen. Maybe the sound of their cooing comforted him. Maybe he liked knowing that in the face of death he could nurture and sustain life. I don't know this. Only that Grandpa left here for good about forty years ago, and that no one has lived here since.

Gradually the forest has grown to absorb the house. Gradually the house has started falling back to nature. I doubt that my dad, who brought us here occasionally when we were little just to check up on things, would have let this place, this land, end up in such a state.

The next day, three hours away, we walk through the backyard of the house where I grew up, in Wichita. It, too, is overgrown and tangled and messy, vines all over the smashed-down long grass, snagging us like barbed wire. The old shed has fallen into a scrap heap of metal and chickenwire, and the half of the yard once given to a garden has weeds up to my hips. Some of the gooseberry bushes have survived, and the cherry tree apparently still produces fruit; rotting cherries roll under our feet. As we walk, we keep kicking the heads off dandelions, scattering more seeds.

This is the yard that my dad mowed every week, with a woodpile here, a flower bed there, the swingset over there, the shed, the purple martin house, the small orchard, the garden. When I was young I thought of the yard as a house, each section its own room. And now it's been reclaimed by nature, all of it starting to blend together. I can no longer trace the exact lines that distinguished playground from shed, orchard from garden, flower bed from grassy lawn. The yard is all tangled vines and weeds and junk, too much to ever sort out; it seems to me beyond repair.

Then, as I kick a vine aside, I see something red, and I lean closer. It takes me a second to identify it, I'm so not expecting to see these fat scarlet clusters of fruit dangling from neglected, drooping vines. When dad planted grapes years ago, he told me that I would be at least twelve before there was any fruit, and that seemed so impossibly far away. And then it never happened, or so I thought. I was disappointed. Grapes are hard to grow, he said by way of apology.

But now I have a daughter who is twelve, a daughter who cooks marbles to shatter their insides, because of the way that, all broken up, they sparkle in the sun, full of their own glittery light. In the sun, these grapes are plump and soft. We pluck them off the vine and taste them. They are warm but sweet, sweeter than fruit from a grocery store.

It's a process my dad could explain but that is mysterious to me, something I have to look up. Sometime when no one was looking, tiny buds swelled, grew shoots that then sprouted tiny leaves and produced small flower clusters like buttons that then transformed into berries. Somehow in this backyard, cold and windy in the winter, rainy and often flooding in the spring and summer, terrible conditions for grapes, these grape berries grew, first green and hard, then ripening.

And now, impossibly, unbelievably, a profusion of red clusters spreads before us, an abundance of sweet fruit, like another of my dad's magic tricks, this last, unexpected gift.

I reached out to Susan Neville right before our first Father's Day without fathers. Susan's father and my father both died in the same year, so, consequently, the subject of fathers and daughters was on our minds. She wrote this essay specifically for this collection. Susan's father was a tail gunner in the Air Force during WWII, a tall man used to low levels of oxygen, a war hero. In Susan's patient, poetic depiction of her father as a kind of fallen Icarus, it is nearly impossible not to recall "the black flak and the nightmare fighters" from Randall Jarrell's famous five-line poem, "The Death of the Ball Turret Gunner." Indiana University Press released Susan's Butler's Big Dance, a book of nonfiction about Butler University and the NCAA men's basketball tournament. The book was dedicated to her father, a graduate of Butler and life-long basketball fan.

Oxygen

MY FATHER ASKS his son, the doctor, if he has had a stroke. The son, my brother, asks his father to raise his left hand and smile. It seems our father's smile isn't stroke-like, as my brother says "well, perhaps you've had a stroke, but I think it's more likely your oxygen level."

Hypoxia, the father says to his son. The oxygen is not getting to the receptors on the hemoglobin, my father says. That's what you mean when you say 'chronic lack of oxygen'.

He likes to catch my brother by surprise like this. He likes to catch us treating him like he's old. Several weeks ago he was caught smoking in the rehab unit. Then they found his scotch and his chocolate. All contraband. Cigarettes, scotch, and chocolate: the three things they gave him after every mission.

My father has two clear worms of rubber running at all times from his nose to a large oxygen concentrator when he's in his bed or to a portable tank when he's in his wheelchair. The part of the rubber that fits in his nostrils looks something like a crab or like bird's feet, and the claws have made calluses on either side of the septum in his nose, so he'll move the crab to the side for a bit and his skin turns even greyer.

He has stood in the bathroom looking at himself in the mirror, on the good days when he can stand, and he has played with watching the color fade from his skin when he removes the tube. I have watched him do this. Sometimes when he stands like that he just falls and we don't know why, so someone is always watching him.

~

Sometimes the portable tank runs out, so my father holds the crab tips up to his ear and listens for the hiss before he changes from the large tank to the small portable one. When the small tank is full, smoke swirls around the bottom of it, and the smoke is cold. He knows to hold the strap on one side and to tilt the tank so he can see the meter.

If he holds the strap by both hands, the tank always looks empty. You can only tell if it's full when it's on a tilt.

It's best when he sets the oxygen level to six, he says. His life has been reduced to numbers, as he knew it eventually would be.

~

When it comes to the concentrator by his bed, my father has to rely on other people to check the number because sometimes getting up from the bed and transferring to the wheelchair requires more energy than might have been required of him, when he was younger, if he chose to swim through the air to the moon, something that might be possible if there were, in the entire universe, enough energy and will.

However. In order to go home to his wife again, which they say is possible but which he fears is not unless he works to convince them he is better than he is, he is going to have to manage that transfer from the bed to the wheelchair on his own. Not just occasionally, they say. Routinely. And yet, and yet he is under certain restrictions that mean he has to press the red button and get an aide into his room in order to attempt the transfer, even if he feels able to do it, so he will not be able to do it on his own even if he says to the nurse to stay back, because it was he who called for her.

~

When he was a young man, my father was in the Air Force. He was a tail gunner. He was in a hurry to grow up and then he did and this is where it landed him.

I have a photo of him wearing the dress uniform in front of his high school. He is seated on a bench. His mother took the photo. The dress uniform was to impress the mothers and fathers. He is wearing the dress uniform in the photo where he is sitting on the bench before he left for training. He is looking at his mother holding the camera. He was so inno-cent. He was so young. He is so innocent. I am just now recognizing this.

Even in photographs, the uniform has the texture of linen. The but-tons are brass. There are buttons on the epaulets, patches on the shoul-ders, a cap covering his blonde hair. The dress uniform was worn at home. These photos are like high school graduation photos. Every family has the photos in a shoe box in a closet. During the war, they were framed and put on top of the piano or on a table in the entry hall. The handsome boys.

The dress uniforms were for marching in parades. The dress uniforms would be worn at funerals. The dress uniforms were brown or blue. The dress uniforms seemed to always make it home, even when the body did not. The dress uniforms hung in closets next to wedding and christening dresses. The going-away dress uniform was not necessarily the same as the one kept in the closet. The dress uniform did not travel with his body as it flew over Yugoslavia, over Innsbruck, Rosenheim, over Verona and Vienna, over Amstettin and Wiener-Neustadt, through Brenner Pass.

When the body flew, it wore a leather jacket lined with wool. It was cold in the fuselage. It was very cold. There was little oxygen.

The dress uniform will still be hanging in his closet when my father dies. Was his body ever that small?

~

I always thought my father was very tall. I thought he was the tallest man I'd ever known. He said he was six feet tall, and I believed him.

In fact he was at the most five-foot-ten.

I only learned this, or even thought about his height because after a life of utter silence about the Second World War he became obsessed, in his last few years, with nothing else. And so we learned, or perhaps we knew but paid no attention to the fact that he was the tail gunner in a plane referred to after the war as the Flying Coffin. I later found out the tail gunner was the shortest man in the unit.

My father, when he was a tail gunner, rode in a glass turret at the back of the plane. When planes went down and landed on the tail, as they often did, the tail gunner was smashed to bits.

When I was a child and we went on long trips in our station wagon, I would complain about sitting in the rear seat, facing backward. I claimed it made me ill. My father did not launch into a story then, though that was the perfect opportunity. That was the direction he faced all through the war. How many years was it since he'd been in the plane? Less than a decade. A handful of years. My age plus five. No time at all.

~

The explosions of light and metal went through the metal skin of the plane and through the skin of other men and into flesh. Planes around them hit the mountains and exploded into fountains of fire, into a lava of machine and body, and it did not seem real. He was too young to be afraid, he said. His pilot was skilled. His pilot was twenty-one, an old man. His pilot was the oldest in the crew. The pilot would not let them down. Above them, the skies were beautiful. Anvil shaped clouds. It was both real and not-real, all of it. Uncanny. They were boys.

~

Stock cars interest him now, and golf and baseball, but basketball games sometimes make him cry. You can see the faces, the pick and roll of bodies moving together, like the twist of a plane. The intensity on the boy's faces, the occasional center that is knocked down over and over, the head hitting the wooden floor or the pole so hard you can hear the crack way up in the stands. Will he get up? The boy gets up and the crowd applauds! He sits out for a play but his legs shake with the adrenalin. Despite his dilated pupils, he's in again, running hard up and down the floor until smack he's knocked down again under the basket. But he gets up. He runs again.

~

Twice they crash-landed in Italy, but they were inside Allied lines.

His entire crew made it home. Ten years ago six of eight of them were alive. It's down to two now, he says. His pilot died recently. His pilot carried them. The pilot was, throughout his life, the real father. He brought them through. No matter what else he did in his life—the job, the retirement, the two wives, the two children and stepchildren, the music (and he loved that, the music) there was this relationship underpinning it: that of the pilot and tail gunner, of the crew. It was the real life and everything that followed was a dream.

~

Five years after he came home from the war he would become a father himself. To me. To the woman who is writing this essay, the woman who knows what her father was thinking because for the first time in his life, toward the end, he talked to her seriously.

~

He wants to phone the other gunner who's still alive but doesn't know his number. Perhaps he's dead? Perhaps my father simply hasn't been informed? They're all dying. His own mother is dead. His father is dead, his sister, his best friends, his cousins. When he was young, he didn't notice that happening: the dying off, the battle toward the end. Sonofabitch. How had this happened? The children churned out like foam along the beaches. Don't talk about it.

Because he was, just yesterday, a tail gunner in a B-24. He was a lover and a husband and a father and he was a businessman, but the crew is all he wants to think about now. Why is that? his wife asks him. Why not all those years we spent traveling? Why not the years we fell in love? Why not the children, yours and mine, the ones we worked so hard to get to love both of us? They were angry for a while, he remembered, but they got over it.

He can't say. He can't say. Perhaps it's the oxygen tank. It's always with him. When his levels go down, they move from the nose catheters to the mask. He wore a mask just like that in the crew.

~

The rear turret was so small he couldn't wear a parachute. He kept the chute to the left, by his feet. He was always cold. He wore a leather mask. He was eighteen and his pilot was twenty-one. He missed his mother. He misses her now, if truth be told. Twice the plane crashed near Italy, but it was a smooth crash and the tail wasn't smashed into the ground like it is in photographs. That was his captain's skill.

When the missions were over, he flew home. Was he happy? It was a different kind of happy. Was he more mature? No, he can truthfully say he was not. He got back to the States and then took a train from the base in California to the Midwest. They neglected to hand him a necessary form in California and he had taken the train back to California to retrieve it. A thousand miles. It didn't matter. He had all the time in the world. It was a sooty ride, but he was not in the cold. Neither was he in the tail of an airplane. He could do what he wanted. There's not much he can say about that particular time, when he was free. He was not himself quite, but in retrospect, perhaps, he was completely happy.

Because he had been a soldier and had a mechanic's license he could go to any base and borrow a jeep for joyrides. He joyrode up and down the coast. He joyrode drunk, looking down over cliffs into the ocean. How is it possible that he lived through all those joyrides? He had. He could jump into the jeep without opening the door. When he was a young man, he could fly, or so it now seems to him.

⁓

My father wonders what it means when you say all hell is breaking loose. His wife came in and said it to him.

When she said that about hell it was one of those moments when something you've heard a million times suddenly seems weird and he spent the rest of the day trying to parcel it out. Or parse it. When I came in later, he asked me.

Why breaking loose? And from what? He wonders if hell is there in everything, like God is supposed to be, and if God spends all his time holding things together so it won't break loose, holding on to the hell in the leaf in that tree outside his window, to the bit of hell in the wooden frame on the hideous picture of that waterfall across from his bed, to the fresh hell in the chipped paint on the heater. And if he tires now and then the hell balloons out of the paint or the leaf or the frame and it becomes this room he's living in, the wife who already slips talks about 'other widows,' the beloved stepson checking into his jail cell, the crash on the television screen. The pilot. The crew.

There were days in his life when he could truthfully have said all heaven is breaking loose. He didn't, at the time, appreciate it. Probably nothing ever breaks loose, it's all a tug of war. Right now hell seems to hold most of the rope because it feels like it's breaking loose. But heaven will prevail. The good will prevail.

And that is what I think about God, he said.

And what, as a child, I thought about fathers, I say.

~

We've all heard about a man who smoked while breathing oxygen and blew his nose right off his face. An accident. I'm not that stupid, my father says. He moves the catheter away from his nose while he smokes.

~

For a year he refused to wear the oxygen around his children or around his friends. He would get weak. His skin would get a lavender tinge. He had seen the old women in the grocery store with their tanks in the caged seat made for children and more often used for purses or fragile things like eggs or cut flowers and for the doddering old people's oxygen tanks. He vowed he would never be one of them. But oh, he felt like he was inhaling such sweetness so he relented at home, at times, and then when he was out, at times, and then finally all of the time, the plastic tubing following him through the house, criss-crossing the floors, going right over the tubes with the wheels of his walker.

His wife straightened the cords like a bride's maid straightening the bride's train.

~

Before the mission they had their photograph taken. The wedding party. The groomsmen. Before getting in the B-24, they retrieved their parachutes. They treated the parachutes like their lovers, their someday children.

In the pictures of his crew, he's one of the men wearing a sheepskin-lined leather jacket. His children thought he was handsome in those pictures. He didn't tell them how cold it was, how his eyelids froze together at times so he couldn't see until he pressed them so tight that the flesh cells created its own heat and he could open his eyes, that the greatest danger to him personally, after being hit by flak, was frostbite.

The plane had neither heat nor pressure. What good would it do if it had? They occupied an empty cloud of air within a metal skin, and the skin of the plane was perforated by shrapnel each mission. It went through the skin and sometimes buried itself in human flesh. It was a war of attrition.

They carried their own oxygen, in those yellowish round tanks that looked like zeppelins, that looked like bombs.

~

The lifting off was half the fear, and once it lifted it took, it seemed, hours to reach altitude and that's when the temperature dropped to 30 to 40 below, the flesh so cold in the gloves, in the jacket. He put on the oxygen tank then and breathed in the pure air. The metal tank stayed by him. His parachute was at his feet. He wore an oxygen mask over his face, a leather helmet. There were times his gloves froze to the guns.

~

Sometimes the flak was white. Sometimes it was black. The bombs had a fuse set to explode at impact or at a certain altitude. Which was best for them? Neither one was best. There was the sense that perhaps they could float above or below the ones set for altitude, that they could dodge the ones certain to go off at impact.

When the bombardier lifted the bomb bay doors and dropped the ordnance, they all could feel the upward buck, the sudden rise, like a fishing lure that had lost the fish from the hook and bobbed back to the surface. In this case the surface was high, high in the air, up in the cold where they could be out of reach of the anti-aircraft artillery, where they could head back to San Pan and hope they made it at least as far as Yugoslavia where there were ways of getting the American soldiers back into Italy.

~

The tail gunner could see the sun glisten off all the planes in the formation. On good days, he could see the explosions from their own bombs.

It was an odd feeling, hurtling backwards through the air. If it were a cowboy movie and they were the cowboys heading into a building for safety, he would be the one at the rear, walking backward into the bank, his guns blazing toward the street. That was him, that one.

〜

The B-24's wings were so fragile that once he saw a plane to their left get hit and the wings fold upward. It fell from the sky with those wings folded, looking like a butterfly.

〜

The brain is the first part of the body to reflect a diminished oxygen supply. Hypoxia. The first evidence is an increase in the rate of breathing. Then there's the light-headedness. And then the joy! The overwhelming joy that makes you want to leap into the air if the ball in the turret or the ball in the hip joint is still strong and you are still young. Where are you going?

〜

So this is the death floor. There is no longer any talk of going home. Who knew there was such a thing as the death floor? It is a Catholic hospital and the chimes play "Jesus Loves You" whenever there's a birth in the building. I'm dead, my father said. Sonofabitch. He hasn't hasn't said another thing since he announced his own death. It appears his last word may have been "sonofabitch."

We're all gathered in the death room. Suddenly I notice that my father's eyes are an icy blue. What color were Dad's eyes I ask my brother, ask my stepsister and my stepmother. I ask my son. They're talking to each other, looking at the monitor tracking the heart rate, looking at the oxygen level. The mask on my father's face is like a white hockey mask.

Still. I can see his eyes and can't seem to communicate the eeriness of them. Something has happened, I say. Really, something horrible has happened! Don't you see it? It's his eyes.

My stepmother stares at his eyes.

What's happened? she asks. She is rubbing lotion on her husband's hands, swabbing his mouth with gel. The room smells like the fruity hand lotion and hand sanitizer and alcohol preps and some other sick sweet smells that I can't identify but will never forget.

My father sucks at the cotton swab like a baby at a nipple. Now and then his arm rises up like he's giving a benediction or like he's trying to hug someone. He seems to be in contact with the world. His breathing sounds like a scuba diver's.

His eyes, I say again. Look at them. What color were his eyes? You saw them every day, I say to my stepmother. And I grew up with them.

I'm not sure, the wife says. She looks into his eyes again. Blue I guess, she says. See? His eyes are blue.

No, I say.

Looking out of my father's skull now are eyes as blue as a baby's, as blue as glacial ice, as blue as a wolf's eyes. His entire life his eyes were green like mine but here he is now with an alien looking through the eye holes. The viscous gel of the eye, the irises have turned an eerie icy blue where they float above the oxygen mask, like a doll's eyes.

The oxygen mask and now the weird eyes. The electrical socket with that same uncanny look; slash/slash mouth, and the two eye holes.

I call my brother over to the bed. Our father's eyes have turned blue, I say. He looks closely. What color did they used to be? Even my brother hadn't noticed the change from green to atmospheric blue, from grass to sky, the eyes of the old man now as blue as the snow underneath the surface of snow.

Because the thing is, the thing is that his eyes have lost all color and no one, not one of us noticed it when it happened nor could anyone recall anything like it happening before. Something as big as that.

What color were his eyes a week ago, his entire life? They were a greenish brown, a hazel just like mine, I say. And like yours, I say to my brother, and like all of our children with the exception of one. How did it happen, and when? Was it gradually happening all the time we were staring at the monitor? What if he had been trying to tell us something with those eyes? Did it happen quickly, in just the last minute or two?

Can you live after your eyes have changed color? I ask. Is he alive right now? Is his brain dead? What does it mean to be alive? A second ago he had grasped my hand purposefully, I was sure of it, but his eyes are now the color of a doll's and he is no longer talking but he is breathing and waving his hands in the air and now and then he makes a sound that sounds like a word but isn't and he had shaken his head "no," I had thought, when I tried to say the Lord's Prayer over him, so I had stopped.

Has he been dead all along? I ask. We all look at the monitor. He's stable, according to the monitor. His arm raises up in the air again, and he moves a purple leg toward the side of the bed. His wife continues rubbing lotion on his hand. The sun sets outside the window.

~

I have agreed to stay the night so the others can get some rest. Soon I will be alone with my now blue-eyed father. I will swab the mouth and rub the hands with lotion. I will not sleep. Once an hour or so I will panic and press the call button. The first time I do this the nun and the nurse will swoop in wearing disposable gowns and plastic gloves and masks. After the first time, they will not wear the mask and gown. They will turn him, check the fluids, attempt to comfort me. They have seen all of this before, every night, all up and down the hallways. What kind of duty is this? I will not sleep at all.

The oxygen mask and the eyes and the electrical outlets will become more human as the night progresses. I will have entered some alternate universe I never knew existed. My father will not be there with me.

Poems run through my head. They are no comfort. Do not go gentle. Yes, do go gentle. Please go gentle. Buffalo Bill. How do you like your blue-eyed boy?

~

And so the one who flew all those missions, the tail gunner with his leather mask and the cylinder of oxygen by his feet, the smallest one in the troop, the trombonist, he would fly into his life and it would be as though it was he who leapt from the plane. He would fly toward his marriages and his children and friendships, toward his work and music, into old age, and eventually into the wing of a hospital where the ground has always been rushing up toward him.

I am a fly boy, he will say. I will always be a fly boy. Have you had a stroke? His eyes have changed from green to blue. He is part of the sky. It is only the lack of oxygen. It is only, he will say, *hypoxia*.

My husband, Pat O'Connor, first introduced me to his friend Susan at a writers' reunion in Fayetteville, Arkansas, and later, I was deeply moved by the brave, funny, and powerful stories in her collection Who I Was Supposed to Be. Susan Perabo is one of those gifted young writers who raced out of the MFA gates into a publishing contract and a wonderful teaching position at Dickinson College. In "What He Worked For," Susan writes about her dad and his work in the American Midwest, back when families took summer vacations together in station wagons, and actually stopping for lunch at a familiar orange-roofed Howard Johnson's. Here, Susan reconsiders and re-appreciates her father, his natural generosity, their relationship, her family, their lives, and a time when being together was simply enough. Susan sent a favorite picture, in which she sits with her father in front of Pleasant Lake in New London, New Hampshire.

SUSAN PERABO

What He Worked For

S UMMERS were for family car trips, first in our old red Ford and later in the wood-paneled station wagon you see when you close your eyes and picture 1977. My mother typed up song sheets with lyrics to "Little Boxes," "One Tin Soldier," "This Land is Your Land." We played Penny for a Red Car and Auto Bingo and did the Yes&Know books (ages 9-99!) until our invisible pens ran dry. We stopped at Stuckeys for lunch and souvenirs, and at dusk pulled into a squat orange Howard Johnson's in Ohio or Mississippi, went for a leisurely swim in the sun-warmed pool, then headed to the HoJo's restaurant, where my sister and I would order the hot dog kid's meal and follow it up with a giant hot fudge sundae. It was spectacular, this sundae, served in a tall, chilled glass big enough for a bouquet of flowers, three scoops of peppermint ice cream already starting to melt under the hot fudge, a generous pile of whipped cream—not a little dollop like you might get at home, but a swirling, majestic tower—a handful of peanuts, a cherry, of course. I could never finish this monstrous sundae. In point of fact, I could hardly make it past the whipped cream. After a few spoonfuls of wonderfully melty peppermint I'd lay down my long, thin spoon and announce that I was stuffed full and could not eat another bite. The third or fourth time this happened, my practical mother suggested that maybe next time I shouldn't order the giant hot fudge sundae, a suggestion my father immediately waved off, insisting, "This is what I work for." This being a sundae, hardly begun, and his seven-year-old daughter getting what she wanted, even if it was something she had no chance of finishing. Just those few magnificent bites—that was enough for me, and so that was enough for him.

We weren't spoiled, my sister and I, not in the common usage of the word anyway. We did not have lots of expensive toys, the latest electronics, or ponies at our birthday parties. We did not go on lavish trips or wear designer clothes. But it was my father's wish and obvious pleasure, reflected in indulgences like hot fudge sundaes, that we have things he did not have as a child, things that were not exactly luxuries but also far from necessities, things that he could provide for us because of his own hard work and his and my mother's thoughtful, careful planning. The family joke is that, as a boy, my father's only toys were "a stick and a string." In truth his situation was not quite so bleak, but the point was not lost on my sister and me: we knew that my father was never the recipient of a giant Howard Johnson's hot fudge sundae. He worked hard so he could give those things to us. That much, at seven, I understood.

As for what exactly his work was, I had absolutely no idea. All I knew was this: every weekday morning around 7:25 my father would appear in the kitchen showered and shaved and holding two ties; my mother (buttering toast, mixing oatmeal) would point to one, he'd put it on, give everyone a quick kiss good-bye, and go out in the world to earn the money that provided me with ice cream. My father worked at Ralston Purina, under the Checkerboard Square in the heart of downtown St. Louis. He didn't make dog food, that much I knew, but beyond that I was pretty clueless. He was trained as a lawyer, so this was what I always wrote on school questionnaires that asked what my father's occupation was, but by the time I was eight or nine he was no longer practicing law. He worked, from what I gathered, in something called Community Affairs, but that was not something you could write on a questionnaire. Whatever it meant—and I didn't spend time wondering—he pulled into the driveway between 5:15 and 5:30, most nights of my childhood, and the four of us had dinner together around the dining room table, except for the rare, thrilling evenings we got to eat on tray tables in front of the television. I had friends whose fathers traveled, or played golf on the weekends, or went out with their buddies to watch sports or bowl a few games. My father did none of these things. At the end of the day, when he came home from work, he came *home* from work.

As my sister and I got older, the memorable mini-extravagances my father was able to provide took on different forms. Non-essential food items —appetizers and desserts—remained a constant, but far more important to me were the post season baseball tickets he was able to obtain for us throughout the 1980s—again courtesy of his job, but this time in a different way than simply giving him purchasing power. The work my father did in the St. Louis community was often acknowledged with small gifts from the agencies he worked with—in the 1970s, the gifts were usually coffee mugs, umbrellas, and tee-shirts. In the 1980s, the gifts suddenly became the equivalent of Perabo gold: Cardinals tickets. He also had a lot of friends at Ralston who had (in the purest sense of the word) "connections." My father actually became something of a playoff ticket shark, in fact—totally inconsistent with his generous personality but completely consistent with his lifelong love of the Cardinals—trading pairs of tickets throughout each game day to ensure that we wound up with the best seats possible. In the seventh game of the 1982 World Series, we were close enough to leap over the first base wall when the Cardinals won.

A few years later, when my sister and I went to college, my parents not only paid our tuition in full but also gave us a small spending allowance. It wasn't a jaw-dropping amount of money by any means, just a couple hundred dollars a month, but it was enough that we didn't have to hold down a job while we went to school, enough that we could put gas in our cars, go out to dinner with our friends, go to the movies (which, as a film major, I did on a weekly basis). My father had painted houses and worked in the cafeteria to help pay his way through Amherst, and most of my friends in college did work-study to help pay the bills. At twenty, I was finally starting to recognize how fortunate I was. It wasn't that my father didn't want us to think about money—that would have been irresponsible—but that he didn't want us to *worry* about money.

And that's what it came down to, really, in the end. My father just didn't —just doesn't—want us to worry. As a parent, there was so little he could control, even when we were young, but by god he could control sundaes and baseball tickets and dinner with friends, could control them merely by the act of providing them. I understand this now, as a parent, both the desire to provide and the futility of the desire. My father wanted to relieve my sister and me from worry one little moment at a time, wanted to provide a respite from unpleasantness or unhappiness. Once, after we'd both graduated from college, we were talking about the number of our friends who'd been forced to move home for one reason or the other, often to the disappointment and/or embarrassment of their parents. My father shook his head adamantly. We were welcome in their home, he said, "any time, at any age, and under any circumstances." This became another Perabo family joke—my sister and I still make up the most outrageous circumstances we can imagine—but at its heart it's not a joke at all. It's the ultimate stability in a perpetually unstable world, a safety net in case something goes terribly wrong. Any circumstances. *Any circumstances.* This was, above all, what he worked for, this lifelong promise. Forget expensive toys and lavish vacations; this may be the only good kind of spoiled there is.

My father retired from Ralston Purina the year I turned thirty. We attended his farewell reception as a family. People whose names I'd heard, but most of whom I'd never met, talked about my father's work in the St. Louis community, about his dedication to urban renewal, his devotion to various charities, his reputation as a trusted colleague and boss. This is what my father had been doing all those years, in those hours he was not at home—his job, Director of Community Affairs, gave him the means to use corporate money to help rebuild poverty-stricken neighborhoods in downtown St. Louis, to support children's charities, to promote education initiatives, to help increase communication and cooperation among groups with deep divisions. He had worked for something in addition to us, it turned out, touched the lives of thousands of people I would never know. Generosity, the thing that came to him so naturally, was his job. Some of this, of course, I had come to realize in my young adulthood. But that afternoon at the retirement reception, as the affection and accolades rained down, I was sorry, and a little embarrassed, that I had not known all he'd done, that I had not thought to ask more about his important work, that I was too busy eating ice cream and watching the World Series to pay as much attention as I should have. But this admission, too, my father would have happily waved off. No time for apologies. We had dinner reservations. His treat, of course.

The closest I have come to meeting Antonya Nelson was once when I stepped out of an elevator at a writer's conference, and she stepped in. Years later, when one of her former students published one of my stories in his journal, I felt justified in requesting Antonya's friendship on Facebook. In writer circles, surely that's not considered stalking. In "Do You See What I See?" Antonya focuses on her father, an English professor, and she wonders about his mind and how much he really can see despite the recent diagnosis of Parkinson's. In the family photograph she sent, he is the young father, looking very much like a brave action hero right after a tornado touched down, lifted the family while they were in a car, then dropped them to the ground in Wichita, Kansas. This photo of her father carrying the young Antonya to an ambulance appeared in the local newspaper.

ANTONYA NELSON

Do You See What I See?

O NE CHRISTMAS holiday when my psychologist sister was still in graduate school, she performed Rorschach tests on our whole family (aged parents, five siblings, numerous offspring, some game in-laws). She set up at the kitchen table and interviewed us individually, placing the famous cards before each of us, scratching away on a notepad as we commented, encouraging us with a steady murmuring "Uh-huh, uh-huh."

My sister was serious in her efforts as administrator of the diagnostic tool, but my family prizes a wisecrack over a felt sentiment any day of the week. With us, it's a kind of competitive sport, witticisms and one-liners, tall tales and hyperbole; we'll sacrifice a great deal of veracity in favor of the better story. One after another we sat across from my poor sister and tried to be funny and/or sarcastic. "Gnomes playing patty-cake!" one of my brothers said; when my sister rotated the card, as per psychiatric practice, the image became a vagina. "Batman!" he would say; then "vagina." This brother reported the same finding for every single image: cartoon figures right-side-up; female genitalia upside-down.

Another brother (the outdoorsman among us, he who has no hearing in his right ear from shooting guns, he with the fishhook scar in his eyebrow) saw a lot of road-kill. "Dead turtle, dead squirrel, dead Bigfoot, dead skinny giraffe, dead eagle digesting a dead mouse," etc.

"Dancing fairies," said my niece, an apprentice irritant. All the pictures were of dancing fairies.

My mother and I (teachers, know-it-alls) both critiqued the instrument, those idiotic pictures that any four-year-old could have made at

225

a craft table using folded paper napkins and food coloring. Along with being amateurishly rendered, they also seemed embarrassingly dated by blatant racist and sexist qualities. Rather than submit to the process, we wished to evaluate its faults, find it lacking merit, be superior to its design and execution, remark dismissively and cattily at its crudeness. My sister sat on the other side of the table sighing, her note-taking at a dead stop.

At this point in his life, my English professor father was slowly succumbing to Parkinson's. Prior to the diagnosis, he'd been the leader of our bratty mocking pack, final judge of a story's success as worthy material. Normally a reticent, ironic, vaguely muttering person, when it was his turn to take the ink-blot test, he became a veritable slap-happy chatterbox. In recent times, we'd all noticed that his mental alacrity had been waning—his long-term memory still sharp, his short-term a little shaky, so that he could quote the pitch-perfect Shakespeare or Dickens or Wilde bon mot without a problem, but not actually recall whether or not he'd bid yet at the Bridge table. His responses to the Rorschach images, alone among the group of us, seemed truly revelatory. True, and revealing.

What did they reveal? Well, something about his inner life. On and on he went, one elaborate whimsical vision after another, whole maniacal tales unfurling with the appearance of every new card. "Those are the gatekeepers, and on either side here come the insurgents, little blistering buggers, attempting to breach the gap!" He gasped, he pointed, he pulled from thin air a chaotic panoply of fantasy. Had there been ten more cards, I have no doubt he could have kept going. My sister took notes furiously, both stunned and delighted by his loquaciousness. Right side up, upside down, it didn't make any difference; there was no stopping his unleashed impressions.

I wonder now if the test didn't offer a kind of pleasant middle ground for him to inhabit, a place free of confident knowledge, a place in which neither memory nor action was necessary; neither sanity nor senility, but simple liberating play. Faced with a Rorschach, you don't have to know; you have merely to respond. Obviously he was having fun. The rest of us, I'm certain, had been lying when we encountered the tests, disingenuous at best; but for all his silliness and random sidebars, I think my father was telling the truth.

And the truth was that he was slipping from the shared world into the private one of his impending dementia and hallucination. A few years after that Christmas, he confided to me that he understood the difference between those two worlds, the one we all occupied together, and the one he alone navigated, but unfortunately he still had to perform in both. It was very hard to do, he said; it took a lot of energy to keep both of them up and running. Especially hard, he added, because he had to keep them separate; the occupants of each were unknown to the other except by him, the go-between.

So given the opportunity to disengage, it wouldn't be surprising to discover that he was having a great time. "Oh look at that sinister fellow!" I can still hear him crowing at the kitchen table ten Christmases ago. "He's a sneaky one, out there in the alley with the kitty cats and the nasty bats, tiptoeing around, peeking in the windows, sniffing at the garbage!" The image before him was clearly just a simple smear of black ink sitting in the middle of a white page—Roadkill Sasquatch; some female private part; perhaps a dancing fairy—but to him it might have seemed like a map of his mental territory, and he was delightedly pointing out the landmarks.

One April at the Conference for the Book, my dad sat next to Lee Smith at City Grocery, a restaurant in Oxford, Mississippi. In between the soft-shelled crabs and the shrimp and grits, my dad later told me Lee was as funny, brilliant, and charming as her novel, Oral History, which we had both read. He also said he wished I'd been there and I admitted that I did too. When I approached Lee, she said she remembered meeting my dad, so, she sent this essay about her dad right away. "Daddy's Dime Store" is very much about Lee's father of course, but it is also about an aging America, dwindling small towns, and the disappearance of family-run businesses. Lee sent this wonderful picture of her together with her dad inside his shop in Grundy, Virginia.

⌒ LEE SMITH

Daddy's Dime Store

I COULD DRIVE this road with my eyes closed, or almost—Route 460 as it winds through the mountains of far southwest Virginia from Richlands to Grundy, my home town. I go over the heart-stopping Shortt's Gap. I pass the huge Island Creek tipple, long shut down; innumerable "yard sales" held in no yard, but right along the roadside; a storefront with a big sign that says "We Buy Ginseng"; several houses turned into the kind of freelance churches where you get to scream out and throw your baby.

Today there is lots of traffic as I get closer to Grundy, and the large hollers spill out into the main road: Big Prater, Little Prater, Watkins Branch, Hoot Owl. An old high school friend in a neighboring truck rolls down his window and says, "Hi Lee, when did you get in?" and we talk until we can move on again.

I am always struck by that "in." Driving into Grundy is literally like coming into a bowl, producing that familiar sense of enclosure which used to comfort me and drive me crazy all at once when I was a teenager. These rugged and almost perpendicular mountains nestle Grundy "like a playpretty cotched in the hand of God," as an old woman once described it to me. The mountains are so steep that the sun never hit our yard directly until about eleven o'clock, so steep that a cow once fell off a cliff straight into my Aunt Bess and Uncle Clyde's kitchen. This is true.

Founded at the confluence of the Levisa River and Slate Creek, Grundy became the county seat of Buchanan County in 1858, enduring cycles of fire and flood, boom and bust ever since as lumber and coal businesses came and went. Perhaps its isolation and its constant struggles made its citizens so close to each other, so caring and generous—the "best people in the world," my daddy always said, and this is true too. I was lucky to grow up here, to hear the stories I heard in my father's dimestore (who was pregnant, who was getting married, who had got saved, who was mean to her children or made the best red velvet cake) and in my grandaddy's office in the gray stone courthouse across the street, where he was county treasurer (who was in debt or out of a job or had set his house on fire just to collect the insurance money). I lived on these stories.

But today I've come to say good-bye. Grundy is poised to make history as it relocates to "higher ground"—just like in the old gospel song. I park in front of the courthouse and stand on the sidewalk watching men board up the windows of the dimestore—this is the last time I will ever see it.

Many of my favorite memories of Grundy take place here, where I literally grew up. As a little girl, my job was "taking care of the dolls." Not only did I comb their hair and fluff up their frocks, but I also made up long, complicated life stories for them, things that had happened to them before they came to the dimestore, things that would happen to them after they left my care. I gave each of them three names: Mary Elizabeth Satterfield, for instance, and Baby Betsy Black.

Upstairs in my father's office, I got to type on a typewriter and observe the whole floor of the dimestore through the two-way glass window. I reveled in my own power—nobody can see me, but I can see everybody! I witnessed not only shoplifting, but fights and embraces as well. Thus I learned the position of the omniscient narrator, who sees and records everything, yet is never visible. It was the perfect early education for a fiction writer.

I always went down to check on the goldfish in their basement tank. Every spring I looked forward to the arrival of the pastel-colored Easter chickens. But my favorites were the little round turtles with roses painted on their shells. I used to wear these turtles to school on my sweaters, where they clung like brooches. I bought jellied orange slices and nonpareils, those flat chocolate discs covered with little white balls of sugar, from Mildred who presided over the popcorn machine and the candy counter at the front of the store. My friends were surprised to find that I never got anything free; despite my protests, I had to save my allowance and pay just like everybody else.

By fall, the Ben Franklin will be gone, demolished along with three dozen other Main Street stores and a score of homes as part of the $177 million Grundy Flood Control and Redevelopment Project, a historic collaboration among the U.S. Army Corps of Engineers, the Virginia State Department of Transportation, and the Town of Grundy itself, population 1100. They'll move the railroad and rebuild US 460 on top of a fourteen-foot levee running where these buildings now stand.

"Doesn't it make you sad?" friends ask. Well, yes and no.

Old Grundy was a ghost town anyway, due to its continued flooding—nine major floods since 1929, and still counting. In 1957, I remember a huge catfish flopping down the dimestore stairs into the water-filled toy section. The flood of 1977 devastated ninety per cent of the downtown businesses and caused $94 million damage countywide.

I remember how Daddy never slept when it rained. He was always out back with his flashlight, "watching the river…"

He closed this dimestore in 1992 at age 83, due to lack of business. The building has been used as a teen center since. Unfailingly civic, my father always loved Grundy, and I know he would have supported any plan to save it.

But…WalMart? already promised for the new town site.

I snap some more pictures, remembering one cold, dark Sunday afternoon, several weeks before Easter. Daddy has taken me down to the dimestore with him to "help make the Easter baskets," which didn't come pre-made and packaged in those days. Many of the women who work in the store are there, too, and lots of little stuffed rabbits, and lots of candy Easter eggs. The women form themselves into an informal assembly line, laughing and gossiping among themselves. They're wearing slacks and tennis shoes. They're drinking coffee. It's almost a party atmosphere. As a "helper," I don't last long. I stuff myself with marshmallow chickens and then crawl into a big box of cellophane straw where I promptly fall asleep while the straw shifts and settles around me, eventually covering me entirely, so nobody can find me when it's time to go.

"Lee!" I hear my daddy calling. "Lee!" The overhead fluorescent lights in the dimestore glow down pink through the cellophane straw. It is the most beautiful thing I have ever seen. "Lee!" they call. I know I have to answer soon but I hold this moment as long as I can, safe and secure in this bright pink world, listening to my father call my name.

Watching him close the dimestore after forty-seven years in business was one of the saddest things I have ever witnessed; in a way, it was fitting that he died on the last day of his going-out-of-business sale.

The merchandise was all gone, and somebody had just come to haul off the last of the fixtures. Daddy fell at home that same night, breaking some ribs; by the time I got to Grundy, he was at the hospital, hemorrhaging internally. All I could do was kiss him good-bye. My father never wanted to retire or leave Grundy, and I can't imagine what he would have done with his days when his beloved dimestore was gone.

Now, his kind of business may be gone forever.

I take a few more pictures of all the boarded-up stores down Main Street, and then I'm gone, too.

233

When she was a student, Johanna Gohmann majored in theater. But then her hilarious, bold, and moving fiction and nonfiction began to win so many awards, she switched majors. After she graduated, "Jo" became a friend and a colleague. She traveled, worked odd jobs, wrote, moved to Ireland, married an Irishman, then returned to the United States and had a son. In "Balloons," Jo stops time, as though life itself and her close relationship with her father is all going by too fast, aging, and, consequently, floating away from her grasp. Jo captures the quiet beauty in a moment, a moment that might be made more beautiful because she knows it is fading. Johanna's husband, David Boyle took her recent picture, and Ernesto Rodriguez photographed her dancing with her father at her wedding.

JOHANNA GOHMANN

Balloons

NINE YEARS AGO, I am twenty-seven, and I am home in New Albany, Indiana visiting with my family. There is a birthday party for one of my seven siblings, and there are the usual hot dogs, and paper plates, and perspiring cans of soda. My mother has brought in a big bunch of brightly colored helium balloons as decoration.

The morning after the party, I am up in my childhood bedroom, and when I look out the window, I see my Dad standing in the front yard, alone in the quiet of a spring morning. The dewy grass is giving a sheen to his leather shoes, and he is holding the big bunch of balloons in his large hands. I watch as he struggles to carefully separate the strings, then he releases the balloons to the sky one at a time. He stares at each one as it drifts up and away, until it becomes just a tiny pinprick of color.

It is a rather odd sight—this six-foot-five grandfatherly figure, clad in impeccable dress slacks and a sport coat, playing with a handful of children's balloons. Watching him, I feel something inside me twist tightly. I slip on some shoes and go outside to join him. When he sees me, he smiles a distracted smile.

"I like watching these balloons float away, Josey."

We stand together, and he releases the string on the last balloon. It drifts skyward, joining the other tiny dots of color in the sky. We watch silently as it sails up into the clouds, fading into the blue. It is a rare, quiet bit of togetherness for us, and should be a sweet moment. But watching those balloons drift away fills me with a strange, anxious kind of melancholy. I don't like watching them go.

When I am thirty-five, my Dad is diagnosed with Alzheimer's. The diagnosis isn't a surprise. He is seventy-seven, and I have seen the shift in him—his confusion with numbers and dates...the way he repeats stories within minutes of each other, sometimes transposing the names of people and places. And yet, when my oldest brother calls me with the news, it still feels improbable. As if my commanding, in-charge father never would allow such a thing to happen to his solid, intelligent mind.

For a while, medication seems to slow things down, but then a full year later, it's undeniable that my dad is slowly coming uncoiled. It becomes the norm for him to appear wearing a shirt inside out, or sporting two pairs of pajama pants beneath his dress slacks, even in the heat of August. I buy him a beeping gadget to help him locate his constantly misplaced glasses and keys. He loses the gadget.

At thirty-six, I am pregnant with my first child. When I talk on the phone to my Dad, I can feel my baby rolling back and forth in my belly, his strong kicks and punches occasionally making the fabric of my dress hitch and jerk. I listen to my father struggle through the conversation, and I try to float, relaxed and easy, through his tide of tangled words. I rub at the patch of flesh over my flailing baby, and I try to imagine my Dad holding my son as he did his other grandchildren—bouncing him gently on his knee, letting him teethe on his heavy silver wristwatch.

As I watch my Dad slowly lose bits and pieces of himself, I think about those long ago released balloons. I know the bright shades of my father are fading with each passing day. They are drifting further and further away from me. And I can feel myself scrabble to contain them... trying to grip the tangled strings of them tightly in my fists...struggling to somehow make them stay.

He spent his life as a successful insurance salesman. This makes him sound staid and dull, but in reality, he is a big, playful personality. His large blue eyes perch above a smirking mouth, and as a younger man, he bears a striking resemblance to Chevy Chase. As he grows older, his features crack and curl, and he suddenly begins to look and sound like Gene Hackman—the same knowing, smiling eyes—the same gruff voice. Once while watching a movie, I hear Gene Hackman tell someone to "shag ass", and it's as though my dad has been transported to the big screen. Shag ass means "to hurry," and the only other person I've ever heard say this is my father.

He has large, mitt-like hands, and their Shrek-like size renders certain tasks comical, such as when he struggles to use scissors, or when he reaches to pet his tiny terrier that he calls "Princess." He has a tiny bit of shrapnel from the Korean War imbedded into the thumb of his right hand, and as children we probe this tiny black pellet with wide-eyed fascination.

He is, as my mother says, "full of foolishness." In one of my favorite photos of him, he is in a Freddy Krueger hat and sweater, brandishing a pair of rubber knives, and giving a hilariously hideous snarl to the camera. As kids, he often tells us about pranks he pulled as a child. When he was a young boy, he and a friend took Limburger cheese (a product whose smell can only be described as fecal) and hid slices in their palms. They went up and down the stairs of their Catholic grade school, quietly greasing the banisters with the stink. When people came down the stairs, they walked away sniffing their hands with disgust. As a little girl, I am enthralled by this prank, and my friends and I reenact it on our last day of school. The cheese is gooey and the smell makes me gag, but I love feeling mischievous like my father.

He likes teasing us—his children—most of all. One warm May night we are all gathered watching "The Incredible Hulk", and my dad comes into the living room and looks at us with a grave, stricken face. He tells us that he's just seen a special news report, and he has some terrible news. President Reagan has decided children simply aren't learning enough, and he is cancelling summer vacation all across the United States. At first we just roll our eyes at him, but he keeps his face so stone cold serious, we become panicked. We begin pacing the house and shouting. One of us anxiously flips through channels trying to find the "special report." We groan on like this for almost half an hour, until some of us begin crying and shouting our hatred for stupid President Reagan. My dad finally breaks down, and admits that he's only joking. We pile on top of him - half furious, half laughing—and try to punch him with our tiny fists.

When we are young, he is gone a lot. He goes on business trips and golf trips, which are often one and the same. He leaves the house in a dark suit, toting a scuffed leather duffle and a rattling bag of clubs. When I kiss his cheek good-bye, my lips come away lightly greased with his aftershave.

When he is home for long stretches, it is an event, and the house buzzes nervously with his presence. At dinner, my six brothers and my sister and I sit around our large kitchen table passing plates of Shake and Bake pork chops and spilling milk. My dad shouts out "reports!" Which means we are to share any interesting events from the day. My mind always goes blank at this, and I feel as if I never have anything worthy of reporting.

After dinner he helps my mother bathe us. We call bath time "souping," because my Dad adores the nonsense words and nicknames that come out of our mouths as toddlers.

When a little one refers to bathing as "souping," he makes it part of our permanent lexicon. The same for "goosing," which means teeth brushing. He is forever asking us if we have "goosed our teeth."

The best part of souping is when Dad comes in, a giant bath towel in hand, and slings one of us inside the towel, then carries us on his back like a hobo sack. He hauls us to our respective rooms and deposits us on the bed with a bounce. We call this "geeking", and we all beg to be "geeked." When it is my turn, he drapes the rough towel beneath my underarms, then throws me over his broad shoulder. I travel down the long hallway bumping damply against his broad back, slick as a seal tucked into a papoose.

After our baths, he comes into my brothers' bedroom and stretches his long frame out on the carpet. We excitedly cluster around him in footed pajamas, shouting for a story. He tells us made up, ghostly tales that are always designed to teach us a moral. There is the smug "Simon Cigarette," who chokes to death on cigarette smoke. Or "Reginald Reservoir", the bratty boy who ignores his parents' pleas to never go near the deep reservoir, and of course meets a terrible fate. And then, the favorite, "Little Sally Go to Church," about a little girl who doesn't want to go to church, and instead wants to stay at home and eat junk food. Sally's lack of piety is always punished by a visit from the Sunday Monster—a giant beast who jumps out of nowhere with a horrific roar. My dad roars in his deep baritone, and we all scream with terrified delight, beg him to stop, then quickly beg him to do it again.

When I am small, he calls me "Josey Lamb," because when I'm around the rowdy swirl of my siblings I appear shy and quiet: gentle as a lamb. He continues to call me this even after I am fully-grown, and have become loud and opinionated, and decidedly less lamb-like. But he does so ironically, with a glint in his eye.

He tears up easily. Which seems funny for a man with such a large, commanding presence. But certain songs and movies leave his eyes pink-rimmed and glistening, and when I am growing up, I actually see him cry more times than my mother. On my wedding day I select "Someone to Watch Over Me" for our father-daughter dance, because it's a song I know he likes. But he refuses to slow dance, and just keeps shimmying around the floor, making goofy faces. A few bars in I ask him what exactly is wrong and he says, "Josey! This music is too sad!" Flustered, I go up to the DJ and request that she instead put on Supertramp's "The Logical Song," another favorite of my father's. He is thrilled, and in my wedding photos we are both spinning and laughing, giving high, jubilant kicks.

When I am in my twenties, I chafe at his politics, and what I consider his small-town small-mindedness. He is a staunch Republican and extremely conservative, whereas I consider myself very liberal. We have heated arguments at the dinner table that leave us both red-faced and shouting, and make my mother flutter nervously around the kitchen. My other siblings never engage with my father in this way, and they find it hilarious the way we shout at each other about Clinton, and both Bushes.

Sometimes, to gall me, he tapes conservative news articles to the lamp hanging above my place at the table. I come down for breakfast and find Karl Rove's smiling face torn from the paper, dangling in front of me from a piece of Scotch Tape. I sleepily look to my father, and he smirks at me over his bowl of Raisin Bran.

With the Alzheimer's, the days of political debates and discussions come to an end. There is no longer any real, lasting talk of the present. My father's mind becomes stuck in the past, like a wheel that can't quite push over, and he speaks to me about long ago events, as though he is plucking dusty photos from an album in his mind, and holding them up to me, saying, "Here. See?"

He tells me several times about how his father once gifted him a new baseball glove. He says he loved the glove so much he oiled it every single night.

Or he recounts the time he found a dead body on the golf course. He describes how he and a friend were playing on New Year's Day, and were the only ones stomping their spiked shoes though the frosted grass, knocking around balls. When my dad rounded a sand trap, he spied the man—gray-faced and frozen, a bottle of whiskey at his side.

He talks about his time in the Korean War. About how frightened he was lying on the floor of a cargo plane, traveling further from his Indiana home than he'd ever been in his life. One night in camp he polished his army boots white, as a sort of goofy mini-protest, and he was soundly punished for it by the colonel.

And he talks about Lynne Anne, the oldest child and sister I never knew. She died when she was five of meningitis. He fingers the tattered prayer card that he still, thirty-eight years later, carries in his wallet, and he tells me in a low, quiet voice how delicate and beautiful her hands were. He talks about her golden hair.

I listen to him talk, and feel overwhelmed by how much there is about him that I don't know, or can't really fathom. His life stretches behind him full of heartbreaks and triumphs and mysteries that I will never really grasp. And through him I learn that understanding people, and loving them, sometimes have very little to do with one another.

Now, when I am home visiting, he really likes to give me things. He has always delighted in giving gifts, but now, each time I am there, he gives me funny things—strange bits of odds and ends. He has taken to handing me the smallest of trinkets, the kinds of treasures a small child might hide away in a cigar box.

"Here Josey," he says. "You can take that home with you."

And he hands me an old golf tee, or a tiny, pretty seedpod that he's spied on the ground. A St. Anthony prayer card. Old fishing hooks. A tattered *National Geographic*. I save all of it. I bring it back to New York with me, and I tuck it into jewelry boxes and special drawers, hidden away like clues.

Losing someone in this way—this subtle losing, piece by piece—is its own unique kind of sadness. It's a mean, cruel kind of grief that I feel could drag me under if I let it. And so I try to focus on the fact that my father is still here with me. He still makes me laugh. He still loves to tell stories. And he still loves to tease. Even now, he still calls me up and holds the phone up to the radio, so that when I get back to my apartment I have a voicemail that is nothing but Rush Limbaugh ranting away. I play back these voicemails, and I picture my Dad huddling in the background, struggling to hold in his laughter. Just like the trinkets, I save these garbled voicemails. And I try to focus on the father I still have...on the bright shades of him that remain.

I can't ever bring myself to think of when that final dot of color finally fades from sight, completely out of my view. Until then, I steadily train my eye on what I can still see. I take in every last glimpse.

Phillip Lopate came to my university as a Writing Fellow for the Lila Wallace–Reader's Digest Foundation years ago. He was always up for an adventure, a party, or a game of tennis, but I think it's safe to say, he missed New York when he lived in Indiana. He and I taught writing together, shopped for antiques (I bought an old "pie chest," which I still cherish) and we watched a lot of movies. Through the years, we've stayed in touch. When Phillip's daughter Lily was a newborn, my husband and I were in New York, and called to see if he could have lunch. Over the phone, Phillip sounded tired and anxious. He could not get away because Lily was in ICU, unable to digest food properly. Later, Phillip wrote about this difficult time. Lily not only survived, she thrived, and her essay here is a testimony to the close relationship she continues to share with her father. Cheryl Cipriani took these beautiful pictures of Lily alone and with her father, Phillip in Brooklyn.

A Relationship of Words

I OFTEN WONDER, when I meet my first real boy-friend or even years into the future when I am engaged to my fiancé, how I will describe my father? How will I give my guy a glimpse into our unique relationship? How will I narrate the experience of being a daughter and the influence of having a writer as a father? What liberties will I take in framing him as a character? Who's to know the parts I'll omit, the parts I'll embellish?

Would I dare to embark on an accurate portrayal? And how will I know if this guy sitting across from me in a café asking about my life story is worth it? Say, we date for two months and as we drive on the turnpike to meet my parents he probes for some family background. He wants stories that showcase how I am a product of my parents. Will I make the effort to reveal the complex narrative of my father and me? Sup-posing he's a swell guy with a decent IQ, a man I imagine myself to be semi-in-love with, I decide to take the gamble. Tell the guy, as my father would say, "the truth." But where to begin?

My Father: A Man About Town

As a kid, I saw my father through a series of movements and actions. Like a tall man with an egg-shaped head he engaged with inanimate ob-jects and moved through space. He rushed to catch the ringing phone. As wardrobe assistant in the daily production of dressing up our Abyssinian cat, he leapt up in haste to answer the doorbell, still with remnants of the feather boa and drop earrings I had festooned on him. He sets time aside to peruse the mail and drink coffee from a glass mug like a Russian.

Ate everything-bagels with cream cheese and lox, leaving residues of onion and sesame seeds on the wooden cutting board. He was also a man of habit, announcing "I'm going into town," where he'd screen films at the Angelika or Film Forum or meet a friend for lunch.

For years I thought his two linked occupations in life were to "buy dolls and write books" because on each of his writing trips to lecture or teach a workshop, he'd bring me back a doll. A porcelain fur-capped one from Russia, a brown paper bag one from Bulgaria, a ramshackle babushka from Poland, a slim kimono-dressed one from Japan, a flamenco dancer with fishnets from Spain and my favorite, a teal-and-gold skirted French Barbie from Paris with pearl studs and a sassy attitude.

The Eccentric

Like anyone, my father has his share of idiosyncrasies. I feel it is my duty as his daughter to dispel the illusion that he is an ideal specimen. I take pleasure in revealing to the world his abnormalities and flaws. For instance, he has a disproportionate fear about butter spoiling, which I can only assume derived from childhood. With swift urgency he is keen to put the butter back in the fridge so that it does not grow rancid. He has a dislike for the rain and like a little boy will exclaim: "I don't like to get wet." In Paris, Karlovy Vary, or Brooklyn, he takes cover under a storefront until the downpour clears.

My father chews his tongue. In a state of deep rumination or pensiveness, careful not to bite too hard he gnaws on the pink saliva muscle at an even rhythm. As he bats spells of boredom at a holiday dinner or is forced to endure a lecture on his lack of domestic skills, he will recline in his chair so it teeters on the back two legs. Suspended at an angle, he will pull at a section of his cheek near his jowls. Akin to pinching yourself to stay awake, he hopes stretched skin will reinvigorate new brain cells, summon up strands of tolerance. It's in these moments when the outside viewer believes him to be "in deep thought," that the scrutinizing daughter knows he is in fact acting out an odd compulsion.

Every morning my father does the *Times* crossword puzzle. It is something of supreme importance to grapple with 5-down and 7-across.

This morning ritual is always done with a black ballpoint pen because pencil is too light for his eyesight, he claims.

The Conversationalist

My father is above all else easy to talk to. He engages you in stimulating conversation, proposes theories and facets about your character, and responds to your stories with playful interest. Mid-sentence he furrows his brows and a cunning smile forms at his lips. My father, always a proponent of words, aims for a higher level of conversing and believes any interaction can be wielded towards maximum amusement. He is also a grammarian, drilling me about the uses of "I and me," "neither and nor" and subject-clause agreements. When I increased the number of "likes" I used in my sentence, he mocked: "do you mean you like arrived at the house, or you arrived at the house?" He was unimpressed when I said the reason for using "likes" was generational. "Be above your generation," he bellowed.

My father is a non-conformist. He never wears jeans because he feels they are ubiquitous. He questions flaunting "Abercrombie & Fitch" across your breast pockets.

Fashion-forward or not, these are his principles. Unlike him, I conform, to an extent. I strive for normalcy. He, on the other hand, argues: "Normal is not an option. Is that your highest goal, to strive for normalcy? Attempt to be like everyone else?" I worry if I break from the fabric of my generation, I will be too isolated, a castaway on my own island. My dad is far too stubborn to have this social anxiety. At seventy, he is a man who's made peace with himself. "What's so bad about being alone? Great things can come from learning to live with yourself?" I don't know if I'm ready for that lesson in isolation. My self is not cultivated enough yet to find contentment in my own company.

Words have created such an open dialogue between us, he never has to work too hard to pry information out of me. He confesses when his teaching has lost its energy or he struggles to sustain a friendship and I complain about my fellow twenty-something's and their skittish hesitance to speak a sentence that conveys what they're thinking. I expect words to carry meaning, be surprising, embody a certain lyricism, but not everyone is a skilled conversationalist.

Words can solve the mystery many parents seem to face, wondering what their kids are thinking. Even in a wordless exchange, my father can prove psychic. Am I just that predictable? It's unnerving how quickly and accurately my father can read me. His analysis of my contradictions, ambivalences and yearnings are spot on. He knows I frequently check my internal temperature and hover around a base-line of dissatisfaction.

I worry my face gives all my secrets away. He sees right through my feigned attempts at easy-going flexibility, especially when I meet new people. While I waited for my college roommate to be assigned, I speculated and he succinctly summarized my wariness as: "I'm prepared to dislike you. Expose yourself." Even if he can guess, he still continues to ask what I'm thinking. It's a question that's been bred into me, I ask it to myself. I answer honestly, knowing he will appreciate the unsettled ambiguity of my thoughts.

On Boys and Self-Presentation

"Have you re-invented yourself yet? Cobbled together an alternate identity?" my father asks, lifting his head from the pages of a 900+ John Ruskin biography. I spent time before college "renovating" my profile on Facebook to make myself appear more fun-loving and appealing. My father called it the "ad agency of Lily." Pictures of cats were swapped for group shots of quasi-friends with their arms strewn across each other. I scoured my I-Photo for images that would convey "a night to remember." My father laughed at the photo-editor in me, so invested in the act of construction.

Similarly, on the topic of boys, he loves to mock my misjudgments, the cycle of unrequited crushes I had growing up, all of whom I felt I could improve: airheads with potential. "Well, Lily, you really know how to pick 'em," he'd say. But he confessed to similar infatuations. In his late thirties, a therapist told him: "Phillip, if only you could apply a tiny percentage of your intelligence to your choice of women..." So now he advises: "Have you ever considered a more bookish boy, maybe one who shares your sense of humor?" It's such a radical proposal. I may need another round of airheads before I take it to heart.

Our Competitive Streak

My father and I are slightly competitive. Since he is my encyclopedia, my literary database, I weigh my intelligence against his. We joke that years into the future, we will challenge each other to a trivia game spanning a multitude of subjects—from books to geography, philosophy and religion—with a pad of paper to keep score. I used to try and forecast the age when my brain would ripen just enough so that I could trump him in certain areas. Today at nineteen, I know more about Descartes and Gilbert Ryle, TI-84 calculators and computer systems, he says, than he ever did. I'm filled with a giddy sense of victory when I know an answer to a crossword clue about movies, music or pop culture. Before I acquired my competitive drive, he practiced the art of losing. When I was a little kid, he'd always cheat so I'd win our games of War and Go Fish. He'd pretend to cry, wrinkling his cheeks and balling up his fists—praising my cunning card strategy. I'd wipe his fake tears and he'd tickle me with his long fingers.

My dad can transition from confidant to Father Knows Best adviser to professor. He is a mentor but not a friend. He is the coach for whom I aim to excel. I play devil's advocate, asking him: "If I wasn't your daughter would you still think I'm smart?" It's a trick question with an impossible answer. His response never lets me see how much his unconditional love may cloud an otherwise critical, unbiased judgment: "You are smart. And you are my daughter." There is a code of respect, which prevents us from speaking as equals. And yet, we raise awareness about each other's flaws, shortcomings or deficiencies. Sometimes we "agree to disagree," arguing like great debaters—poking holes in each other's logic and demanding substantiating evidence.

My Father: The Editor

My father is my primary reader. More so than my friends, I trust his opinion. I also trust myself enough to disagree with his opinion. He is also a valued editor: he has a way with sentences. Now, I e-mail him attachments, but when I was younger we'd edit side-by-side. The sessions had a teacher-student dynamic, resembling a scene out of *My Fair Lady*, where Professor Higgins drills Eliza Doolittle: "Lily, the only time you use an apostrophe in its is if you are connecting two words: it is. As in, it's a shame you won't be coming to the party." I continued to think the word "its" looked naked without its accessorized apostrophe. He'd critique my shifts of tenses and misuse of words, and push me to pin down what I was really saying: "What is this garble, Lily?" Hours spent, combing each sentence of my seventh grade NYC Housing project paper, marked my enrollment in the school of Lopate. The kitchen table was our shared workspace, and until I went off to college, every good paper was written in his company.

"I don't just want to write for the sake of expression, Dad. I want to write well, really try to master the craft"

"I'll teach you everything I know." His eyes gave a generous smile. "If you're willing to roll up your sleeves and put in the time you can make words do anything you want them to." So I started to put in the time, spending double the hours of my peers on papers and essays, I endeavored to shape my prose into something elegant.

For every teacher I ever experienced, my father offered a counter-angle of exposure. If his teaching contradicted theirs, I felt forced to meld the two practices together. When a teacher in high school imposed a requirement of one-sentence long theses, my father disagreed: "That is absolute poppycock that you have to limit your thesis to only a few words." Teachers wanted you to insert road maps and previews, and my dad felt those aids condescended to your reader, and robbed the piece of surprise. If I followed his advice, it was an affront to my teacher—an ethical dilemma. Who was I to believe, him or them? I usually chose him but it made for a longer process. Now the test was separating my dad's rules from my own. The takeaway from him was less syntax than psychology: to write honestly, lean towards discomfort, attempt to delve into unresolved tangled territory and engage with humor.

My Father's Credo: To Read and Never Stop

If nothing else, my father wants me to read. Arguing for the accumulation of material, he preaches: "Lily, you must develop your reading muscles, strengthen your vocabulary, harness your absorption skills—

endurance, patience!" When my eyes wander towards easier contemporary reads like vampire trilogies and beach romances, he is the cheerleader telling me to finish an Austen, Bronte or Dostoyevsky. For my dad, reading is a religion. It is a tactic of survival. In his view, we are all lonely and great works of literature, written by writers who wrestled with that same hollowness, are a consolation.

Sometimes my father's views are too heavy. I don't always opt for the existential or intellectual. I can enjoy the trivial. A disillusioning book can make it harder to engage lightheartedly with the everyday. So if I endeavor to know suffering I can't as easily divorce from it. Learning is a lifestyle—you read for life, there's no one moment when you transition from ignorance to self-assured knowledge. Higher-quality literature stimulates greater self-awareness and forces you to confront your own limits. My dad takes comfort in knowing his limits. He is a realist. I am only a partial realist. The other part of me is an idealist, taking stock in the possibility of becoming a limitless person.

My Father and His Fame

"They loved me! Lily—I'm a star" he reports, elated with the success of his recent reading. When my father returns home from a successful writing gig he is on cloud nine. Always happy to be back in New York, he feels invigorated. When he walks through the door, he encounters real life: I type on my laptop, the cats lounge by the window, my mom folds laundry. It is a lackluster environment full of family members who are not hankering for his autograph. He announces himself at the doorway, beaming in his blue Armani suit, "The crowd just ate me up!"

"That's great, honey," my mom will reply in an automated voice as she flips through her calendar and offers him a beer.

"You are a star, Dad—shine bright shine far," I offer sarcastically.

"Phillip, I want to hear more about your trip but could you take out the garbage?" my mom says, walking upstairs. Out of the corner of my eye I can see my dad's face deflate. These moments are an endorsement of his career, why should he have to surrender them so quickly to the daily round? He pets his favorite tabby cat on the head, propped on the edge of our kitchen counter and nudges her delicate ear with his thumb:

"I know you don't believe it but it's true. Your dad's a celebrity of sorts."

"Hey, you're no Justin Timberlake or Rachel McAdams," I say.

"True," he would agree, "I'm just myself. Outside of the tiny world of essay-writers, no big deal." His honest, self-deprecating humility always had a way of turning my wave of gloating into guilt.

The idea that my father was a well-known public figure in the essay world seemed at first too bizarre to take seriously. Seeing his books on the shelves of my professors was always strange and made me oddly skeptical. Can't they find another father-figure of the essay? Why are they photocopying excerpts from his book? Once a gorgeously handsome Spaniard came to interview my dad about a project and I asked after he left, "What did he want with you?" Marveling at the Spaniard's chiseled chin, I found it hard to grasp why he would seek the company of someone like my dad over myself.

Until a rave review was printed in the *Times* for his new book, I denied my dad's fame. He didn't deserve the continual applause, in my mind, because the public perception of "Phillip Lopate" was not all he was. I like to think his identity is not solely wrapped up in his profession, but rather is a découpage of influences, from dead authors to baseball to city sidewalks to whitefish, latkes and kasha varnishkes and, above all, us.

I've grown to adopt a facetiously cool air: "Who? Oh that guy, Phillip Lopate? Yeah I know him." In a creative nonfiction class, his book was assigned as our primary textbook. In the campus bookstore my friend grabbed two copies off the shelf. "Here, don't you need one?"

"You know, strangely enough I have one already." The girl nodded as if impressed with my organizational skills. I felt no need to brag about the autographed copy that rested on my windowsill or the intimacy with which I knew the author.

When his essay "Against Joie de Vivre" was recently ranked in the top ten essays since 1950, alongside James Baldwin and Susan Sontag, I couldn't help but kid him: "Congrats, Dad. I guess I should read that essay, must be some good shit." In reality, I am his biggest secret fan.

On Similarities and Differences

I have my father's hands, with long lean fingers that can stretch a full scale on the piano. I have my father's toes, especially a stubby middle one that is crooked and hides shyly behind the others. Up until the age of fourteen, I chewed my tongue just like him. We both grasp the air with our hands when we're struggling to express an idea. Our lips move subtly when we type. We both print and kill trees regularly. We justify a fear of the unknown by thinking about the story it will give us to tell. Neither of us pushes moral platitudes. But unlike him, I am more likely to screen a call, less abrupt in ending a phone conversation, less concise in e-mails and less decisive when shopping. I do not promise I will never tell white lies. We are both liberal Democrats, New Yorkers and contemplatives. I am my father, and I am also a very distinct being—myself.

On Small Victories and Daily Disappointments

My dad understands far better than anyone my degrees of discontentment. I often find myself identifying with the Chekhov character Masha in *The Seagull* who announces solemnly: "I am in mourning for my life!" He listens when I tell him how I feel some essential element is lacking in my life, and he reminds me of Peggy Lee singing "Is that all there is?" as an account of unmet expectations.

I tell him I have a bittersweet mentality I can't seem to shake. He gives me a look with kind eyes and tells me: "That's the trouble with sensitive people. You're always thinking, you're exposed to life. But even in moments of loneliness or emptiness, a sensitive person's best bet is to find amusement in the crevices of discontentment." I ask him if he thinks happiness is a construct. He pulls at a roll of his chin and offers: "I don't believe it's a complete fabrication. You just need to redefine your expectations to better fit a more reasonable ideal."

"But I don't want to lower my standards. I want to experience the extraordinary." "Yes but happiness isn't like a burst of confetti, it's more like a groundhog—you have to entertain the possibility of seeing its shadow, come across it and let it influence you." I pause, digesting his words. I feel enlightened and displeased with his offering. "Lily, I have to finish some e-mails. I don't know what to tell you, find hope in the idea of rare moments of happiness…"

When I stress about the future and speculate what society will make of me—he tells me there is no sense in prediction. "Why do you always ask me these impossible questions? What makes you think I have the answers? You want a guarantee or a movie trailer for what your life will be like? Enjoy the suspense of not-knowing."

Still I push further: "People say just be yourself, but that's not very specific." "People? Who are these people, Lily? People employ a vague vocabulary when they themselves don't know. Why be so gullible?" I laugh at the thought of fully-grown adults bumbling around with neon question marks suspended above their heads.

"Maybe I should go out and find myself?" I ask wistfully.

"I hate that expression 'find yourself.' What a cop-out! Your identity isn't a misplaced glove that you dropped on the subway platform. You never lost yourself to begin with, so what do you expect to find?"

When I was in graduate school, Jayne Anne Phillips' Black Tickets was required reading for any writer. Jayne Anne's pioneer-like father is bigger-than-life, taming and tending the land in this essay, "Burning the Trees." There is a dreamy, haunting quality to this piece and the two sweaty brothers, the pick-up trucks, all that manual labor, the bows and arrows, and those fruit trees laced with spider webs. Jayne Anne tried to find an earlier photograph of her father, when she says he was "movie star handsome." Here she is pictured in the 1980s with her still handsome father, Russell Randolph Phillips. Appropriately, they stand outside, with all that land stretched out behind them.

JAYNE ANNE PHILLIPS

Burning the Trees

THE YEAR HIS first child was born, my father
purchased the land for our house from the
farmer across the road. Behind our acre of yard lay fields planted with
hay and corn, the creek, the wooded hills. My father designed the house,
oversaw its construction, erected the wire fence that marked the bound-
ary of his property. Always he tended that demarcation, pulling up milkweed and thistles, clipping back the grass. He put in a hedge out front
along the two-lane road, then the hemlocks, and a lone dogwood. When
I was still young, he worked at the ground, fertilizing and seeding. Still,
the row of fruit trees he'd planted far down in the back yard got caterpil-
lars every spring. By July their limbs were spun with a gossamer webbing
that looked fibrous and illumined from a distance. Summers then were
a long, spooled dream, a collective dream shared with my two brothers.
I stood between them, the middle child, but they are far from me now.
Literally, they moved deeper into the South as I moved north; they followed my father into a personal mythology in which men were defined
by their work, strengthened and honed by physical labor, their independence expressed in deliberate, nearly telegraphed oral communication.
The power of women was expressed in talk and domicile; the power of
men in quiet and mobility, in the painstaking care of implements, ma-
chinery, vehicles: modes of work and transport. My parents' embattled
marriage ended as we children left home. Separately, they lived a mile
from each other, saw their children into their early thirties, and died
three years apart. They burned out like stars and left an emptiness. The
past is their story and their legacy. My brothers' lives embodied the story

as I stood apart to articulate it, ensuring my separation from the circle that enclosed us all.

Forty years ago, inside that story, my father called me "Princess"; he called the boys by their names. My brothers, the older and the younger, were already engaged in work and speed. I stood still, looking and listening. The older one, christened with our father's heavy name, dressed like a man even as a child; he wore crisply ironed open-necked shirts and creased pants for dress, belted dungarees and tucked, striped T-shirts for play. He was tall and skinny for his age no matter his age, with narrow, almond-shaped eyes; he wore his hair slicked up high like James Dean and rocketed over the hilly lawn on his chrome two-wheeler, peeling rubber in the driveway and leaping off the bike to turn and catch the handlebars with one deft hand.

My younger brother was muscular and compact, a blond blue-eyed towhead whose skin tanned deeply golden as his close-cropped hair bleached white; he drank so much water in the heat that his stomach distended and sloshed when he moved. He seldom wore a shirt at all and his knees were permanently grass-stained. He was the one I played with. Our older brother rode the fence line like a sentry, but my younger brother rode his own transport, a yellow tractor-like vehicle that trundled low to the ground, too heavy for any of us to lift. He called it The Tractor and hauled things in a metal cart that attached to a knob under the seat. He rode the long driveway to the road and back, pedaled the sidewalk that ran the length of our ranch-style brick house, drove onto the concrete back porch where I abided with my dolls. He "came home from work" and rode away again.

School ended on the first of May and started again in September. My mother, a teacher, was home, working in her flower beds, raising kids, cooking, cleaning, living. She gave me books: weekly trips to the library and packages arriving from mail-order book clubs. I gave you all books, she would say later, but the boys looked once and threw them down. There were no camps or lessons for us in summer, no agenda but summer itself, and nowhere to go but across the glistening two-lane to the three or four houses that shared our rural road, or into the yard, the fields, the woods. The boys played Little League baseball some years; there was no soccer, no sports for girls at all, no academic enrichment, no jockeying to get into this or that exclusive school. There were no exclusive schools. There were no drama camps or dance classes. Even 4-H and Scout camps started later, when kids were teenagers. Young kids just played; on our road, siblings played together.

On hot afternoons, mothers took their children to Hinkle's Pool, a business owned by the mayor. Fifty cents to swim for the day; kids over ten could be dropped off alone. The pool provided all the "structured" programming that existed, other than scattered weeks of Bible school at this or that church. The mayor's kids, five teenagers, were the lifeguards, and they were strict. Running, shoving, splashing got you benched; the older kids lazed against each other on their towels and swam during breaks, when the younger kids were ordered out and lined up at the snack bar to buy popsicles.

We were eight, nine and eleven; our mother took us to the pool a few times, but my older brother was already embarrassed by her presence and she didn't relish spending hours in "that cacophony." Finally, she announced we kids wouldn't go to the pool until we could all go without her. Instead she sprayed us with the garden hose while we ran into each other, shrieking, or she took us to swimming holes and ponds she knew about —cool, shaded water out long dirt roads, across train trestles we walked in single file. She'd been a child in the town herself, an adolescent, a teenager. We knew we'd live in the town always, as she had, graduate from the high school she and my father had attended almost a generation apart. The town library was "down by the college" where she'd taken her teaching degree; maybe we saw ourselves on the same leafy Methodist campus, sitting at desks in imposing brick buildings with matching columns. Our father had attended classes there for a semester—this we couldn't fathom. When a great-aunt told us he'd won fifty silver dollars in his high school elocution contest, we couldn't believe it. Elocution? What was elocution? Oh yes, he started college, she told us, but he quit and went to work. Nineteen twenty-nine, she said, as though numbers settled the question, and went on with her sewing.

We went on playing. The days were long, hot, luxurious, timeless. My father was gone, buying and caretaking and selling huge machines that shook the ground when they moved: front loaders with immense shovels and back loaders with blades as broad as cars; cement mixers with chutes and rumbling drums. He built roads and sidewalks for the town. My brothers built roads in the "garden," which was not a garden at all but the lower right corner of the yard, gone to weeds. It seemed a huge expanse, tangled and wild. Squash and pumpkin vines snaked through knee-high dandelion and sticky milkweed. Up by the house, my mother grew flowers, lettuce and herbs in carefully manicured beds, but left us to dig in the garden. My brothers moved all their biggest dump trucks out there for the summer, a fleet of vehicles that seemed toy replicas of what our father drove and sold. The trucks were mostly bright yellow; their beds raised and lowered with cranks and their visages looked snaggled and real. Their tires were big-treaded, double wide, scaled to size; they bumped over the lumpy ground loaded down with dirt and stones and clods of earth. We dug the roads out with shovels. This was interesting, but what my brothers loved was moving dirt from one end of their network to the other. They filled the trucks and drove the trucks along, moving beside them on all fours, making engine sounds, stalling sounds, rev-'em-up sounds; the roads grew more and more intricate, curving and looping back, crossing one another. My brothers excavated, filled in, sheared curves, widened turnarounds. Insects buzzed and the days grew hotter and hotter. The garden steamed. I went up to the house to read. My brothers kept at it, oblivious, sweat bees the size of houseflies raising itchy welts along their legs and arms, between their fingers, in the creases of their necks. Boys! my mother would call down to them. Lunch! They ignored her.

Finally, they dug up a nest that swarmed and hovered like a cloud over the garden for days. The cloud contained itself, whining almost inaudibly, but the garden was impenetrable. A hard rain would have settled the bees, but it seldom rained. It might not rain for weeks. Perhaps this was why my father dragged the archery set out of the shed; real bows and arrows someone at work had given him, and a plastic-covered bull's-eye target four feet across, backed with bound straw. He propped the target against the shed and showed my brothers how to use their wrist guards. He drew a line across the grass with lime. Stand here, everyone behind the line. Retrieve your own arrows before the next person shoots. Hit the target or the shed, nothing else.

My arrows faltered, studding the ground or falling at my feet. My brothers sneered, perfecting their stances. The older one stood sideways, squinting one narrow eye as he took aim, his arm tensed and still before the release. The younger one faced the target squarely, considering before he raised the bow into position. He was short and his arrows hit low, but he was stronger, like a little bull. He kept shooting and shooting.

Over the next day or two, the insect cloud in the garden floated higher and lower, emitting a thin tone almost like music. The boys rode their vehicles up the hill and down the hill, walked through the field to fish in the creek, took up their positions before the target by afternoon. After supper, they shot some more. My father was working in the yard near the shed. Maybe I called out to my younger brother; maybe he turned because he heard a dog bark, or saw a shape move to his left. The arrow flew wide. Suddenly my father leaned down and grabbed his ankle. The arrow protruded from his boot; I saw him pull it out and drop to his haunches. I called my mother. She drove the car off the driveway into the yard and backed it down the hill to my father. He was so careful of the grass; it was odd to see the blue and white Mercury sitting in the yard down by the shed and the garden. We watched our father wrap his shirt around the wound as the shirt darkened with blood. He lifted himself into the passenger seat and they were gone.

My father knew how to grow a lawn. The grass was so thick and green that it sprang back almost immediately after they'd driven off, as though the car had never sat there at all. We kids were home alone for the first time we could remember. The concrete porch ran the length of the house, a foot off the ground; we sat and waited. I shot my father, my younger brother said, I should run away. The older one nodded. I would if I were you, he said, before they get back. You could take the apples and the bread, I said. But we didn't move. The sounds in the fields and the trees seemed suddenly distinct, separate from one another, each a realized presence. Locusts singing, the whir of grasshoppers flying and dropping, a whine of bees and gnats, the singed, needling sound of mosquitoes close to our ears. Lightning bugs appeared above the fields, blinking their tiny lights.

The fruit trees at the edge of the yard, four, five, six of them, held their branches aloft. They were young trees, about the height of a grown man. By now, deep into summer, the limbs were edged with transparence, overrun with nesting insects. In the dusk light, they seemed to glow. We walked into the yard to look at them. Up close, the webs squirmed with ravenous, pale gold worms, each lifting its blind head.

My brother stayed home. My father returned from the hospital with a bandage on his ankle. Bled like hell, he told us, but I reckon I'll live. Then he reached out to run his palm softly over my brother's buzz-cut head. The curve of his big hand enclosed the shape of my brother's skull lightly, carefully, as though his fingers framed a world. He leaned in close. For a man 8 years old, he said softly, as though in confidence, you've got yourself a powerful arm. My brother smiled, tremulous, then squared his shoulders and nodded his version of our father's familiar, affirmative gesture. No words, just the colluding, acknowledging glance, masculine and graceful, the raised brow, the rueful exhalation midway between a sigh and a laugh.

Our mother insisted we put the bows and arrows away until next year, or the next. But our father refused to get rid of his boots just because one of them was neatly punctured. He wore the boots a few evenings later when he burned the trees. He performed this ceremony every summer. A bucket of water, a torch made of kerosene-soaked rags. He lit the torch to burn the insects out; the webs would burn quickly, before the limbs caught. We kids sat on the edge of the concrete porch and watched the trees light up a patchy code in the gravid dusk. We were told to keep our distance in case the trees themselves burned, but they only flared at intervals along their branches, as though playing host to roiling stars. My father moved around them, managing each nested blaze. He wore his khaki work clothes and lit the torch with his cigarette lighter; he smoked a cigarette as he did the work. We saw his long form lift the brilliant torch, and in his other hand the cigarette glittered, small and secret, as the worms fell from the trees in ashes. In a dream I have now, the brother closest to me whispers, "Look, their wings are flying up," as singed leaves laced with sparks scatter drowsily higher. We watch my father bend down to douse the torch but it's too late, the coronas of the little trees begin to curl and flare. They bloom with leaping fire and furl like novas, feeding themselves. We don't call for our mother. She has died before him and left us to show him the way. He walks toward us up the hill of the rolling lawn, his pale clothes glowing against the flames, and we all realize he has been gone for many years.

My father and I first read Bobbie Ann Mason's short stories in The New Yorker back in the 1980s. I recall talking about the marvelous ending of her novel In Country with him, and how funny and sad it was when the grandmother takes the geranium out of the car at the Vietnam war memorial to honor her son, all while hoping her slip doesn't show. Bobbie Ann's biography on Elvis is one of the best on the subject, perhaps because of her own personal, southern connection. Bobbie Ann wrote this essay, "My Fathers," in conjunction with her book The Girl in The Blue Beret, which was inspired by her father-in-law's experience in WWII. Pictured here are the men she calls her fathers—her father (above), Wilburn A. Mason, and her father-in-law (below), Barney Rawlings, in an airplane cockpit simulator. Pam Spaulding took the picture of Bobbie Ann.

My Fathers

MY FATHER DIED twenty years ago, but for fourteen years after his death, I had the privilege of having an alternate father—my father-in-law, Barney Rawlings. They were much alike, although they seemed startlingly different. Daddy was a Kentucky farmer who knew all about the earth and cows and dogs, and Barney was a pilot for TWA, living on Long Island, where he could drive easily to Kennedy Airport. He didn't care for cars. The majesty of the airplane was what counted, and he lived to soar through the sky.

For Daddy, a car was his Pegasus. He was fond of small foreign cars, and he bought the first Volkswagen in the county. Over the years he was proud to own a Fiat, a Renault, and a Suzuki, in succession. As a farmer, he was tied to the daily chores, but every day he would jump in his car and hit the road. It was this routine, his "little run" to town, that liberated him, much as Barney's flights to Cairo or London did him. World travel meant for Barney the flight itself, not the Pyramids along the Nile. Daddy felt that freedom in his car. He always knew where home was, and the delight of going away made home worth returning to.

Both fathers served in the Second World War, and the John Wayne stereotype of that generation applied. Barney was affable enough, addressing his passengers from the cockpit, but he was coolly reserved, kept his own counsel, and wasn't close to his family. Daddy was withdrawn, secretive. He found it painfully embarrassing to talk to anyone outside his own community of country people. When I came home from college, I was full of ideas that I could not share. I didn't know how to explain, say, James Joyce's stream-of-consciousness or nature imagery in *Lolita*. The gulf between us widened. But in the last years of his life we found common ground as I gravitated back to the land. We shared a love for animals. He liked to have a small dog with him in his car, so they could go motivating down the road listening to Chuck Berry. I got my musical tastes from him.

Daddy died too soon, and we never got to the point where we could have the ultimate conversation we both wanted. Barney, my father-in-law, was forced to retire from flying at age sixty. This was potentially devastating for him, but he surprised us. Folding his wings wasn't the end of the world. He began writing novels. And he wrote a memoir about what he did in World War Two—his B-17 was shot down and he was guided to safety by the French Resistance. It was a weighty story to have carried around all those years.

He also found time to explore the genealogy of his Missouri family. He had grown up very poor, and flying had been his way out of the hard past. But in his last years he seemed content, despite being grounded. He was settled. He had several cats. And he developed a tenderness I hadn't seen before. In an old newspaper, he found an obituary for a heretofore unknown relative, a child who had died very young. He wept for this little being no one had thought about for perhaps a century.

I remember my last words to him. "I will always honor you," I said.

But it was two years before I was motivated to write a novel inspired by his war experiences. I wondered what would happen if a retired pilot went back to France to look up his wartime helpers.

Father's Day reminds us to honor all our fathers. How I wish I had asked Daddy more about his Navy days in the War. I honor both of my fathers, and I hope they knew how much I loved them.

"Working for a Living" is the cornerstone of this anthology. I sat by my father's bed and read this essay to him in the last month of his life. My father and I loved all of Alice Munro's unadorned, nuanced prose, but this piece was significant and resonated with us because of the author's relationship with her father, their work together, the time they spent together, the way they talked with each other, the details about their farm, and that harsh Canadian cold. I wrote to Alice Munro, requesting this essay, which first appeared in Grand Street. Miraculously, her publisher forwarded the letter to her home in Clinton, Ontario, and Alice phoned me, granting me permission. After a lifetime of writing, Alice thought she'd put down her pen and try living life as an "ordinary person" instead of a constant observer. That lasted about three months. On December 10, 2013, at age 82, she was awarded the Nobel Prize in Literature.

ALICE MUNRO

Working for a Living

IN THE FIRST years of this century there was a notable difference between people who lived on farms and people who lived in country towns and villages. Outsiders—city people—did not understand these differences but the town people and farmers were very sure of them. In general, people in the towns saw people who lived on farms as more apt to be slow-witted, tongue-tied, uncivilized, than themselves, and somewhat more docile in spite of their strength. Farmers saw people who lived in towns as having an easy life and being unlikely to survive in situations calling for fortitude, self-reli-ance, lifelong hard work. They believed this in spite of the fact that the hours men worked at factories or stores or at any job in town, were long, and the wages low, and that many houses in town had no running water or flush toilets or electricity. And to a certain extent they were right, for the people in town had Sundays and Wednesday or Saturday afternoons off, and the farmers didn't. The townspeople too were not altogether mis-taken, for the country people when they came into town to church were often very stiff and shy and the women were never so pushy and confi-dent as town women in the stores, and the country children who came in to go to High School or Continuation School, though they might get good marks and go on to successful careers later, were hardly ever elected President of the Literary Society, or Class Representative, or given the award as Most Outstanding Student. Even money did not make much dif-ference; farmers maintained a certain proud and wary reserve that might be seen as diffidence, in the presence of citizens they could buy and sell.

When my father had gone as far as he could go at the country school

267

he wrote a set of exams called, collectively, the Entrance. He was only twelve years old. The Entrance meant, literally, the Entrance to High School, and it also meant the Entrance to the World, in professions such as medicine or law or engineering, which country boys passed into at that time more easily than later. This was just before the First World War, a time of prosperity in Huron County and expansion in the country, a country not yet fifty years old.

He passed the Entrance and went to the Continuation School in Blyth. Continuation Schools were small high schools, without the final Fifth Form, now Grade Thirteen; you would have to go to a larger town for that.

At Continuation School my father learned a poem:

Liza Grayman Ollie Minus.
We must make Eliza Blind.
Andy Parting, Lee Behinus.
Foo Prince on the Sansa Time.

He used to recite this to us, for a joke, but the fact was, he did not learn it as a joke. This was the poem he heard and accepted. About the same time he went into the stationery store and asked for Sign's Snow Paper. Another joke he told us. But of course he had not done it as a joke. That was what he heard the teacher say.

Sign's Snow paper. Science Note-paper.

He did not hope for such reasonable clarification, would not dream of asking for it. Later he was surprised to see the poem on the blackboard.

Lives of Great Men all remind 'us,
We must make our lives sublime.
And departing, leave behind us
Footprints on the Sands of Time.

He had been willing to give the people at the school, and in the little town, the right to have a strange language, or logic; he did not ask that they make sense of his terms. He had a streak of pride posing as humility, making him scared and touchy, ready to bow out, never ask questions. I know it all very well. He made a mystery there, a hostile structure of rules and secrets, far beyond anything that really existed. He felt a danger too, of competition, or ridicule. The family wisdom came to him then. Stay out of it. He said later that he was too young, he would have stayed in school, made something out of himself, if only he had been a couple of years older. He said he made the wrong choice. But at that time, he said, he did what many boys wanted to do. He began to spend more and more days in the bush. He kept going to school, but not very seriously, so that his parents realized there was not much point in sending him somewhere to take Fifth Form, and write the Senior Matriculation exams, and no hope of university, or the professions. His mother would have liked that for him but it did not matter so much as it would to city people, that he turned his back on education and advancement. They had the farm; he was the only son, the only child.

There was no more wild country in Huron County then than there is now. Perhaps there was less. The farms had been cleared in the period between 1830 and 1860, when the Huron Tract was being opened up, and they were cleared thoroughly. Many creeks had been dredged and the progressive thing to do was to straighten them out, make them run through the flat fields like tame canals. The early farmers had no liking for trees around the buildings or along the fences. They must have loved the look of open land. And the masculine approach to the land was managerial, firm, suspicious. Only women were allowed to care about the landscape, not to think always of its subjugation, productivity. My grandmother was famous for having saved a line of silver maples along the lane. These trees grew beside a crop field, and they were getting big and old, their roots interfered with plowing and they shaded too much of the crop. My grandfather and my father went out in the morning (for my father had to take the manly view of things like this) and made ready to cut the first tree down. But my grandmother saw them from the kitchen window and she flew out in her apron and upbraided and defied them, so that they finally had to take up the axes and the cross-cut saw and go away, and the trees stayed and spoiled the crop at the edge of the field until the terrible winter of 1935 finished them off.

But at the back of the farms the pioneers had to leave a woodlot, a bush, where they cut trees in the early winter before the deep snow. Both for their own use and to sell. Wood of course was the first crop of the country. Rock elm went for ship timbers and white pine for ships' masts, until there were no rock elm or white pine left. Poplar and ash and maple and birch and beech and cedar and hemlock remain; fine trees.

Through the woodlot or bush at the back of my grandfather's farm ran the Blyth Creek, dredged a long time ago, when the farm was first cleared, so that the earth dredged up now made a high, humpy bank with little cedars growing on it. This was where my father started trapping. He eased himself out of school into the life of trapping. He could follow the Blyth Creek for many miles in either direction, to its rising in Grey Township or to the place where it flowed into the Maitland River. In some places, most particularly in the village of Blyth, the creek became public for a mile or so, but for most of its length it ran through the backs of farms, with the bush on either side, so that it was possible to follow it without being aware of the farms, the cleared land, the straight roads and fences; it was possible to imagine you were in the forest, in the Huron Tract just a hundred years ago.

My father had read a lot of books by this time, both at home, and from the Blyth Library, and the Sunday-school library, and he would certainly have read Fenimore Cooper. So he would have absorbed the myths and half-myths about the wilderness that most country boys did not know. Most boys whose imaginations absorbed these myths would live in cities. If they were rich enough they would travel north every summer, with their families, they would learn camping, canoeing; later they would go on hunting trips; if their families were truly rich they would go up the rivers of the far north with Indian guides. That is, if they liked that sort of thing. Many did. There was a whole experience of wilderness which belonged to rich people from cities, a belief in the wisdom of Indian guides, in the value of solitude and danger, in the pure manly joys of hunting and fishing (not then corrupted by ease and convenience), which must have kept some men sane. People who had this experience of the wilderness would travel right through our part of the country without noticing there was any wilderness there. But farm boys from Huron County, not knowing anything about this huge mythical wilderness, the deep romantic north (as it was known for instance by Ernest Hemingway, the doctor's son from Oak Park), nevertheless were drawn, some of them were, for a time, to the strips of bush along the creeks and rivers, where they fished and hunted and built rafts and set traps. They made their forays into this world but soon gave it up, to enter on the real, heavy work of their lives, as farmers. And one of the differences between farmers then and now was that in those days they did not expect either holidays or recreation to be part of that life.

My father being a Huron County farm boy with the extra, Fenimore-Cooper perception, a cultivated hunger, did not turn aside from these boyish interests at the age of eighteen, nineteen, twenty. Instead of giving up the bush he took to it more steadily and seriously. He began to be talked about and thought about more as a trapper than as a young farmer, and as an odd and lonely character, though not somebody that anyone feared or disliked. He was edging away from the life of a farmer, just as he had edged away earlier from the idea of getting an education and becoming a professional man. He was edging towards a life he probably could not clearly visualize, since he would know what he didn't want so much better than what he wanted. The life in the bush, on the edge of the farms, away from the towns: how could it be managed? Even here, some men managed it. Even in this tamed country there were a few hermits, bush-dwellers, men who inherited farms and didn't keep them up, or were just squatters, who fished and trapped and hunted and led nomadic lives; not like the farmers who whenever they left their own areas, traveled by buggy or, more often now, by car, on definite errands to certain destinations.

He was making money now from his trapline. So at home they could not complain. He paid board and he still helped his father when it was necessary. He and his father never talked. They would work all morning cutting wood in the bush and never talk, except when they had to, about the work. His father was not interested in the bush except as a woodlot. It was to him like a field of oats, the crop being wood instead of oats.

My father's mother walked back to the bush on Sunday afternoons. She was a tall woman with a dignified figure, but she still had a tomboy's stride. She would bunch up her skirts and climb a fence; put one foot up on the wire and her hand on the fence post and swing her leg over.

He showed her the snares where he was catching fish. She was uneasy, because he was catching fish on Sunday. She was very strict, and this strictness had a peculiar history. She had been brought up in the Anglican church, called locally the Church-of-England; Anglicanism was thought of, in that country, as being next door to Popery but also next door to free-thinking. It was hardly religion at all, just a business of bows and responses, short sermons, easy interpretations, pomp and frivolity. Her father had been a drinker, a story teller, a convivial Irishman. When she married she wrapped herself up in her husband's Presbyterianism, getting fiercer in it than most; she took on the propriety competition like the housework competition, with her whole heart. But not for love; not for love. For pride's sake she did it, so that nobody could say she regretted anything, or wanted what she couldn't have.

But she stayed friends with her son in spite of the Sunday fish, which she wouldn't cook. She would look at the skins he had got and hear how much he got for them and she washed his smelly clothes. The smell was from the fish-bait he carried as much as from the animal pelts. She could be pleased and exasperated with him as if he were a much younger son; maybe he seemed younger to her, with his traps, his treks along the creek. He never went after girls; he grew less and less sociable. His mother did not mind. Perhaps it helped her bear the disappointment that he had not gone on to school to be a lawyer or a minister; she could imagine that he would still do that, the plans were not forgotten but merely postponed. At least he was not just turning into a farmer, a copy of his father.

As for the father he passed no opinion, did not say whether he approved or disapproved. He lived a life of discipline, silence, privacy. His grandfather had come from Scotland, from the Vale of Ettrick, on a sailing-ship in 1818, to Quebec and then to the Scotch Block settlement in Halton County. The family grew there and some of the sons came on to Morris Township, in Huron County, in the early eighteen-fifties. They were Grits, Presbyterians; they were against the English Church and the Family Compact, Bishop Strachan, and saloons; they were for universal suffrage (but not for women), free schools, responsible government, the Lord's Day Alliance. Of the young men who came to Huron County, one was killed by a falling tree while they were clearing the bush. The other two lived to be old, and founded families, and kept the family notions going.

Family photographs commemorated them: the seated father, bearded, vigorous, with his luxuriant beard and commanding eyes; the drained, flattened, bleak and staring wife, the scared or faintly sullen or ominously dutiful children. For that was what it came to; the powerful fathers died out and the children had learned obedience so thoroughly there was not much room for anything else. They knew how to work till they dropped, but not how to take any risk or manage any change, they lived by hard routines, and by refusals. Not every one of them, of course. Some went away, to California, Iowa, dropped from sight. My grandfather diverged a little, learned to play the violin, married the tall, temperamental Irish girl with eyes of two colors. That done, he reverted; for the rest of his life he was diligent, orderly, silent. They prospered. But prosperity was not pursued in the same way as it is now. I remember my grandmother saying, "When we needed something done, if it was time to paint the house or when your father went into Blyth to school and needed new clothes and so on, I would say to your grandfather, 'Well, we better raise another calf and get some extra.'" Now, if they could get "some extra" when they needed it, by raising a calf or whatever, it seems they could have got that extra all along. That is, in their ordinary life they were not always making as much money as they could have, not stretching themselves to the limit. They did not see life in those terms. Nor did they see it in terms of saving at least part of their energies for good times, as some of their Irish neighbors did. How, then? I believe they saw it mostly as ritual, seasonal and inflexible, work done for its own sake. This must have been what my father's father had in mind for him without mentioning it. And what my grandmother in spite of her own submission to it was not altogether sorry to see him avoid.

The animals he trapped were muskrats, marten, mink, now and then a bobcat, otter, foxes. Most foxes in the wild are red. Occasionally a black fox will occur there as a spontaneous mutation. But he had never caught one. Some of these animals had been caught elsewhere, and bred selectively to increase the show of white hairs along the back and tail. They were called silver foxes, and in the early nineteen-twenties silver-fox farming was just starting in Canada. In 1925 my father bought a pair, a silver-fox male and female, and put them in pens on his father's farm. At first they must have seemed just another kind of animal being raised on the farm, rather more bizarre than the chickens or the pigs, something interesting to show the visitors. When my father bought them and built pens for them, it might even have been taken as a sign that he meant to stay, to be a slightly different farmer than most, but a farmer. The first litter was born, he built more pens. He took a snapshot of his mother holding three little pups. He sent off his first pelts. The prices were very good. The trapline was becoming less important than these animals he raised in captivity.

A young woman came to visit them, a cousin on the Irish side, from Eastern Ontario. She was a school-teacher, lively, importunate, good-looking, and a couple of years older than he. She was interested in the foxes, and not, as his mother thought, pretending to be interested in order to entice him. (Between his mother and the visitor there was an almost instant antipathy, though they were cousins.) The visitor came from a much poorer home, a poorer farm, than this. She had become a school-teacher by her own desperate efforts, and the only reason she had stopped there was that school-teaching was the best thing for women that she had run across so far. She was a popular hardworking teacher but some gifts she knew she had were not being used. These gifts had something to do with taking chances, making money. They were as out-of-place in my father's house as they had been in her own though they were the very gifts (less often mentioned than the hard work, the perseverance) that had built the country. She looked at the foxes and did not see their connection with the wilderness; she saw a new industry, the possibility of riches. She had a little money saved, to help buy a place where all this could get started. She became my mother.

∼

When I think of my parents in the time before they became my parents, after they had made their decision but before their marriage had made it (in those days) irrevocable, they seem not only touching and helpless, marvelously deceived, but more attractive than at any later

heading for Highway 21, up and down the long hills, after sunset and before dark, I thought and talked about what long car trips used to be like, how arduous and uncertain. I described to my husband—whose family, more realistic than ours, considered themselves in those days too poor to own a car—how the car's noises and movements, the jolting and rattling, the straining of the engine, the painful groans of the gears, made the crowning of hills, the covering of miles, an effort everybody in the car had to share. Would a tire go flat, would the radiator boil over, would there be a breakdown? The use of the word breakdown, made the car seem frail and skittish, with a mysterious almost human vulnerability.

"Of course people who could afford newer cars, or could afford to keep them in good repair, wouldn't have trips like that," I said. "Their trips would be more or less like today's, only slower and shorter."

Then it came to me why we could have been driving to Muskoka through this part of Bruce County. I was not mistaken after all. My father didn't dare take the car through any town or on a main highway; there were too many things wrong with it. It shouldn't have been on the road at all. It was a time when my father could not afford repairs. He did what he could to fix it himself, to keep it running. Sometimes a neighbor helped him. I remember my father saying of this neighbor, "The man's a mechanical genius," which makes me suspect he was no mechanical genius himself. Now I knew why I could remember such a feeling of risk and trepidation, as we found our way over the unpaved sometimes ungraveled roads, with their one-lane bridges. As things came back to me I could even remember my father saying that he had had only enough money for gas to get up to the hotel where my mother was, and that if she didn't have any money he didn't know what they were going to do. He didn't say this to me at the time, of course; he bought me the ice-cream cone, he told me to push on the dashboard when we were going up the hills, he seemed to be enjoying himself. He said it, long after my mother was dead, remembering some times they had gone through together.

The furs my mother was selling to American tourists at the summer hotel (we always spoke of American tourists, perhaps acknowledging that they were the only kind who were of any use to us) were tanned and dressed. Some skins were cut and sewn together in short capes, others were left whole and made into what was called scarfs. A fox scarf was one fox skin, a mink scarf was two or three skins. The head of the animal was left on and was given golden-brown glass eyes and artificial jaws. Fasteners were sewn on the paws. Many of the capes had a fox head sewn on, in the middle of the back.

Thirty years later these furs would have found their way into secondhand clothing stores, and would be bought and worn as a joke. Of all the mouldering and grotesque fashions of the past this wearing of animal skins would seem the most amusing and barbaric.

My mother sold the fox scarfs for twenty-five, thirty-five, forty, fifty dollars, depending on the quality of the fur and the number of white guard hairs, the "silver," it had. Capes cost fifty, seventy-five, perhaps a hundred dollars. My father had started raising mink as well during the late nineteen-thirties, but my mother was selling only fox, because the number of mink we raised was small and we had been able to dispose of them without taking a loss.

At home the colony of fox pens stretched from behind the barn to the high bank overlooking the river flats. The first pens were built of fine wire on a framework of cedar poles, and they had earth floors. Those built later had raised wire floors. All the pens were set side by side like the houses of a town inside the high guard fence, and because the building had been done at different times and not all planned out in the beginning, there were all the differences there are in a real town: some wide streets and some narrow streets, some spacious earth-floored old original pens and some smaller wire-floored modern pens which seemed less well-proportioned even if more sanitary. There were even two long apartment buildings, called The Sheds. The New Sheds had a covered walk between two facing rows of pens with slanting wooden roofs and high wire floors. The Old Sheds had just one short row of pens and was rather primitively patched together. The New Sheds was a hellishly noisy place full of adolescent foxes, due to be pelted, most of them, before they were a year old. The Old Sheds was indeed a slum and contained disappointing breeders who would not be kept another year, a fox who had been crippled, even for a time one red fox. I don't know where it came from; it may have been a sport in a litter.

When the hay was cut in our field some of it was spread on top of the pens, to keep the foxes from suffering too much from the heat, and to protect their fur which otherwise would turn quite brown. They looked very scruffy and shabby anyway, in the summertime, with their old fur falling out and the new fur just starting. By November they were resplendent, the tips of their tails snowy and the back fur deep and black with its silver overlay. Then they were ready to be killed, skinned, the skins stretched, cleaned, sent off to be tanned, sent to the auctions.

Up to this time everything was in my father's control, barring illness and the chanciness of breeding. Everything was of his making: the pens, the wooden kennels inside them where the foxes could hide and have their young, the metal water-dishes that tipped from the outside and were filled twice a day with fresh water, the tank that brought the water from the pump, the feed-trough in the barn where the feed of meal and water and ground horse-meat was mixed, the killing-box with the chloroform. Then when the pelts were shipped away nothing was in his control any more. There was nothing to do but wait; wait to see what the pelts were sold for, far away in Montreal, in great auction sheds he had never seen. The whole year's income, the money to pay the feed bill, the money to pay the bank, as well as the loan he had from his mother, had to come from that. Some years the price was fairly good, some years not too bad, some years terrible. The truth was, though nobody could see it at the time, that he had got into the business just a little too late, and without enough capital to get going in a big way in the first years when the profits were good. Before he was fairly started the Depression came. The effect of the Depression on the market was erratic, not steadily bad as you might think, but in ten years there was more bad than good. Things did not pick up much with the beginning of the war; in fact the price in 1940 was one of the worst ever. During the Depression bad prices were not so hard to take; my father could look around and see that he was still doing better than many other people; but now, with the war jobs opening up, and the country getting prosperous again, it was very hard to have worked as he had, and come up with next to nothing.

He said to my mother that he was thinking of pelting and selling all his stock, by Christmas of 1940. He meant to get out, change his life. He said he could go into the army as a tradesman, he was not too old for that. He could be a carpenter, a butcher.

My mother had another idea. She suggested that they keep out all the best skins, not send them to the auctions, send them instead to be dressed—that is, made into scarfs and capes, provided with eyes and claws—and then take them out and sell them. People were getting some money now. And though we were off the beaten track for tourists, she knew about them. She knew they were up in the hotels and shops of Muskoka, they had come from Detroit and Chicago with money to spend on bone china, Shetland sweaters, Hudson Bay blankets. Why not silver foxes?

There are two kinds of people, when it comes to changes, invasions, upheavals. If a highway is built through their front yard, some people will be affronted, mourning the loss of privacy, peony bushes, lilacs, and a dimension of themselves; the other sort will see their opportunity and build a hot-dog stand, get a fast-food franchise, open a motel. My mother was the second sort of person. The very idea of the tourists and their money flocking to the northern woods filled her with vitality.

In the summer, then, the summer of 1941, she went off to Muskoka with a trunk-load of furs. My grandmother, my father's mother, arrived, magnificent with foreboding, to take over the house. She hated what my mother was doing. She said that when she thought of American tourists all she could hope was that none of them ever came near her. She was a widow, now. She disliked my mother and my mother's outlook on life so much that when we were all together she withdrew into a harsh and timid version of herself, but after my mother had been gone a day she thawed out, forgave my father his marriage and the predictable failure of his exotic venture, and he forgave her the humiliation of owing her money. She baked bread and pies and cooked good meals (though we had no money we were not in want; the garden flourished, the hens laid, we had a Jersey cow) and cleaned and mended and served up more comfort than we were used to. In the evenings she carried pails of water to the flower border and to the tomato plants. Then we all sat out in the yard

and looked at the view. Our nine-acre farm, no farm at all by my grandmother's standards, had an unusual location. To the east was the town,
the church towers and the Town Hall visible when the leaves were off
the trees, and on the mile or so of road between us and the main street
there was a gradual thickening of houses, a turning of dirt paths into
sidewalks, an appearance of street lights that got closer together, so that
you could say that we were at the town's very furthest edge, though half
a mile beyond its municipal boundaries. But to the west there was only
one farmhouse to be seen, and that one far away, at the top of a hill almost at the midpoint of the western horizon. We called it Roly Grain's
house, but who Roly Grain might be, or what road led to his house, I
never asked or imagined it; it was too far away. The rest of the view was
a wide field and river-flats sloping down to the great hidden curve of the
river, a pattern of overlapping bare and wooded hills beyond. It was very
seldom that you got a stretch of country as empty as this, in our thickly
populated county. It is changed now, there is more to watch; the field in
our side of the river has become the town's airport.

When we sat there after supper my father smoked and he and my
grandmother talked about the old days on the farm, their old neighbors,
and my younger brother and sister pestered my grandmother to let them
look in her window. My grandmother's eyes were hazel, but in one of
them she had a large spot, taking up about a third of the iris, and this
spot was blue. People said her eyes were of different colors; that was not
quite true. We called the blue spot her window. She would pretend to
be cross at being asked to show it, she would duck her head and beat off
whoever was trying to see, or she would screw her eyes shut, opening the
good one a crack to see if she was still being watched. She was always
caught out in the end and had to sit with her eyes wide open, being
looked into. The blue was pale and clear without a speck of other colors
in it, pure as the sky.

~

My father and I turned into the hotel driveway in the early evening.
We drove between the stone gateposts and there ahead of us was the hotel, a long stone building with gables and a white verandah and hanging

pots overflowing with flowers. The semi-circular drive took us closer to the verandah sooner than we might have expected. People were sitting there, in lawn chairs and rocking chairs, with nothing to do but look at us.

We parked in a gravel lot beside the tennis court, and got out of the car. The hot wind we made as we drove along had been blowing in my hair all day. My father saw that something was wrong about me, and asked me if I had a comb. I found one down behind the car seat. It was dirty and some teeth were missing. I tried, he tried, but we had to give it up. Then he combed his own hair, frowning and bending to look in the car mirror. We walked across the lot and my father wondered out loud whether we should try the back or the front door. He seemed to think I might know what to do, something he had never thought in any circumstances before. I said we should try the front, because I wanted to get another look at the lily-pond in the semi-circle of lawn bounded by the drive. There was an elegant toy bridge over it, and an artificial frog as big as a cat at the edge.

"Run the gauntlet," said my father softly, and we went up the steps and entered the lobby. It was very dark after outside, the walls and ceiling paneled in dark oiled wood. To one side was the dining-room, with the glass doors shut and the little tables covered with white cloth, each one with a bouquet of flowers; to the other side a long room with a huge stone fireplace at the end, and the skin of a bear on the wall.

"Look," said my father. "She's here somewhere."

In a corner of the lobby was a waist-high display case, and behind the glass was a fox cape, beautifully spread out on white velvet. A sign on top of the case said Silver Fox, the Canadian Luxury, in a flowing script done with white and silvery paint on a black board.

"Here somewhere," my father said. We looked into the room with the fireplace. A woman with bobbed hair, writing at a desk, looked up and said, "I think if you ring the bell somebody'll come." It sounded strange to me to hear someone you had never seen before speak to you so easily. I even wondered if she were somebody my father knew.

We backed out and crossed to the glass doors of the dining-room. Across an acre of white tables with their silver and turned-down glasses and bunches of flowers and napkins peaked like wigwams we saw two

figures, ladies, seated at a table by the kitchen door, finishing a late supper or drinking evening tea. My father turned the door knob, and they
looked up. One of them rose and came towards us between the tables.
The moment in which I did not realize this was my mother was not long,
but there was a moment. I saw not my mother but a woman in an unfamiliar dress, a cream-colored dress with a pattern of little red flowers,
a pleated skirt, a belt. The material was crisp and glowing. The woman
who wore it looked brisk and elegant, her dark hair parted in the middle
and pinned up in a neat coronet of braids. Even when I knew it was my
mother and when she put her arms around me and kissed me, spilling
an unaccustomed fragrance, I felt that she was still a stranger. She had
crossed effortlessly into the world of the hotel; indeed it seemed as if she
had always been living there. I felt at first amazed and betrayed, then
excited and hopeful, my thoughts running on to what could be got out of
this situation for my own enjoyment.

The woman my mother had been sitting with was the dining-room
hostess, a fair-haired, tanned, tired-looking woman with heavy red lipstick, who was subsequently revealed to have many troubles, which she
had talked about to my mother. She was immediately friendly—there
seemed to be no normal warming-up period with people in the hotel—and she brought fresh tea from the kitchen and a very large dish
of ice cream for me, because I had told my mother at once about the
ice-splinters. Then she went away and left us alone, the three of us, in
that splendid dining-room. My parents talked but I took in little of the
conversation. I interrupted from time to time. They never told me not to
and answered me with such cheerfulness and patience it seemed as if
they, too, had taken on the hotel demeanor. My mother said we would
sleep tonight in her cabin. She had a little cabin, with a fireplace. She said
we would eat breakfast here in the morning. They said that when I was
finished I could go and look at the frog.

That must have been a happy conversation; relieved, on my father's
side; triumphant, on my mother's. She had done well, she had sold just
about everything she had brought, the venture was a success. Vindica-
tion; salvation. He must have been thinking of what had to be done at
once: what bills to pay; whether to get the car fixed here or chance it

again on the back roads and take it to the garage in Wingham, to somebody he trusted. She would have been thinking of the future, of how they could try this in other hotels, of how many furs they should get made up, of whether it could be made into a year-round business. She couldn't have foreseen how soon the Americans were going to get into the war, and how that was going to keep them at home.

She would talk afterwards about how she had done it, how she had known the right way to go about it, never pushing anybody, showing the furs with as much pleasure to those who could not think of buying as to those who could. A sale would seem to be the last thing in her head. She had to show the people who ran the hotel that she would not cheapen the impression they gave; she had to show them that she was a lady, no huckster; she had to become a friend. That was no chore for her. She had the true instinct for mixing friendship and business considerations, that all good salespeople have. She never had to calculate her advantage, and coldly act upon it; she did everything naturally and felt a true warmth where her interest lay. She who had such difficulty with my father's relatives, who was thought stuck-up by our neighbors and somewhat pushy by the women at the church, had found a world of strangers in which she was at once at home.

When she was recalling this summer, and insisting on the gifts she had, later on, I was not sympathetic. I soon came to dislike the whole idea of putting your whole self to use in that way, making yourself dependent on the response of others, employing flattery however subtle, and all for money. I thought it shameful, and took it for granted that my father, and of course my grandmother, must feel the same way. I would not grant that those gifts were anything to be proud of. When I thought of the fox-farm, after it was gone, I thought of the layout of the pens, all the details of that small self-contained kingdom. I thought of the foxes themselves, and their angry golden eyes, their beautiful tails, and as I grew away from childhood and country ways I began for the first time to question their captivity, their killing, their conversion into money, which had all seemed so natural and necessary. (I never got so far as regretting this for the mink, who seemed to me mean-spirited, rat-like, deserving of no better fate.) I mentioned this lightly to my father, in later years, and he said there was some religion in India that believed all the animals went to Heaven too; think, he said, if that were true, he would be met when he got there by packs of snarling foxes and the other fur-bearers he had trapped, and the mink, and a herd of thundering horses he had killed and butchered for their food.

Then he said, not so lightly, "You get into things, you know, you don't realize what you're getting into."

It was in those later years that he would speak of my mother's salesmanship, and how she had saved the day, and say that he didn't know what he was going to do, that time, if she hadn't had the money when he got there.

"But she had it," he said, and the tone in which he said this made me wonder about the reservations I had assumed he shared. Such shame now seemed shameful. It would be a relief to me to think he hadn't shared it.

~

On a spring evening in 1949, the last spring, in fact the last whole season, I lived at home, I was riding my old bicycle, now mostly ridden by my brother and sister, to the Foundry, to give a message to my father.

My father had started working at the Foundry in 1947. It had become apparent the year before that not just our fox-farm but a whole industry was going downhill very fast. Perhaps the mink could have tided us over, if we had not owed so much money already, to the feed company, to my grandmother, to the bank. Mink prices were not good enough to save us. My father had made the mistake many fox-farmers had made, in the mid-forties. He had invested borrowed money in new breeders, a Norwegian platinum and a Pearl Platinum male. It was thought that as the popularity of silver foxes declined, that of the new platinums must spectacularly rise. But the fashion went against long-haired furs altogether.

When my father went looking for a job he had to find a night job, because he had to work all day at going out of business. He had to pelt all the stock and sell the skins for what he could get, he had to tear down the pens. I suppose he did not have to tear them down, immediately, but he must have wanted them gone. He got a job as a night-watchman at the Foundry, covering the hours from five in the afternoon till ten in the evening. There was not much money in that but he was able to do piece-work as well.

He did something called "shaking down floors." He did some of this after his regular shift was over, and often he would not get home until after midnight or one o'clock.

The message I was taking to my father was important in the family's life, but not serious. It was simply that he must not forget to call in at my grandmother's house on his way home from work, no matter how late it was. My grandmother lived in Wingham now. She tried to be useful to us, she baked pies and bran muffins and mended my father's and brother's socks. My father was supposed to call and pick up these things but often he forgot. She would sit up knitting, dozing under the light, listening to the radio, until the Canadian stations signed off at midnight and she would find herself picking up distant news reports, American jazz. She would wait and wait and my father wouldn't come. She had done this last night and tonight she had phoned at suppertime and said, "Was it tonight or last night your father was planning to come?"

"I don't know," I said. I always felt that something had been done wrong, or not done at all, when I heard my grandmother's voice. I felt that our whole family had failed her. She lived alone, and was still strong enough to carry armchairs up and down stairs, but she needed more company, more gratitude, than she ever got.

"I sat up last night but he didn't come."

"He must be coming tonight, then."

I told my mother what the call was about and she said, "You better ride up and remind your father, or there'll be trouble."

When she had to deal with a problem like this—my grandmother's touchiness—my mother seemed to brighten up, as if for a moment she had got back her competence. She had Parkinson's disease. It had been overtaking her for years, with evasive symptoms, but had only lately been diagnosed, so that she knew it was hopeless. Its progress took up more and more of her attention. She could no longer walk or eat or talk normally, she was stiffening out of control. She had a long time yet to live. When she said something that showed a concern for other people or even for the housekeeping, and did not follow it with a reference to herself (and that will upset me) I felt my heart soften towards her. Most of the time I was angry at her, for her abdication, and self-absorption. We argued. She would rally her strength and struggle with me, long after she had given up on ordinary work and appearances.

I had never been to the Foundry before in the two years my father had worked there and I did not know where to find him. Girls of my age did not hang around men's workplaces. I did not have much interest either. I mourned the passing of the fox-farm, as my mother did. I had never thought it might make us rich but I saw now that it had made us unique and independent. It made me unhappy to think of my father working in the Foundry. I felt as if he had suffered a great defeat. But when my mother said, "He's too fine for that," meaning more or less the same thing, I had to argue, and say she was a snob. The first Christmas he worked there we received a large basket of fruit, nuts and candy. All the employees got one. My mother could not bear to think of herself being on the receiving and not the distributing end of things, when it came to Christmas baskets, and so we were not allowed to break the cellophane to eat one grape. We had to put the basket in the car and drive down the road to a family she had picked out as suitable recipients. By the next Christmas her authority had waned. I broke the cellophane and said it was despicable to be proud, and she wept. I pretended to be greedy. The chocolate was brittle and going grey.

I could not see any light in the Foundry buildings. The windows were painted blue on the inside. I almost missed the office, which was an old house at the end of the long main building. I saw a light there, behind the Venetian blinds, and I thought someone must be working late. I thought that I could knock and ask where to find my father. But when I looked through the little window in the door I saw that it was my father in there. He was alone, and he was scrubbing the floor.

I had not known that scrubbing the floor every night was one of the watchman's duties. This does not mean that my father had made a point of keeping quiet about it. I was surprised, for I had never seen him do any of this sort at home. Now that my mother was sick, I did it, or let it go. He would never have had time. Besides, there was men's work and women's work. I believed that, and so did everybody else I knew.

My father's scrubbing apparatus was unlike anything anybody had at home. He had two buckets on a stand, on rollers, with attachments on the side to hold various mops and brushes. His scrubbing was vigorous and efficient; it had no resigned, feminine, ritualistic rhythm. He seemed to be in good humor.

He had to come and let me in.

"I thought it was Tom," he said. Tom was the Foundry manager; all the men called him by his first name. "Well. You come up to see if I'm doing this right?"

I gave him the message, and sat on the desk. He said he was almost finished here, and if I waited he could show me around the Foundry.

I said I would wait.

When I say that he was in a good humor here, I don't mean that his humor at home was bad, or sullen or irritable. But it did seem as if his cheerfulness was submerged, there, as if he thought it inappropriate. Here there was a weight off him.

When he had finished the floor to his satisfaction he stuck the mop on the side, and rolled the apparatus down a slanting passage-way into the main building. He opened a door that said Caretaker.

"My domain."

He dumped the buckets into an iron tub and the water gurgled away. There on a shelf among piles of unfamiliar things—tools, rubber hose, fuses, window-panes—was his familiar lunch-bucket, that I packed every afternoon when I got home from school. I filled the thermos with strong black tea and put in buttered bran muffins and pie if we had any, and three thick sandwiches of fried meat and ketchup. The meat was cottage roll ends, the cheapest thing you could buy and the only meat I remember us having in the house over a period of two or three years.

He led the way into the main building. The lights burning there were like street-lights; that is, they cast a little light at the intersections of the passage-ways, but didn't light up the whole inside of the Foundry, which was so large and high that I had the sense of being in a forest with thick dark trees, or in a town with tall, even buildings. My father switched some more lights on and things shrank a bit, as they do; you could now see the brick walls blackened on the inside and the windows not only painted over but covered with black wire mesh. What lined the passage-ways were bins, stacked one on top of the other, and elaborate, uniform metal trays. My father pointed out a pile of castings disfigured by lumps like warts or barnacles.

"Those aren't cleaned yet. They put them in a contraption that's called a wheelabrator and it blasts shot at them, takes all that off."

"That looks like coal dust but you know what it is? It's green sand."

"Green sand?"

"They use it for moulding. It's sand with a bonding agent, like clay, or sometimes they use linseed oil. Are you anyway interested in this?"

I said yes, for pride's sake, and courtesy's. And it was true, I was interested, but my interest kept flying away from the particular explana-tions my father began to provide me with, to general effects: the gloom, the fine dust in the air; the idea of there being places like this all over the country, with their windows painted over. You went past and never thought about what was going on inside; the never-ending time-consum-ing life-consuming process.

"Like a tomb in here," my father said, as if he had an inkling of my thoughts. But he meant something different.

"Compared to the daytime. The racket then, you wouldn't believe it. They try to get them to wear ear-plugs but nobody does."

"Why not?"

"I don't know. Too independent. They won't wear the fire-aprons either. See. Here's the cupola."

This was a huge black pipe which did have a cupola on top. He showed me where they made the fire, in the bottom of it, how the metal passed through, in a pipe, the pipe going through a hole in the brick which was now plugged up with clay. He showed me the ladles they used to carry the molten metal and pour it into the molds. He showed me chunks of metal that were like grotesque stubby limbs. He said those were the cores, the solid shapes of the hollows in the castings. He told me all these things with satisfaction in his voice, as if he were revealing something that gave him a serious pleasure.

We turned a corner and came on two men working, wearing work pants and undershirts.

"Here's a couple of good hard-working fellows," my father said. "You know Ferg? You know George?" I did know them, or at least I knew who they were. George had a daytime job on the bread-wagon but worked in the Foundry to make extra money, because he had ten children. Ferg had been in the war and had not settled down to any regular daytime job.

"She's seeing how the other half lives," said my father, making a delicate apology. Then, still aware of them, he said in a louder and more humorous voice than necessary, "Now. You see what shaking down floors is all about."

Working carefully together, using long, strong hooks, the two men lifted a heavy casting out of a box of sand.

"That's still plenty hot, it was cast today," he said. "Now they have to work the sand around and get it ready for the next casting." We moved away.

"Those two fellas always work together. I work on my own."

"It must be heavy."

"It is. It's considered the heaviest job there is here. It took me a while to get used to. But it doesn't bother me now."

Much that I saw was soon to disappear: the cupola, the hand-lifted ladles, the killing dust. Many particular skills and dangers were soon to go. With them went the everyday risks, the foolhardy pride, the random ingenuity and improvisation. The processes I saw were probably closer to those of the Middle Ages than to those of today. And with this I imagine the special character of men who work in the Foundry will have changed; they will not be so different now from men who work in the factories or at other jobs. In those days the men who worked in the Foundry were rougher and stronger and had more pride, were perhaps more given to self-dramatization, than the men whose jobs were not so dirty and hazardous. They were too proud, in fact, to demand any protection, or to use what was provided. They belonged to no union. Instead, they stole from the Foundry.

"Tell you a story about George," my father said, as we walked along. (He was "doing a round" now, and had to punch clocks in different parts of the building.) "You know he likes to take a bit of stuff home with him. The odd bit of whatever he thinks might come in useful. So the other night he had a sack of such stuff, and he went out before dark and hid it under the office steps, where it'd be handy for him to pick up when he got off. And he didn't know, but Tom was in the office watching him. Tom didn't have the car parked outside, he'd walked. His wife had the car. Well, he saw what George was up to and after George went back inside, Tom came out and got the sack and he put it in the back of George's car. Then he waited, he stayed late and turned out the lights and finally George came back and was poking around under the steps, and Tom just watched him, never let on, then just as George was going off he came out and said, would you mind giving me a ride home? George nearly dropped. They got in the car and still Tom never gave a sign, but George had seen the sack right off and apparently he could hardly get the key in the ignition. He's still in the dark."

It would be easy to make too much of this story and to suppose that between the management and the workmen there was an easy familiarity, tolerance, even an appreciation of each other's dilemmas. There was that, but it didn't mean there wasn't also plenty of rancor, and stunning callousness, and deceit. But jokes were always important. The men who worked in the evenings, shaking floors, would gather in my father's room, the Caretaker's room, to smoke and talk—on Friday nights they might have a bottle—and there they talked about jokes that had been played years ago and recently. They talked about jokes played by and on people long dead. They talked seriously, too. They discussed whether there were such things as ghosts, and who had seen them. And money, they talked about that; who had it, in town, what they did with it, where they kept it. My father told me about these talks years later. One night somebody asked: what is the best time in a man's life?

When is a person the happiest?

Some said, when you're a kid and can fool around all the time and go down to the river and go skating in the winter and that's all you think about, having a good time.

When you're a young fellow and haven't got any responsibilities.

When you're first married if you're fond of your wife, and a little later too when the children are small and running around and don't show any bad characteristics yet.

Then my father said, "I don't know, I think maybe right now." They asked him why.

He said because you weren't old yet, but you could see ahead to when you would be, and you could see that a lot of the things you used to think you wanted out of life you would never get. It was hard to see how you could be happy in such a situation, but sometimes he thought you were.

When he told this to me, he said, "Those were some of the best fellows I ever met. We used to have some great old discussions. It was a whole new revelation to me because up to then I was always on my own, and I never knew you could enjoy it so much, working with other people."

~

He also told me that one night not long after he started work at the Foundry he came out at twelve o'clock or so and found a great snowstorm in progress. The roads were full, the snowplows would not be out till dawn. He had to leave the car where it was. He started to walk home. This was a distance of about two miles. The walking was heavy, in the freshly drifted snow, and he was walking in a south-westerly direction, with the west wind coming against him. He had done several floors that night and he was just getting used to the work. He wore a heavy overcoat, an army greatcoat, which one of our neighbors who had fought in the war had given him. Usually he wore a windbreaker. He must have put the coat on because the wind was so cold, and there was no heater in the car.

He felt dragged down, pushing against the storm, and about a quarter of a mile from home he found he wasn't moving. He was standing in the middle of a drift, and he could not move his legs. He could hardly stand against the wind. He was worn out. He thought perhaps his heart was giving out. He thought of his death. He would die leaving a sick crippled wife who could not even take care of herself, an old mother full of disappointment, a younger daughter whose health had always been delicate, an older girl who was often self-centered and mysteriously incompetent, a son who seemed to be bright and reliable but who was still only a little boy. He would die in debt, and before he had even finished pulling down the pens; they would be there to show the ruin of his enterprise.

"Was that all you thought about?" I said when he told me this.

"Wasn't that enough?" he said, and went on to tell me how he pulled one leg out of the soft snow, and then the other, he got out of that drift, and there were no others quite so deep, and in a while he was in the shelter of the windbreak of pine trees he himself had planted. He had got home.

But I had meant, didn't he think of himself; of the boy who had trapped along the Blyth Creek, and asked for Sign's Snow Paper; the young man about to be married who had cut cedar poles in the swamp to build the first fox-pens; the forty-year-old man who had thought of joining the army? I meant, was his life now something that only other people had a use for?

~

My father always said that he didn't really grow up until he went to work in the Foundry. He never wanted to talk much about the fox-farm, until he was old and could talk easily about anything that had happened. But my mother, as she was being walled in by increasing paralysis, often wanted to talk about her three weeks at the Pine Tree Hotel, the friends and money she had made there.

Contributors

JANE SMILEY is the Pulitzer Prize–winning author of *A Thousand Acres*. She has written thirteen novels, four books of nonfiction, and the collection of short stories *The Age of Grief*, which was made into the movie *The Secret Lives of Dentists*. She is a member of The American Academy of Arts and Letters. Her newest novel, *Some Luck*, is the first volume of a trilogy.

PATRICIA HENLEY is the author of two chapbooks of poetry, four short story collections, two novels, a stage play, and a novel for young adults, *Where Wicked Starts*, co-authored with Elizabeth Stuckey-French. Patricia lives in Cincinnati, Ohio.

BLISS BROYARD's *One Drop: My Father's Hidden Life-A Story of Race and Family Secrets* became a New York Times Notable Book and won a number of awards. Bliss is also the author of the bestselling story collection, *My Father, Dancing*, which received the Louisiana Endowment for the Arts Humanist Book of the Year award and was a finalist for the Essence and Books for a Better Life awards. She has written for the *New York Times*, *The New Yorker*, *Elle*, *More*, and *Real Simple*, among others. She is at work on a novel set on Martha's Vineyard called *Happy House*.

MAKO YOSHIKAWA is the author of the novels *One Hundred and One Ways* and *Once Removed*. Her work has been translated into six languages and she has received a Radcliffe Fellowship. As a literary critic she has published articles that explore the relationship between incest and race in twentieth-century American fiction. Her essays have appeared in the *Missouri Review*, *Harvard Review*, and *Best American Essays 2013*. She's a professor of creative writing at Emerson College in Boston.

NANCY JAINCHILL is a psychologist residing in Woodstock, New York, practicing there and in New York City. She earned her doctorate in psychology from New York University and has a Master's Degree in Women's Literature from Goddard College. She has published extensively in the field of adolescent drug treatment research, and most recently she has edited and been a contributor to the volume, *Understanding and Treating Adolescent Substance Use Disorders* (2012). She is completing an MFA in Creative Writing at Bennington College.

JILL McCORKLE is the author of four story collections and six novels, most recently *Life After Life*. Her work has appeared in *The Atlantic*, *The American Scholar* and *Ploughshares*, as well as *Best American Short Stories* and *Best American Essays*. Jill has received the New England Book Award, The John Dos Passos Prize for Excellence in Literature, and the North Carolina Award for Literature. She is currently a professor in the MFA in Creative Writing program at North Carolina State.

JOYCE MAYNARD has been a reporter and columnist for *The New York Times*, a syndicated newspaper columnist whose "Domestic Affairs" column appeared in over fifty papers nationwide, and a regular contributor to NPR, *Vogue*, *O*, *Newsweek*, *The New York Times Magazine*, MORE, and *Salon*, among many other magazines. As a fiction writer, she has been a fellow at the Mac-Dowell Colony and Yaddo. Maynard is the author of fifteen books, including the novel *To Die For* and the best-selling memoir, *At Home in the World*. Her latest novel, *After Her* was released in 2013. Her novel, *Labor Day*, became a motion picture in 2014.

JESSICA WOODRUFF's work has appeared in *Relief*, *The New Purlieu Review*, *Catfish Creek*, *Jet Fuel Review*, and *Mangrove Literary Journal*. She is currently working on a memoir about her experience living in foster homes.

JANE FRIEDMAN co-founded and co-edits *Scratch*, a magazine exploring the intersection of writing and money and named a top website for writers. Her work has appeared or is forthcoming in anthologies from Seal Press, the University of Chicago, and Milkweed. She writes a blog about the publishing industry at JaneFriedman.com, and she speaks around the world at such events as BookExpo America, Frankfurt Book Fair, and Digilit. Jane also teaches digital publishing and media at the University of Virginia, and is currently working on a series of lectures on publishing for The Great Courses.

MELORA WOLFF's work has appeared in *The Normal School*, *The New Brick Reader*, *The New York Times*, *Best American Fantasy*, *Brick*, *Gettysburg Review*, and *Salmagundi*. She was named a Notable Essayist in *Best American Essays 2012*, and received Special Mention in Nonfiction in *The Pushcart Prizes 2014*. She has received fellowships in nonfiction from The New York Foundation for the Arts, the Corporation of Yaddo, and the MacDowell Colony for the Arts. She teaches at Skidmore College in Saratoga Springs, New York.

Contributors

MAXINE HONG KINGSTON has received many honors, including a Guggenheim fellowship, the National Humanities Medal in 1997, and the John Dos Passos Prize for Literature. She has written the novels *Tripmaster Monkey, His Fake Book*, and *Hawaii One Summer*. Most recently she returned to nonfiction with *The Fifth Book of Peace*. Maxine edited a collection of nonfiction pieces from people touched by war in *Veterans of War, Veterans of Peace*, culled from some of her writing workshops. She is a Professor Emeritus at the University of California–Berkeley.

BARBARA SHOUP is the author of eight novels, including *Night Watch, Wish You Were Here, Stranded in Harmony, Faithful Women, Vermeer's Daughter, Everything You Want, An American Tune*, and *Looking for Jack Kerouac*. She is also co-author of *Novel Ideas: Contemporary Authors Share the Creative Process* and *Story Matters*. Barbara was the 2006 PEN Phyllis Naylor Working Writer Fellow, and she lives in Indianapolis, where she is the executive director of the Writers' Center of Indiana.

ANN HOOD is the author of the bestselling novels *The Obituary Writer, The Knitting Circle*, and *The Red Thread*. Among her honors are two Pushcart Prizes, two Best American Food Writing Awards, a Best American Spiritual Writing Award and a Best American Travel Writing Award. Ann is a regular contributor to the *New York Times* and NPR's "The Story." Her new novel, *An Italian Wife*, was published in September 2014.

ALEXANDRA STYRON is the author of the memoir *Reading My Father* and a novel, *All The Finest Girls*. A graduate of Barnard College and the MFA program at Columbia University, her work has appeared in *The New Yorker, The New York Times, Vanity Fair, The Financial Times*, and *The Wall Street Journal*. She teaches memoir writing in the MFA program at Hunter College, and lives with her husband and two children in Brooklyn, New York.

NANCY MCCABE has written four books of creative nonfiction, including *From Little Houses to Little Women: Revisiting a Literary Childhood; Meeting Sophie: A Memoir of Adoption*; and *Crossing the Blue Willow Bridge: A Journey to my Daughter's Birthplace in China*. Her work has won a Pushcart Prize for memoir, and her essays have appeared in *Newsweek, Writer's Digest, Fourth Genre, Crazyhorse, Massachusetts Review*, and *Crab Orchard Review*, among others. She directs the writing program at the University of Pittsburgh at Bradford and teaches in the brief-residency MFA program at Spalding University.

SUSAN NEVILLE is the author of four works of creative nonfiction: *Indiana Winter; Fabrication: Essays on Making Things and Making Meaning; Twilight in Arcadia; Iconography: A Writer's Meditation;* and *Sailing the Inland Sea*. Her short fiction includes *In the House of Blue Lights*, winner of the Richard Sullivan prize and listed as a Notable Book by the Chicago Tribune, and *Invention of Flight*, winner of the Flannery O'Connor Award for Short Fiction. Her stories have appeared in the *Pushcart Prize* anthology and in *Extreme Fiction* and *The Story Behind the Story*.

SUSAN PERABO is the author of a novel, *The Broken Places*. Her fiction has been anthologized in *Best American Short Stories, Pushcart Prize Stories,* and *New Stories from the South*, and has appeared in numerous magazines, including *One Story, Glimmer Train, The Iowa Review, The Missouri Review,* and *The Sun*. Her new collection of short stories is forthcoming from Simon and Schuster. She is Writer-in-Residence and Professor of English at Dickinson College in Carlisle, Pennsylvania.

ANTONYA NELSON's short stories have appeared in *Esquire, The New Yorker, Quarterly West, Redbook, Ploughshares, Harper's* and other magazines. Several of her books have been *New York Times Book Review* Notable Books: *In the Land of Men, Talking in Bed, Nobody's Girl: A Novel, Living to Tell: A Novel,* and *Female Trouble*. In 1999, *The New Yorker* selected Nelson as one of "the twenty best young fiction writers in America today." She is the recipient of the Rea Award for Short Fiction, a 2000-2001 NEA Grant, and a Guggenheim Fellowship. She is currently a professor of English at the University of Houston, and she also teaches in the Warren Wilson MFA program.

LEE SMITH has received many writing awards, such as the O. Henry Award, the American Academy of Arts and Letters Award for Fiction, and the North Carolina Award for Literature. Her novel *The Last Girls* was listed on the *The New York Times* bestseller's list and won the Southern Book Critics Circle Award. *Mrs. Darcy and the Blue-Eyed Stranger*, a collection of new and selected stories, was published in 2010. Since 1968, she has published fifteen novels, including *Family Linen*, and *Saving Grace*, as well as four collections of short stories, and has received eight major writing awards.

LILY LOPATE is currently a student at Bryn Mawr College, has been a staff writer, columnist and managing editor at *Bi-College News* (Bryn Mawr and Haverford Colleges), and editor-in-chief of the literary magazine, *Reflections*. She has received national recognition for her personal essays and poetry from the Scholastic Art & Writing Awards and the Columbia Press Association. She has also published in the e-zine *Mr. Beller's Neighborhood*, which features New York stories.

JOHANNA GOHMANN has combed the slush pile as an assistant at Writer House Literary Agency, edited the "true stories" in *True Story* magazine, worn a tuxedo and served steak to stock brokers, been an assistant editor at *Elle*, reviewed both nightclubs and erotic novels, worked as a reporter in Queens, New York, and Dublin, Ireland, and written blurbs for Scholastic books. She has contributed to numerous publications, including *Salon*, *The Morning News*, *The Chicago Sun-Times*, *Babble*, and *Curve*. She is a regular writer for *Bust* magazine. Her essays have been anthologized in *A Moveable Feast: Life-Changing Food Adventures Around the World*, *Joan Didion Crosses the Street*, *The Best Sex Writing 2010*, and *The Best Women's Travel Writing 2010* and 2015. She lives in Brooklyn with her husband and son.

BOBBIE ANN MASON's first book of fiction, *Shiloh & Other Stories* won the PEN/ Hemingway Award and was nominated for the American Book Award, the PEN/ Faulkner Award, and the National Book Critics Circle Award. She received a Guggenheim Fellowship and a grant from the National Endowment for the Arts, and she received an Arts and Letters Award for Literature from the American Academy of Arts and Letters. *In Country* was made into a film starring Bruce Willis. Both *Feather Crowns* and *Zigzagging Down a Wild Trail* won the Southern Book Critics Circle Award. Her memoir, *Clear Springs*, was a finalist for the Pulitzer Prize.

JAYNE ANNE PHILLIPS is the author of five novels—*Quiet Dell, Lark and Termite, Motherkind, Shelter, Machine Dreams*—and two widely anthologized collections of stories, *Fast Lanes* and *Black Tickets*. *Quiet Dell* was a *Wall Street Journal* Best Fiction of 2013, and a Kirkus Reviews Best of 2013, selection. *Lark & Termite*, winner of the Heartland Prize, was a Finalist for the 2009 National Book Award, the National Book Critics Circle Award, and the *Prix de Medici Etranger*. Jayne Anne's works are published in nine languages. She is the recipient of a Guggenheim Fellowship, two National Endowment for the Arts Fellowships, a Bunting Fellowship, the Sue Kaufman Prize (1980) and an Academy Award in Literature (1997) from the American Academy and Institute of Arts and Letters. She is Distinguished Professor of English and Director of the MFA Program at Rutgers University-Newark, the State University of New Jersey.

ALICE MUNRO's first collection of stories was published as *Dance of the Happy Shades*. In 2009, she won the Man Booker International Prize. That same year, she published the short-story collection *Too Much Happiness*. Her work frequently appears in magazines including *The New Yorker*, *The Atlantic Monthly*, and *The Paris Review*. On December 10, 2013, she was awarded the Nobel Prize in Literature.

PHILLIP LOPATE is the author of several personal essay collections, including *Bachelorhood*, *Against Joie de Vivre*, and *Portrait of My Body*. He has also written two novels, three poetry collections, a memoir, a collection of movie criticism, and several other books. In addition, he has edited *The Art of the Personal Essay*; *Writing New York*; *Journey of a Living Experiment*, a best essays of the year series, *The Anchor Essay Annual*; and *American Movie Critics*. His essays, fiction, poetry, film and architectural criticism have appeared in *The Best American Short Stories*, *The Best American Essays*, several Pushcart Prize annuals, *The Paris Review*, *Harper's*, *Vogue*, *Esquire*, *Film Comment*, *Threepenny Review*, *Double Take*, *New York Times*, *Harvard Educational Review*, *Preservation*, *Cite*, *7 Days*, *Metropolis*, *Conde Nast Traveler*, and many other periodicals and anthologies. Phillip is currently the director of the nonfiction graduate program at Columbia University.

MARGARET McMULLAN is the author of six award-winning novels including *Aftermath Lounge*, *In My Mother's House*, *Sources of Light*, *How I Found the Strong*, and *When I Crossed No-Bob*. Her stories and essays have appeared in *The Chicago Tribune*, *Ploughshares*, *Southern Accents*, *TriQuarterly*, *Michigan Quarterly Review* and *The Sun* among several other journals and anthologies. She has received an NEA Fellowship in literature and a Fulbright award to teach at the University of Pécs in Pécs, Hungary. She holds the Melvin M. Peterson Endowed Chair in Literature and Writing at the University of Evansville in Evansville, Indiana.